Constance Fenimore Woolson

The front yard

And other Italian stories

Constance Fenimore Woolson

The front yard
And other Italian stories

ISBN/EAN: 9783741181597

Manufactured in Europe, USA, Canada, Australia, Japa

Cover: Foto ©Andreas Hilbeck / pixelio.de

Manufactured and distributed by brebook publishing software (www.brebook.com)

Constance Fenimore Woolson

The front yard

"'MADEMOISELLE NEED GIVE HERSELF NO UNEASINESS'"

THE FRONT YARD

AND

OTHER ITALIAN STORIES

BY

CONSTANCE FENIMORE WOOLSON

AUTHOR OF "ANNE" "HORACE CHASE" ETC.

ILLUSTRATED

NEW YORK
HARPER & BROTHERS PUBLISHERS
1895

NOTE

OF the stories contained in this volume, "In Venice" was originally published in the *Atlantic Monthly*, "The Street of the Hyacinth" in the *Century Magazine*, and the other four stories in *Harper's Magazine*.

CONTENTS

	PAGE
THE FRONT YARD	1
NEPTUNE'S SHORE	50
A PINK VILLA	91
THE STREET OF THE HYACINTH	137
A CHRISTMAS PARTY	194
IN VENICE	234

ILLUSTRATIONS

"'MADEMOISELLE NEED GIVE HERSELF NO UNEASINESS'"	*Frontispiece*	
"''TWOULD BE SOMETHING TO CELEBRATE THE DAY WITH, THAT WOULD'"	*Facing p.*	2
"NOUNCE TOO CAME OUT, AND SAT ON THE WALL NEAR BY, LISTENING"	"	22
"STILL HOLDING NOUNCE'S HAND, SHE WENT ROUND TO THE FRONT OF THE HOUSE"	"	42
"'YOU KNOW I AM YOUR SLAVE'"	"	58
AZUBAH ASH	"	68
THE OLD WATCH-TOWER	"	86
"THE CART WAS GOING SLOWLY ACROSS THE FIELDS, FOR THE ROAD WAS OVERFLOWED"	"	88
"'MRS. CHURCHILL, LET ME PRESENT TO YOU MR. DAVID ROD'"	"	100
SORRENTO	"	102
ON THE WAY TO THE DESERTO	"	112
AT THE DESERTO	"	114
"SHE SAT DOWN AND GATHERED HER CHILD TO HER BREAST"	"	128
"FANNY PUT OUT HER HANDS WITH A BITTER CRY"	"	134
"A SMALL CHILD PERCHED ON EACH OF HIS SHOULDERS"	"	214

THE FRONT YARD

"WELL, now, with Gooster at work in the per-dairy, and Bepper settled at last as help in a good family, and Parlo and Squawly gone to Perugia, and Soonter taken by the nuns, and Jo Vanny learning the carpenter's trade, and only Nounce left for me to see to (let alone Granmar, of course, and Pipper and old Patro), it doos seem, it really doos, as if I might get it done *sometime;* say next Fourth of July, now; that's only ten months off. 'Twould be something to celebrate the day with, that would; something like!"

The woman through whose mind these thoughts were passing was sitting on a low stone-wall, a bundle of herbs, a fagot of twigs, and a sickle laid carefully beside her. On her back was strapped a large deep basket, almost as long as herself; she had loosened the straps so that she could sit down. This basket was heavy; one could tell that from the relaxed droop of her shoulders relieved from its weight for the moment, as its end rested on a fallen block on the other side of the wall. Her feet were bare, her dress a narrow cotton gown, covered in front to the hem by a dark cotton apron; on her head was a straw bonnet, which had behind a little cape of brown ribbon three inches deep, and in front broad strings of the same brown, carefully tied in a bow, with the loops pulled out to their full width and pinned on each side of her chin. This bonnet, very clean and decent (the ribbons had evidently been washed more than once), was of old-fashioned shape, projecting beyond the wearer's forehead and cheeks. Within its tube her face could be seen, with its deeply browned skin, its large irregular features, smooth, thin white hair, and blue eyes, still bright, set amid a bed of wrinkles. She was sixty years old, tall and broad-shouldered. She had once been remarkably erect and strong. This strength had been consumed more by constant toil than by the approach of old age; it was not all gone yet; the great basket showed that. In addition, her eyes spoke a language which told of energy that would last as long as her breath.

These eyes were fixed now upon a low building that stood at a little distance directly across the path. It was small and ancient, built of stone, with a sloping roof and black door. There were no windows; through this door entered the only light and air. Outside were two large heaps of refuse, one of which had been there so long that thick matted herbage was growing vigorously over its top. Bars guarded the entrance; it was impossible to see what was within. But the woman knew without seeing; she always knew. It had been a cow; it had been goats; it had been pigs, and then goats again; for the past two years it had been pigs steadily—always pigs. Her eyes were fixed upon this door as if held there by a magnet; her mouth fell open a little as she gazed; her hands lay loose in her lap. There was nothing new in the picture, certainly. But the intensity of her feeling made it in one way always new. If love wakes freshly every morning, so does

"'TWOULD BE SOMETHING TO CELEBRATE THE DAY WITH, THAT WOULD'"

hate, and Prudence Wilkin had hated that cow-shed for years.

The bells down in the town began to ring the Angelus. She woke from her reverie, rebuckled the straps of the basket, and adjusting it by a jerk of her shoulders in its place on her back, she took the fagot in one hand, the bundle of herbs in the other, and carrying the sickle under her arm, toiled slowly up the ascent, going round the cow-shed, as the interrupted path too went round it, in an unpaved, provisional sort of way (which had, however, lasted fifty years), and giving a wave of her herbs towards the offending black door as she passed — a gesture that was almost triumphant. "Jest you wait till next Fourth of July, you indecent old Antiquity, you!" This is what she was thinking.

Prudence Wilkin's idea of Antiquity was everything that was old and dirty; indecent Antiquity meant the same qualities increased to a degree that was monstrous, a degree that the most profligate imagination of Ledham (New Hampshire) would never have been able to conceive. There was naturally a good deal of this sort of Antiquity in Assisi, her present abode; it was all she saw when she descended to that picturesque town; the great triple church of St. Francis she never entered; the magnificent view of the valley, the serene vast Umbrian plain, she never noticed; but the steep, narrow streets, with garbage here and there, the crowding stone houses, centuries old, from whose court-yard doors issued odors indescribable—these she knew well, and detested with all her soul. Her deepest degree of loathing, however, was reserved for the especial Antiquity that blocked her own front path, that elbowed her own front door, this noisome stable or sty—for it was now one, now the other—which she had hated and abhorred for sixteen long years.

For it was just sixteen years ago this month since she had first entered the hill town of St. Francis. She had not entered it alone, but in the company of a handsome bridegroom, Antonio Guadagni by name, and so happy was she that everything had seemed to her enchanting—these same steep streets with their ancient dwellings, the same dirt, the same yellowness, the same continuous leisure and causeless beatitude. And when her Tonio took her through the town and up this second ascent to the squalid little house, where, staring and laughing and crowding nearer to look at her, she found his family assembled, innumerable children (they seemed innumerable then), a bedridden grandam, a disreputable old uncle (who began to compliment her), even this did not appear a burden, though of course it was a surprise. For Tonio had told her, sadly, that he was "all alone in the world." It had been one of the reasons why she had wished to marry him—that she might make a home for so desolate a man.

The home was already made, and it was somewhat full. Desolate Tonio explained, with shouts of laughter, in which all the assemblage joined, that seven of the children were his, the eighth being an orphan nephew left to his care; his wife had died eight months before, and this was her grandmother—on the bed there; this her good old uncle, a very accomplished man, who had written sonnets. Mrs. Guadagni number two had excellent powers of vision, but she was never able to discover the goodness of this accomplished uncle; it was a quality which, like the beneficence of angels, one is obliged to take on trust.

She was forty-five, a New England woman, with some small savings, who had come to Italy as companion and attendant to a distant cousin, an invalid with money. The cousin had died suddenly at Perugia, and Prudence had allowed the chance of returning to Ledham with her effects to pass by unnoticed—a remarkable lapse of the quality of which her first name was the exponent, regarding which her whole life hitherto had been one sharply outlined example. This lapse was due to her having already become the captive of this handsome, this irresistible, this wholly unexpected Tonio, who was serving as waiter in the Perugian inn. Divining her savings, and seeing with his own eyes her wonderful strength and energy, this good-natured reprobate had made love to her a little in the facile Italian way, and the poor plain simple-hearted spinster, to whom no one had ever spoken a word of gallantry in all her life before, had been completely swept off her balance by the novelty of it, and by the thronging new sensations which his few English words, his speaking dark eyes, and ardent entreaties roused in her maiden breast. It was her one moment of madness (who has not had one?). She married him, marvelling a little inwardly when he required her to walk to Assisi, but content to walk to China if that should be his pleasure. When she reached the squalid house on the height and saw its crowd of occupants, when her own money was demanded to send down to Assisi to purchase the wedding dinner, then she understood—why they had walked.

But she never understood anything else. She never permitted herself to understand. Tonio, plump and idle, enjoyed a year of paradisiacal opulence under her ministrations (and in spite of some of them); he was eighteen years younger than she was; it was natural that he should wish to enjoy on a larger scale than hers—so he told her. At the end of twelve months a fever carried him off, and his widow, who mourned for him with all her heart, was left to face the world with the eight children, the grandmother, the good old uncle, and whatever courage she was able to muster after counting over and over the eighty-five dollars that alone remained to her of the six hundred she had brought him.

Of course she could have gone back to her own country. But that idea never once occurred to her; she had married Tonio for better or worse; she could not in honor desert the worst now that it had come. It had come in force; on the very day of the funeral she had been obliged to work eight hours; on every day that had followed through all these years, the hours had been on an average fourteen; sometimes more.

Bent under her basket, the widow now arrived at the back door of her home. It was a small narrow house, built of rough stones plastered over and painted bright yellow. But though thus gay without, it was dark within; the few windows were very small, and their four little panes of thick glass were covered with an iron grating; there was no elevation above the ground, the brick floor inside being of the same level as the flagging of the path without, so that there was always a sense of groping when one entered the low door. There were but four rooms, the kitchen, with a bedroom opening from it, and two chambers above under the sloping roof.

Prudence unstrapped her basket and placed it in a wood-shed which she had constructed with her own hands. For she could not comprehend a house without a wood-shed; she called it a wood-shed, though there was very little wood to put in it: in Assisi no one made a fire for warmth; for cooking they burned twigs. She hung up the fagot (it was a fagot of twigs), the herbs, and the sickle; then, after giving her narrow skirts a shake, she entered the kitchen.

There was a bed in this room. Granmar would not allow it to be moved elsewhere; her bed had always been in the kitchen, and in the kitchen it should remain; no one but Denza, indeed, would wish to shove her off; Annunziata had liked to have her dear old granmar there, where she could see for herself that she was having everything she needed; but Annunziata had been an angel of goodness, as well as of the dearest beauty; whereas Denza—but any one could see what Denza was! As Granmar's tongue was decidedly a thing to be reckoned with, her bed remained where it always had been; from its comfortable cleanliness the old creature could overlook and criticise to her heart's content the entire household economy of Annunziata's successor. Not only the kitchen, but the whole house and garden, had been vigorously purified by this successor; single-handed she had attacked and carried away accumulations which had been there since Columbus discovered America. Even Granmar was rescued from her squalor and coaxed to wear a clean cap and neat little shawl, her withered brown hands reposing meanwhile upon a sheet which, though coarse, was spotless.

Granmar was a very terrible old woman; she had a

beak-like nose, round glittering black eyes set in broad
circles of yellow wrinkles, no mouth to speak of, and
a receding chin; her voice was now a gruff bass, now a
shrill yell.

"How late you are! you do it on purpose," she said
as Prudence entered. "And me—as haven't had a
thing I've wanted since you went away hours upon
hours ago. Nunziata there has been as stupid as a
stone—behold her!"

She spoke in peasant Italian, a tongue which Mrs.
Guadagni the second (called Denza by the family, from
Prudenza, the Italian form of her first name) now spoke
readily enough, though after a fashion of her own. She
remained always convinced that Italian was simply lunatic English, English spoiled. One of the children,
named Pasquale, she called Squawly, and she always
believed that the title came from the strength of his
infant lungs; many other words impressed her in the
same way.

She now made no reply to Granmar's complaints save
to give one business-like look towards the bed to see
whether the pillows were properly adjusted for the old
creature's comfort; then she crossed the room towards
the stove, a large ancient construction of bricks, with
two or three small depressions over which an iron pot
could be set.

"Well, Nounce," she said to a girl who was sitting
there on a little bench. The tone of her voice was
kindly; she looked to see if a fire had been made. A
few coals smouldered in one of the holes. "Good girl,"
said Prudence, commendingly.

"Oh, very good!" cried Granmar from the bed—
"very good, when I told her forty times, and fifty, to

make me an omelet, a wee fat one with a drop of fig in it, and I so faint, and she wouldn't, the snake! she wouldn't, the toad!—toadest of toads!"

The dark eyes of the girl turned slowly towards Prudence. Prudence, as she busied herself with the coals, gave her a little nod of approbation, which Granmar could not see. The girl looked pleased for a moment; then her face sank into immobility again. She was not an idiot, but wanting, as it was called; a delicate, pretty young creature, who, with her cousin Pippo, had been only a year old when the second wife came to Assisi. It was impossible for any one to be fond of Pippo, who even at that age had been selfish and gluttonous to an abnormal degree; but Prudence had learned to love the helpless little girl committed to her care, as she had also learned to love very dearly the child's brother Giovanni, who was but a year older; they had been but babies, both of them. The girl was now seventeen. Her name was Annunziata, but Prudence called her Nounce. "If it means 'Announce,' Nounce is near enough, I guess," she said to herself, aggressively. The truth was that she hated the name; it had belonged to Tonio's first wife, and of the memory of that comely young mother, poor Prudence, with her sixty years, her white hair, and wrinkled skin, was burningly jealous even now. Giovanni's name she pronounced as though it were two words—Jo Vanny; she really thought there were two. Jo she knew well, of course; it was a good New England name; Vanny was probably some senseless Italian addition. The name of the eldest son, Augusto, became on her lips Gooster; Paolo was Parlo, Assunta was Soonter.

The nuns had finally taken Soonter. The step-mother

had been unable to conceal from herself her own profound relief. True, the girl had gone to a "papish" convent; but she had always been a mystery in the house, and the constant presence of a mystery is particularly trying to the New England mind. Soonter spent hours in meditation; she was very quiet; she believed that she saw angels; her face wore often a faraway smile.

On this September evening she prepared a heavily abundant supper for Granmar, and a simple one for Nounce, who ate at any time hardly more than a bird; Granmar, on the contrary, was gifted with an appetite of extraordinary capacities, the amount of food which was necessary to keep her, not in good-humor (she was never in good-humor), but in passable bodily tranquillity, through the twenty-four hours being equal to that which would have been required (so Prudence often thought) for three hearty New England harvesters at home. Not that Granmar would touch New England food; none of the family would eat the home dishes which Prudence in the earlier years had hopefully tried to prepare from such materials as seemed to her the least "onreasonable"; Granmar, indeed, had declared each and all fit only for the hogs. Prudence never tried them now, and she had learned the art of Italian cooking; for she felt that she could not afford to make anything that was to be for herself alone; the handful of precious twigs must serve for the family as a whole. But every now and then, in spite of her natural abstemiousness, she would be haunted by a vision of a "boiled dinner," the boiled corned-beef, the boiled cabbage, turnips, and potatoes, and the boiled Indian pudding of her youth. She should never taste these dainties on earth again. More than once she caught herself hoping that at least the aroma of them would be given to her some time in heaven.

When Granmar was gorged she became temporarily more tranquil. Prudence took this time to speak of a plan which she had had in her mind for several days. "Now that Gooster and the other boys are doing for themselves, Granmar, and Bepper too at last, and Jo Vanny only needing a trifle of help now and then (he's so young yet, you know), I feel as though I might be earning more money," she began.

"Money's a very good thing; we've never had half enough since my sainted Annunziata joined the angels," responded Granmar, with a pious air.

"Well, it seems a good time to try and earn some more. Soonter's gone to the convent; and as it's a long while since Pipper's been here, I really begin to think he has gone off to get work somewhere, as he always said was going to."

"Don't you be too sure of Pippo," said Granmar, shaking her owl-like head ominously.

"'Tany rate he hasn't been here, and I always try to hope the best about him—"

"And *that's* what you call the best?" interrupted Granmar, with one of her sudden flank movements, "to have him gone away off no one knows where—Annunziata's own precious little nephew—taken by the pirates —yam! Sold as a slave—yam! Killed in the war! Oh, Pippo! poor Pippo! poor little Pipp, Pipp, Pipp!"

"And so I thought I'd try to go to the shop by the day," Prudence went on, when this yell had ceased; "they want me to come and cut out. I shouldn't go until after your breakfast, of course; and I could leave cold things out, and Nounce would cook you something hot at noon; then I should be home myself every night in time to get your supper."

"And so that's the plan—I'm to be left alone here with an idiot while you go flouncing your heels round Assisi! Flounce, cat! It's a wonder the dead don't rise in their graves to hear it. But we buried my Annunziata too deep for that—yam!—otherwise she'd 'a been here to tear your eyes out. An old woman left to starve alone, her own precious grandmother, growing weaker and weaker, and pining and pining. Blessed stomach, do you hear—do you hear, my holy, blessed stomach, always asking for so little, and now not even to get that? It's turned all a mumble of cold just thinking of it—yam! I, poor sufferer, who have had to stand your ugly face so long—I *so* fond of beauty! You haven't got but twenty-four hairs now; you know you haven't—yam! I've got more than you twenty times over—hey! *that* I have." And Granmar, tearing off her cap, pulled loose her coarse white hair, and grasping the ends of the long locks with her crooked fingers, threw them aloft with a series of shrill halloos.

"I won't go to the shop," said Prudence. "Mercy on us, what a noise! I say I won't go to the shop. There! do you hear?"

"Will you be here every day of your life at twelve o'clock to cook me something that won't poison me?" demanded Granmar, still hallooing.

"Yes, yes, I promise you."

Even Granmar believed Prudence's yes; her yea was yea and her nay nay to all the family. "You cook me something this very minute," she said, sullenly, putting on her cap askew.

"Why, you've only just got through your supper!" exclaimed Prudence, astonished, used though she was to Granmar's abdominal capacities, by this sudden demand.

"You won't? Then I'll yell again," said Granmar. And yell she did.

"Hold up—do; I believe you now," said Prudence. She fanned the dying coals with a straw fan, made up the fire, and prepared some griddle-cakes. Granmar demanded fig syrup to eat with them; and devoured six. Filled to repletion, she then suffered Prudence to change her day cap for a nightcap, falling asleep almost before her head touched the pillow.

During this scene Nounce had sat quietly in her corner. Prudence now went to her to see if she was frightened, for the girl was sometimes much terrified by Granmar's outcries; she stroked her soft hair. She was always looking for signs of intelligence in Nounce, and fancying that she discovered them. Taking the girl's hand, she went with her to the next room, where were their two narrow pallet beds. "You were very smart to save the eggs for me to-day when Granmar wanted that omerlet," she whispered, as she helped her to undress.

Memory came back to Nounce; she smiled comprehendingly.

Prudence waited until she was in bed; then she kissed her good-night, and put out the candle.

Her two charges asleep, Mrs. Guadagni the second opened the back door softly and went out. It was not yet nine o'clock, a warm dark night; though still September, the odors of autumn were already in the air, coming from the September flowers, which have a pungency mingled with their perfume, from the rank ripeness of the vegetables, from the aroma of the ground after the first rains.

"I could have made thirty cents a week more at the shop," she said to herself, regretfully (she always translated the Italian money into American or French). "In a month that would have been a dollar and twenty cents! Well, there's no use thinking about it sence I can't go." She bent over her vegetables, feeling of their leaves, and estimating anew how many she could afford to sell, now that the family was so much reduced in size. Then she paid a visit to her fig-trees. She had planted these trees herself, and watched over their infancy with anxious care; at the present moment they were loaded with fruit, and it seemed as if she knew the position of each fig, so many times had she stood under the boughs looking up at the slowly swelling bulbs. She had never before been able to sell the fruit. But now she should be able, and the sale would add a good many cents to the store of savings kept in her work-box. This work-box, a possession of her youth, was lined with vivid green paper, and had a colored lithograph of the Honorable Mrs. Norton (taken as a Muse) on the inside of the cover; it held already three francs and a half, that is seventy cents—an excellent sum when one considered that only three weeks had passed since the happy day when she had at last beheld the way open to saving regularly, laying by regularly; many times had she begun to save, but she had never been able to continue it. Now, with this small household, she should be able to continue. The sale of the figs would probably double the savings already in the work-box; she might even get eighty cents for them; and that would make a dollar and fifty cents in all! A fig fell to the ground. "They're ripe," she thought; "they must be picked to-morrow." She felt for the fallen fig in the darkness, and carrying it to the garden wall, placed it in a dry niche where it would keep its freshness until she could send it to town with the rest. Then she went to the hen-house. "Smart of Nounce to save the eggs for me," she thought, laughing delightedly to herself over this proof of the girl's intelligence. "Granmar didn't need that omerlet one bit; I left out two tremenjous lunches for her." She peered in; but could not see the hens in the darkness. "If Granmar'd only eat the things we do!" her thoughts went on. "But she's always possessed after everything that takes eggs. And then she wants the very best coffee, and white sugar, and the best wine, and fine flour and meal and oil—my! how much oil! But I wonder if *I* couldn't stop eating something or other, steader pestering myself about her? Let's see. I don't take wine nor coffee, so I can't stop them; but I could stop soup meat, just for myself; and I will. Thus meditating, she went slowly round to the open space before the house.

To call it a space was a misnomer. The house stood at the apex of the hill, and its garden by right extended as far down the descent in front as it extended down the opposite descent behind, where Prudence had planted her long rows of vegetables. But in this front space, not ten feet distant from the house door, planted directly across the paved path which came up from below, was the cow-shed, the intruding offensive neighbor whose odors, gruntings (for it was now a pig-sty), and refuse were constantly making themselves perceptible to one sense and another through the open windows of the dwelling behind. For the house had no back windows; the small apertures which passed for windows were all in front; in that climate it was impossible that they should be always closed. How those odors choked Prudence Wilkin! It seemed as if she could not respect herself while obliged to breathe them, as if she had not respected herself (in the true Ledham way) since the pig-sty became her neighbor.

For fifty francs the owners would take it away; for another twenty or thirty she could have "a front yard." But though she had made many beginnings, she had never been able to save a tenth of the sum. None of the family shared her feelings in the least; to spend precious money for such a whim as that—only an American could be capable of it; but then, as everybody knew, most Americans were mad. And why should Denza object to pigs?

Prudence therefore had been obliged to keep her longings to herself. But this had only intensified them. And now when at last, after thinking of it for sixteen years, she was free to begin to save daily and regularly, she saw as in a vision her front yard completed as she would like to have it: the cow-shed gone; "a nice straight path going down to the front gate, set in a new paling fence; along the sides currant bushes; and in the open spaces to the right and left a big flowerin' shrub—snowballs, or Missouri currant; near the house a clump of matrimony, perhaps; and in the flower beds on each side of the path bachelor's-buttons, Chiny-asters, lady's-slippers, and pinks; the edges bordered with box." She heaved a sigh of deep satisfaction as she finished her mental review. But it was hardly mental after all; she saw the gate, she saw the straight path, she saw the currant bushes and the box-bordered flower beds as distinctly as though they had really been there.

Cheered, almost joyous, she went within, locking the door behind her; then, after softly placing the usual store of provisions beside Granmar's bed (for Granmar had a habit of waking in the night to eat), she sought her own couch. It was hard, but she stretched herself upon it luxuriously. "The figs 'll double the money," she thought, "and by this time to-morrow I shall have a dollar and forty cents; mebby a dollar fifty!" She fell asleep happily.

Her contentment made her sleep soundly. Still it was not long after dawn when she hurried down the hill to the town to get her supply of work from the shop. Hastening back with it, she found Granmar clamoring for her coffee, and Nounce, neatly dressed and clean (for so much Prudence had succeeded in teaching her), sitting patiently in her corner. Prudence's mind was full of a sale she had made; but she prepared the coffee and Nounce's broth with her usual care; she washed her dishes, and made Granmar tidy for the day; finally she arranged all her sewing implements on the table by the window beside her pile of work. Now she could give herself the luxury of one last look, one last estimate; for she had made a miracle of a bargain for her figs. By ten o'clock the men would be up to gather them.

It was a hazy morning; butterflies danced before her as she hastened towards the loaded trees. Reaching them, she looked up. The boughs were bare. All the figs had been gathered in the night, or at earliest dawn.

2

"Pipper!" she murmured to herself.

The ground under the trees was trampled.

Seven weeks later, on the 16th of November, this same Prudence was adding to her secreted store the fifteen cents needed to make the sum ten francs exactly—that is, two dollars. "Ten francs, a fifth of the whole! It seems 'most too lucky that I've got on so well, spite of Pipper's taking the figs. If I can keep along this way, it 'll *all* be done by the Fourth of July; not just the cow-shed taken away, but the front yard done too. My!" She sat down on a fagot to think it over. The thought was rapture; she laughed to herself and at herself for being so happy.

Some one called, "Mamma." She came out, and found Jo Vanny looking for her. Nounce and Jo Vanny were the only ones among the children who had ever called her mother.

"Oh, you're up there in the shed, are you?" said Jo Vanny. "Somehow, mamma, you look very gay."

"Yes, I'm gay," answered Prudence. "Perhaps some of these days I'll tell you why." In her heart she thought: "Jo Vanny, now, *he'd* understand; he'd feel as I do if I should explain it to him. A nice front yard he has never seen in all his life, for they don't have 'em *here*. But once he knew what it was, he'd care about it as much as I do; I know he would. He's sort of American, anyhow." It was the highest praise she could give. The boy had his cap off; she smoothed his hair. "'Pears to me you must have lost your comb," she said.

"I'm going to have it all cut off as short as can be," announced Jo Vanny, with a resolute air.

"Oh no."

"Yes, I am. Some of the other fellows have had theirs cut that way, and I'm going to, too," pursued the young stoic.

He was eighteen, rather undersized and slender, handsome as to his face, with large dark long-lashed eyes, well-cut features, white teeth, and the curly hair which Prudence had smoothed. Though he had vowed them to destruction, these love-locks were for the present arranged in the style most approved in Assisi, one thick glossy flake being brought down low over the forehead, so that it showed under his cap in a sentimental wave. He did not look much like a hard-working carpenter as he stood there dressed in dark clothes made in that singular exaggeration of the fashions which one sees only in Italy. His trousers, small at the knee, were large and wing-like at the ankle, half covering the tight shabby shoes run down at the heel and absurdly short, which, however, as they were made of patent-leather and sharply pointed at the toes, Jo Vanny considered shoes of gala aspect. His low flaring collar was surrounded by a red-satin cravat ornamented by a gilt horseshoe. He wore a ring on the little finger of each hand. In his own eyes his attire was splendid.

In the eyes of some one else also. To Prudence, as he stood there, he looked absolutely beautiful; she felt all a mother's pride rise in her heart as she surveyed him. But she must not let him see it, and she must scold him for wearing his best clothes every day.

"I didn't know it was a festa," she began.

"'Tain't. But one of the fellows has had a sister married, and they've invited us all to a big supper to-night."

"To-night isn't to-day, that I know of."

"Do you wish me to go all covered with sawdust?" said the little dandy, with a disdainful air. "Besides, I wanted to come up here."

"It *is* a good while sence we've seen you," Prudence admitted. In her heart she was delighted that he had wished to come. "Have you had your dinner, Jo Vanny?"

"All I want. I'll take a bit of bread and some wine by-and-by. But you needn't go to cooking for me, mamma. I say, tell me what it was that made you look so glad?" said the boy, curiously.

"Never you mind *now*," said Prudence, the gleam of content coming again into her eyes, and lighting up her brown, wrinkled face. She was glad that she had the ten francs; she was glad to see the boy; she was touched by his unselfishness in declining her offer of a second dinner. No other member of the family would have declined or waited to decline; the others would have demanded some freshly cooked dish immediately upon entering; Uncle Patro would have demanded three or four.

"I've brought my mandolin," Jo Vanny went on. "I've got to take it to the supper, of course, because they always want me to sing—I never can get rid of 'em! And so you can hear me, if you like. I know the new songs, and one of them I composed myself. Well, it's rather heavenly."

All Tonio's children sang like birds. Poor Prudence, who had no ear for music, had never been able to comprehend either the pleasure or the profit of the hours they gave to their carollings. But when, in his turn, her little Jo Vanny began his pipings, then she listened, or tried to listen. "Real purty, Jo Vanny," she would say, when the silence of a moment or two had assured her that his song was ended; it was her only way of knowing—the silence.

So now she brought her work out to the garden, and sewed busily while Jo Vanny sang and thrummed. Nounce, too, came out, and sat on the wall near by, listening.

At length the little singer took himself off — took himself off with his red-satin cravat, his horseshoe pin, and his mandolin under his arm. Nounce went back to the house, but Prudence sat awhile longer, using, as she always did, the very last rays of the sunset light for her sewing.

After a while she heard a step, and looked up. "Why, Gooster!—anything the matter?" she said, in surprise.

Unlike the slender little Jo Vanny, Gooster was a large, stoutly built young man, as slow in his motions as Jo Vanny was quick. He was a lethargic fellow with sombre eyes, eyes which sometimes had a gleam in them.

"There's nothing especial the matter," he answered, dully. "I think I'll go for a soldier, Denza."

"Go for a soldier? And the per-dairy?"

"I can't never go back to the podere. *She's* there, and she has taken up with Matteo. I've had my heart trampled upon, and so I've got a big hankering either to kill somebody or get killed myself; and I'll either do it here, or I'll go for a soldier and get knifed in the war."

"Mercy on us! there isn't any war now," said Prudence, dazed by these sanguinary suggestions.

"There's always a war. What else are there soldiers

for? And there's lots of soldiers. But I could get knifed here easy enough; Matteo and I—already we've had one tussle; I gave him a pretty big cut, you may depend."

Seventeen years earlier Prudence Wilkin would have laughed at the idea of being frightened by such words as these. But Mrs. Tonio Gnadagni had heard of wild deeds in Assisi, and wilder ones still among the peasants of the hill country roundabout; these singing, indolent Umbrians dealt sometimes in revenges that were very direct and primitive.

"You let Matteo alone, Gooster," she said, putting her hand on his arm; "you go straight over to Perugia and stay there. Perhaps you can get work where Parlo and Squawly are."

"I shall have it out with Matteo here, or else go for a soldier to-morrow," answered Gooster, in his lethargic tone.

"Well, go for a soldier, then."

"It don't make much difference to me which I do," Gooster went on, as if only half awake. "If I go for a soldier, I shall have to get to Florence somehow, I suppose; I shall have to have ten francs for the railroad."

"Is it ten exactly?" said Prudence. Her mind flew to her work-box, which held just that sum.

"It's ten."

"Haven't you got any money at all, Gooster?" She meant to help him on his way; but she thought that she should like to keep, if possible, a nest-egg to begin with again—say twenty cents, or ten.

Gooster felt in his pockets. "Three soldi," he replied, producing some copper coins and counting them over.

"NOUNCE TOO CAME OUT, AND SAT ON THE WALL NEAR BY, LISTENING"

"And there's nothing due you at the per-dairy?"

There was no necessity for answering such a foolish question as this, and Gooster did not answer it.

"Well, I will give you the money," said Prudence. But to-morrow 'll do, won't it? Stay here a day or two, and we'll talk it over."

While she was speaking, Gooster had turned and walked towards the garden wall. The sight of his back going from her—as though she should never see it again—threw her into a sudden panic; she ran after him and seized his arm. "I'll give you the money, Gooster; I told you I would; I've got it all ready, and it won't take a minute; promise me that you won't leave this garden till I come back."

Gooster had had no thought of leaving the garden; he had espied a last bunch of grapes still hanging on the vine, and was going to get it; that was all. "All right," he said.

Prudence disappeared. He gathered the grapes and began to eat them, turning over the bunch to see which were best. Before he had finished, Prudence came back, breathless with the haste she had made. "Here," she said; "and now you'll go straight to Florence, won't you? There's a train to-night, very soon now; you must hurry down and take that."

He let her put the money in his coat-pocket while he finished the grapes. Then he threw the stem carefully over the garden wall.

"And no doubt you'll be a brave soldier," Prudence went on, trying to speak hopefully. "Brave soldiers are thought a heap of everywhere."

"I don't know as I care what's thought," answered Gooster, indifferently. He took up his cap and put it on. "Well, good-bye, Denza. Best wishes to you. Every happiness." He shook hands with her.

Prudence stood waiting where she was for five minutes; then she followed him. It was already dark; she went down the hill rapidly, and turned into the narrow main street. A few lamps were lighted. She hastened onward, hoping every minute to distinguish somewhere in front a tall figure with slouching gait. At last, where the road turns to begin the long descent to the plain, she did distinguish it. Yes, that was certainly Gooster; he was going down the hill towards the railway station. All was well, then; she could dismiss her anxiety. She returned through the town. Stopping for a moment at an open space, she gazed down upon the vast valley, now darkening into night; here suddenly a fear came over her—he might have turned round and come back! She hurried through the town a second time, and not meeting him, started down the hill. The road went down in long zigzags. As she turned each angle she expected to see him; but she did not see him, and finally she reached the plain: there were the lights of the station facing her. She drew near cautiously, nearer and nearer, until, herself unseen in the darkness, she could peer through the window into the lighted waiting-room. If he was there, she could see him; but if he was on the platform on the other side— No; he was there. She drew a long breath of relief, and stole away.

A short distance up the hill a wheelbarrow loaded with stones had been left by the side of the road; she sat down on the stones to rest, for the first time realizing how tired she was. The train came rushing along; stopped; went on again. She watched it as long as she could see its lights. Then she rose and turned slowly up the hill, beginning her long walk home. "My," she thought, "won't Granmar be in a tantrum, though!"

When she reached the house she made a circuit, and came through the garden behind towards the back door. "I don't want to see the front yard *to-night!*" she thought.

But she was rather ashamed of this egotism.

"And they say they'll put me in prison—oh—ow!—an old man, a good old man, a suffering son of humanity like me!" moaned Uncle Pietro.

"An old man, a good old man, a suffering son of humanity like *him*," repeated Granmar, shrilly, proud of this fine language.

Suddenly she brandished her lean arms. "You Denza there, with your stored-up money made from *my* starvation—yam!—mine, how dare you be so silent, figure of a mule? Starvation! yes, indeed. Wait and I'll show you my arms, Pietro; wait and I'll show you my ribs—yam!"

"You keep yourself covered up, Granmar," said Prudence, tucking her in; "you'll do yourself a mischief in this cold weather."

"Ahi!" said Granmar, "and do I care? If I could live to see you drowned, I'd freeze and be glad. Stored-up money! stored-up money!"

"What do you know of my money?" said Prudence. Her voice trembled a little.

"She confesses it!" announced Granmar, triumphantly.

"An old ma—an," said Pietro, crouching over

Nounce's scaldino. "A good old ma—an. But—accommodate yourself."

Prudence sat down and took up her sewing. "I don't believe they'll put you in jail at all, Patro," she said; "'twon't do 'em any good, and what they want is their money. You just go to 'em and say that you'll do day's work for 'em till it's made up, and they'll let you off, I'll bet. Nine francs, is it? Well, at half a franc a day you can make it up full in eighteen days; or call it twenty-four with the festas."

"The Americans are all mercenary," remarked old Pietro, waving his hand in scorn. "Being themselves always influenced by gain, they cannot understand lofty motives nor the cold, glittering anger of the nobility. The Leoncinis are noble; they are of the old Count's blood. They do not want their money; they want revenge—they want to rack my bones."

Granmar gave a long howl.

"Favor me, my niece, with no more of your mistakes," concluded Pietro, with dignity.

"I don't believe they'd refuse," said Prudence, unmoved. "I'll go and ask 'em myself, if you like; that'll be the best way. I'll go right away now." She began to fold up her work.

At this Pietro, after putting the scaldino safely on the stove, fell down in a round heap on the floor. Never were limbs so suddenly contorted and tangled; he clawed the bricks so fiercely with his fingers that Nounce, frightened, left her bench and ran into the next room.

"What's the matter with you? I never saw such a man," said Prudence, trying to raise him.

"Let be! let be!" called out Granmar; "it's a stroke;

and you've brought it on, talking to him about working, working all day long like a horse—a good old man like that."

"I don't believe it's a stroke," said Prudence, still trying to get him up.

"My opinion is," said Granmar, sinking into sudden calm, "that he will die in ten minutes—exactly ten."

His face had indeed turned very red.

"Dear me! I suppose I shall have to run down for the doctor," said Prudence, desisting. "Perhaps he'd ought to be bled."

"You leave the doctor alone, and ease his mind," directed Granmar; "that's what he needs, sensitive as he is, and poetical too, poor fellow. You just shout in his ear that you'll pay that money, and you'll be surprised to see how it 'll loosen his joints."

Mrs. Guadagni surveyed the good old uncle for a moment. Then she bent over him and shouted in his ear, "I'll make you a hot fig-tart right away now, Patro, if you'll set up."

As she finished these words Granmar threw her scaldino suddenly into the centre of the kitchen, where it broke with a crash upon the bricks.

"He's going to get up," announced Prudence, triumphantly.

"He isn't any such thing; 'twas the scaldino shook him," responded Granmar, in a loud, admonitory tone. "He'll never get up again in *this* world unless you shout in his ear that you'll pay that money."

And in truth Pietro was now more knotted than ever.

At this moment the door opened and Jo Vanny came in. "Why, what's the matter with uncle?" he said, seeing the figure on the floor. He bent over him and tried to ease his position.

"It's a stroke," said Granmar, in a soft voice. "It'll soon be over. Hush! leave him in peace. He's dying; Denza there, she did it."

"They want me to pay the nine francs he has—lost," said Prudence. "Perhaps you have heard, Jo Vanny, that he has—lost nine francs that belonged to the Leoncinis? Nine whole francs." She looked at the lad, and he understood the look; for only the day before she had confided to him at last her long-cherished dream, and (as she had been sure he would) he had sympathized with it warmly.

"I declare I wish I had even a franc!" he said, searching his pockets desperately; "but I've only got a cigarette. Will you try a cigarette, uncle?" he shouted in the heap's ear.

"Don't you mock him," ordered Granmar (but Jo Vanny had been entirely in earnest). "He'll die soon, and Denza will be rid of him; that's what she wants. 'Twill be murder, of course; and he'll haunt us—he's always said he'd haunt somebody. But *I* ain't long for this world, so I ain't disturbed. Heaven's waiting wide open for *me*."

Jo Vanny looked a little frightened. He hesitated a moment, surveying the motionless Pietro; then he drew Prudence aside. "He's an awful wicked old man, and might really do it," he whispered; "'specially as you ain't a Catholic, mamma. I think you'd better give him the money if it'll stop him off; *I* don't mind, but it would be bad for you if he should come rapping on your windows and showing corpse-lights in the garden by-and-by."

Prudence brought her hands together sharply — a gesture of exasperation. "He ain't going to die any more than I am," she said. But she knew what life would be in that house with such a threat hanging over it, even though the execution were deferred to some vague future time. Angrily she left the room.

Jo Vanny followed her. "Come along, if you want to," she said, half impatient, half glad. She felt a sudden desire that some one besides herself should see the sacrifice, see the actual despoiling of the little box she had labored to fill. She went to the wood-shed. It was a gloomy December day, and the vegetables hanging on the walls had a dreary, stone-like look; she climbed up on a barrel, and removed the hay which filled a rough shelf; in a niche behind was her work-box; with it in her hand she climbed down again.

She gave him the box to hold while she counted out the money — nine francs. "There are twelve in all," she said.

"Then you'll have three left," said Jo Vanny.

"Yes, three." She could not help a sigh of retrospect, the outgoing nine represented so many long hours of toil.

"Let me put the box back," said the boy. It was quickly and deftly done. "Never mind about it, mamma," he said, as he jumped down. "*I*'ll help you to make it up again. I want that front yard as much as you do, now you've told me about it; I think it will be beautiful."

"Well," said Prudence, "when the flower-beds are all fixed up, and the new front path and swing gate, it *will* be kind of nice, I reckon."

"Nice?" said Jo Vanny. "That's not the word. 'Twill be an ecstasy! a smile! a dream!"

"Bless the boy, what nonsense he talks!" said the step-mother. But she loved to hear his romantic phrases all the same.

They went back to the kitchen. The sacrifice had now become a cheerful one. She bent over the heap. "Here's your nine francs, Patro," she shouted. "Come, now, come!"

Pietro felt the money in his hand. He rose quietly. "I'm nearly killed with all your yelling," he said. Then he took his hat and left the house.

"We did yell," said Prudence, picking up the fragments of the broken scaldino. "I don't quite know why we did."

"Never mind why-ing, but get supper," said Granmar. "Then go down on your knees and thank the Virgin for giving us such a merciful, mild old man as Pietro. You brought on his stroke; but what did he do? He just took what you gave him, and went away *so* forgivingly—the soul of a dove, the spice-cake soul!"

In January, the short, sharp winter of Italy had possession of Assisi.

One day towards the last of the month a bitter wind was driving through the bleak, stony little street, sending clouds of gritty, frozen dust before it. The dark, fireless dwellings were colder than the outside air, and the people, swathed in heavy layers of clothing, to which all sorts of old cloaks and shawls and mufflers had been added, were standing about near the open doors of their shops and dwellings, various prominences under apron or coat betraying the hidden scaldino, the earthen dish which Italians tightly hug in winter with the hope that the few coals it contains will keep their benumbed fingers warm. All faces were reddened and frost-bitten. The hands of the children who were too young to hold a scaldino were purple-black.

Prudence Guadagni, with her great basket strapped on her back, came along, receiving but two or three greetings as she passed. Few knew her; fewer still liked her, for was she not a foreigner and a pagan? Besides, what could you do with a woman who drank water, simple water, like a toad, and never touched wine —a woman who did not like oil, good, sweet, wholesome oil! Tonio's children were much commiserated for having fallen into such hands.

Prudence was dressed as she had been in September, save that she now wore woollen stockings and coarse shoes, and tightly pinned round her spare person a large shawl. This shawl (she called it "my Highland shawl") had come with her from America; it was green in hue, plaided; she thought it still very handsome. Her step was not as light as it had been; rheumatism had crippled her sorely.

As she left the town and turned up the hill towards home, some one who had been waiting there joined her. "Is that you, Beppo? Were you coming up to the house?" she said.

"Yes," answered Beppa, showing her white teeth in a smile. "I'm bringing you some news, Denza."

"Well, what is it? I hope you're not going to leave your place?"

"I'm going to leave it, and that's my news: I'm going to be married."

"My! it's sudden, isn't it?" said Prudence, stopping.

"Giuseppe doesn't think it's sudden," said Beppa, laughing and tossing her head; "he thinks I've been ages making up my mind. Come on, Denza, do; it's so cold!"

"I don't know Giuseppe, do I?" said Prudence, trudging on again; "I don't remember the name."

"No; I've never brought him up to the house. But the boys know him — Paolo and Pasquale; Augusto, too. He's well off, Giuseppe is; he's got beautiful furniture. He's a first-rate mason, and gets good wages, so I sha'n't have to work any more—I mean go out to work as I do now."

"Bepper, do you *like* him?" said Prudence, stopping again. She took hold of the girl's wrist and held it tightly.

"Of course I like him," said Beppa, freeing herself. "How cold your hands are, Denza—ugh!"

"You ain't marrying him for his furniture? You love him for himself — and better than any one else in the whole world?" Prudence went on, solemnly.

"Oh, how comical you do look, standing there talking about love, with your white hair and your great big basket!" said Beppa, breaking into irrepressible laughter. The cold had not made her hideous, as it makes so many Italians hideous; her face was not empurpled, her fine features were not swollen. She looked handsome. What was even more attractive on such a day, she looked warm. As her merriment ceased, a sudden change came over her. "Sainted Maria! she doubts whether I love him! Love him? Why, you poor old woman, I'd die for him to-morrow. I'd cut myself in pieces for him this minute." Her great black eyes gleamed; the color flamed in her oval cheeks; she gave a rich, angry laugh.

It was impossible to doubt her, and Prudence did not doubt. "Well, I'm right down glad, Beppa," she said, in a softened tone—"right down glad, my dear." She was thinking of her own love for the girl's father.

"I was coming up," continued Beppa, "because I thought I'd better talk it over with you."

"Of course," said Prudence, cordially. "A girl can't get married all alone; nobody ever heard of that."

"I sha'n't be much alone, for Giuseppe's family's a very big one; too big, I tell him—ten brothers and sisters. But they're all well off, that's one comfort. Of course I don't want to shame 'em."

"Of course not," said Prudence, assenting again. Then, with the awakened memories still stirring in her heart: "It's a pity your father isn't here now," she said, in a moved tone; "he'd have graced a wedding, Beppa, he was so handsome." She seldom spoke of Tonio; the subject was too sacred; but it seemed to her as if she might venture a few words to this his daughter on the eve of her own marriage.

"Yes, it's a pity, I suppose," answered Beppa. "Still, he would have been an old man now. And 'tain't likely he would have had a good coat either—that is, not such a one as I should call good."

"Yes, he would; I'd have made him one," responded Prudence, with a spark of anger. "This whole basket's full of coats now."

"I know you're wonderful clever with your needle," said the girl, glancing carelessly at the basket that weighed down her step-mother's shoulders. "I can't think how you can sew so steadily, year in, year out; I never could."

"Well, I've had to get stronger spectacles," Prudence confessed. "And they wouldn't take my old ones in exchange, neither, though they were perfectly good."

"They're robbers, all of them, at that shop," commented Beppa, agreeingly.

"Now, about your clothes, Bepper—when are you going to begin? I suppose you'll come home for a while, so as to have time to do 'em; I can help you some, and Nounce too; Nounce can sew a little."

"No, I don't think I'll come home; 'twouldn't pay me. About the clothes—I'm going to buy 'em."

"They won't be half so good," Prudence began. Then she stopped. "I'm very glad you've got the money laid up, my dear," she said, commendingly.

"Oh, but I haven't," answered Beppa, laughing. "I want to borrow it of you; that is what I came up for to-day—to tell you about it."

Prudence, her heart still softened, looked at the handsome girl with gentle eyes. "Why, of course I'll lend it to you, Bepper," she said. "How much do you want?"

"All you've got won't be any too much, I reckon," answered Beppa, with pride. "I shall have to have things nice, you know; I don't want to shame 'em."

"I've got twenty-five francs," said Prudence; "I mean I've got that amount saved and put away; 'twas for—for a purpose—something I was going to do; but 'tain't important; you can have it and welcome." Her old face, as she said this, looked almost young again. "You see, I'm so glad to have you happy," she went on. "And I can't help thinking—if your father had only lived — the first wedding in his family! However, *I'll* come—just as though I was your real mother, dear; you sha'n't miss that. I've got my Sunday gown, and five francs will buy me a pair of new shoes; I can earn 'em before the day comes, I guess."

"I'm afraid you can't," said Beppa, laughing.

"Why, when's the wedding? Not for two or three weeks, I suppose?"

"It's day after to-morrow," answered Beppa. "Everything's bought, and all I want is the money to pay for 'em; I knew I could get it of you."

"Dear me! how quick! And these shoes are really too bad; they're clear wore out, and all the cleaning in the world won't make 'em decent."

"Well, Denza, why do you want to come? You don't know any of Giuseppe's family. To tell the truth, I never supposed you'd care about coming, and the table's all planned out for (at Giuseppe's sister's), and there ain't no place for you."

"And you didn't have one saved?"

"I never thought you'd care to come. You see they're different, they're all well off, and you don't like people who are well off—who wear nice clothes. You never wanted *us* to have nice clothes, and you like to go barefoot."

"No, I don't!" said Prudence.

"'Tany rate, one would think you did; you always go so in summer. But even if you had new shoes, none of your clothes would be good enough; that bonnet, now—"

"My bonnet? Surely my *bonnet's* good?" said the New England woman; her voice faltered, she was struck on a tender point.

"Well, people laugh at it," answered Beppa, composedly.

They had now reached the house. "You go in," said Prudence; "I'll come presently."

She went round to the wood-shed, unstrapped her basket, and set it down; then she climbed up on the barrel, removed the hay, and took out her work-box. Emptying its contents into her handkerchief, she descended, and, standing there, counted the sum—twenty-seven francs, thirty centimes. "'Twon't be any too much; she don't want to shame 'em." She made a package of the money with a piece of brown paper, and, entering the kitchen, she slipped it unobserved into Beppa's hand.

"Seems to me," announced Granmar from the bed, "that when a girl comes to tell her own precious Granmar of her *wedding*, she ought in decency to be offered a bite of something to eat. Any one but Denza would think so. Not that it's anything to me."

"Very well, what will you have?" asked Prudence, wearily. Freed from her bonnet and shawl, it could be seen that her once strong figure was much bent; her fingers had grown knotted, enlarged at the joints, and clumsy; years of toil had not aged her so much as these recent nights—such long nights!—of cruel rheumatic pain.

Granmar, in a loud voice, immediately named a succulent dish; Prudence began to prepare it. Before it was ready, Jo Vanny came in.

"You knew I was up here, and you've come mousing up for an invitation," said Beppa, in high good-humor. "I was going to stop and invite you on my way back, Giovanni; there's a nice place saved for you at the supper."

"Yes, I knew you were up here, and I've brought you a wedding-present," answered the boy. "I've brought one for mamma, too." And he produced two silk handkerchiefs, one of bright colors, the other of darker hue.

"Is the widow going to be married, too?" said Beppa. "Who under heaven's the man?"

In spite of the jesting, Prudence's face showed that she was pleased; she passed her toil-worn hand over the handkerchief softly, almost as though its silk were the cheek of a little child. The improvised feast was turned into a festival now, and of her own accord she added a second dish; the party, Granmar at the head, devoured unknown quantities. When at last there was nothing left, Beppa, carrying her money, departed.

"You know, Jo Vanny, you hadn't ought to leave your work so often," said Prudence, following the boy into the garden when he took leave; she spoke in an expostulating tone.

"Oh, I've got money," said Jo Vanny, loftily; "*I* needn't crawl." And carelessly he showed her a gold piece.

But this sudden opulence only alarmed the stepmother. "Why, where did you get that?" she said, anxiously.

"How frightened you look! Your doubts offend me," pursued Jo Vanny, still with his grand air. "Haven't I capacities?—hasn't Heaven sent me a swarming genius? Wasn't I the acclaimed, even to laurel crowns, of my entire class?"

This was true: Jo Vanny was the only one of Tonio's children who had profited by the new public schools.

"And now what shall I get for you, mamma?" the boy went on, his tone changing to coaxing; "I want to get you something real nice; what will you have? A new dress to go to Beppa's wedding in?"

For an instant Prudence's eyes were suffused. "I ain't going, Jo Vanny; they don't want me."

"They *shall* want you!" declared Jo Vanny, fiercely.

"I didn't mean that; I don't want to go anyhow; I've got too much rheumatism. You don't know," she went on, drawn out of herself for a moment by the need of sympathy—"you don't know how it does grip me at night sometimes, Jo Vanny! No; you go to the supper, and tell me all about it afterwards; I like to hear you tell about things just as well as to go myself."

Jo Vanny passed his hand through his curly locks with an air of desperation. "There it is again—my gift of relating, of narrative; it follows me wherever I go. What will become of me with such talents? I shall never die in my bed; nor have my old age in peace."

"You go 'long!" said Prudence (or its Italian equivalent). She gave him a push, laughing.

Jo Vanny drew down his cap, put his hands deep in his pockets, and thus close-reefed scudded down the hill in the freezing wind to the shelter of the streets below.

By seven o'clock Nounce and Granmar were both asleep; it was the most comfortable condition in such weather. Prudence adjusted her lamp, put on her strong spectacles, and sat down to sew. The great brick stove gave out no warmth; it was not intended

to heat the room; its three yards of length and one
yard of breadth had apparently been constructed for
the purpose of holding and heating one iron pot. The
scaldino at her feet did not keep her warm; she put
on her Highland shawl. After a while, as her head
(scantily covered with thin white hair) felt the cold
also, she went to get her bonnet. As she took it from
the box she remembered Beppa's speech, and the pang
came back; in her own mind that bonnet had been the
one link that still united her with her old Ledham re-
spectability, the one possession that distinguished her
from all these "papish" peasants, with their bare
heads and frowzy hair. It was not new, of course, as
it had come with her from home. But what signified
an old-fashioned shape in a community where there
were no shapes of any kind, new or old? At least it
was always a bonnet. She put it on, even now from
habit pulling out the strings carefully, and pinning the
loops on each side of her chin. Then she went back
and sat down to her work again.

At eleven o'clock Granmar woke. "Yam! how cold
my legs are! Denza, are you there? You give me
that green shawl of yours directly; precisely, I am
dying."

Prudence came out from behind her screen, lamp in
hand. "I've got it on, Granmar; it's so cold setting up
sewing. I'll get you the blanket from my bed."

"I don't want it; it's as hard as a brick. You give
me that shawl; if you've got it on, it'll be so much
the warmer."

"I'll give you my other flannel petticoat," suggested
Prudence.

"And I'll tear it into a thousand pieces," responded

Granmar, viciously. "You give me that shawl, or the next time you leave Nounce alone here, *she* shall pay for it."

Granmar was capable of frightening poor little Nounce into spasms. Prudence took off the shawl and spread it over the bed, while Granmar grinned silently.

Carrying the lamp, Prudence went into the bedroom to see what else she could find to put on. She first tried the blanket from her bed; but as it was a very poor one, partly cotton, it was stiff (as Granmar had said), and would not stay pinned; the motion of her arms in sewing would constantly loosen it. In the way of wraps, except her shawl, she possessed almost nothing; so she put on another gown over the one she wore, pinned her second flannel petticoat round her shoulders, and over that a little cloak that belonged to Nounce; then she tied a woollen stocking round her throat, and crowned with her bonnet, and carrying the blanket to put over her knees, she returned to her work.

"I declare I'm clean tired out," she said to herself; "my feet are like ice. I wouldn't sew any longer such a bitter night if it warn't that that work-box 'ain't got a thing in it. I can't bear to think of it empty. But as soon as I've got a franc or two to begin with again, I'll stop these extry hours."

But they lasted on this occasion until two o'clock.

"It don't seem as if I'd ever known it *quite* so baking as it is to-night." It was Prudence who spoke; she spoke to Nounce; she must speak to some one.

Nounce answered with one of her patient smiles. She often smiled patiently, as though it were something which she was expected to do.

Prudence was sitting in the wood-shed resting; she had been down to town to carry home some work. Now the narrow streets there, thrown into shade by the high buildings on each side, were a refuge from the heat; now the dark houses, like burrows, gave relief to eyes blinded by the yellow glare. It was the 30th of August. From the first day of April the broad valley and this brown hill had simmered in the hot light, which filled the heavens and lay over the earth day after day, without a change, without a cloud, relentless, splendid; each month the ground had grown warmer and drier, the roads more white, more deep in dust; insect life, myriad legged and winged, had been everywhere; under the stones lurked the scorpions.

In former summers here this never-ending light, the long days of burning sunshine, the nights with the persistent moon, the importunate nightingales, and the magnificent procession of the stars had sometimes driven the New England woman almost mad; she had felt as if she must bury her head in the earth somewhere to find the blessed darkness again, to feel its cool pressure against her tired eyes. But this year these things had not troubled her; the possibility of realizing her long-cherished hope at last had made the time seem short, had made the heat nothing, the light forgotten; each day, after fifteen hours of toil, she had been sorry that she could not accomplish more.

But she had accomplished much; the hope was now almost a reality. "Nounce," she said, "do you know I'm 'most too happy to live. I shall have to tell you: I've got *all* the money saved up at last, and the men are coming to-morrow to take away the cow-shed. Think of that!"

Nounce thought of it; she nodded appreciatively. Prudence took the girl's slender hand in hers and went on: "Yes, to-morrow. And it'll cost forty-eight francs. But with the two francs for wine-money it will come to fifty in all. By this time to-morrow night it will be gone!" She drew in her breath with a satisfied sound. "I've got seventy-five francs in all, Nounce. When Bepper married, of course I knew I couldn't get it done for Fourth of July. And so I thought I'd try for Thanksgiving—that is, Thanksgiving *time;* I never know the exact day now. Well, here it's only the last day of August, and the cow-shed will be gone to-morrow. Then will come the new fence; and then the fun, the real fun, Nounce, of laying out our front yard! It'll have a nice straight path down to the gate, currant bushes in neat rows along the sides, two big flowerin' shrubs, and little flower beds bordered with box. I tell you you won't know your own house when you come in a decent gate and up a nice path to the front door; all these years we've been slinking in and out of a back door, just as though we didn't have no front one. I don't believe myself in tramping in and out of a front door *every* day; but on Sundays, now, when we have on our best clothes, we shall come in and out respectably. You'll feel like another person, Nounce; and I'm sure *I* shall—I shall feel like Ledham again—my!" And Prudence actually laughed.

Still holding Nounce's hand, she went round to the front of the house.

The cow-shed was shedding forth its usual odors; Prudence took a stone and struck a great resounding

"STILL HOLDING NOUNCE'S HAND, SHE WENT ROUND TO THE FRONT OF THE HOUSE"

blow on its side. She struck with so much force that she hurt her hand. "Never mind—it done me good!" she said, laughing again.

She took little Nounce by the arm and led her down the descent. "I shall have to make the front walk all over," she explained. "And here 'll be the gate, down here—a swing one. And the path will go from here straight up to the door. Then the fence will go along here—palings, you know, painted white; a good clean American white, with none of these yellows in it, you may depend. And over there—and there—along the sides, the fence will be just plain boards, notched at the top; the currant bushes will run along there. In the middle, here—and here—will be the big flowerin' shrubs. And then the little flower-beds bordered with box. Oh, Nounce, I can't hardly believe it—it will be so beautiful! I really can't!"

Nounce waited a moment. Then she came closer to her step-mother, and after looking quickly all about her, whispered, "You needn't if you don't want to; there's here yet to believe."

"It's just as good as here," answered Prudence, almost indignantly. "I've got the money, and the bargain's all made; nothing could be surer than that."

The next morning Nounce was awakened by the touch of a hand on her shoulder. It was her step-mother. "I've got to go down to town," she said, in a low tone. "You must try to get Granmar's breakfast yourself, Nounce; do it as well as you can. And—and I've changed my mind about the front yard; it'll be done some time, but not now. And we won't talk any more about it for the present, Nounce; that 'll please me most; and you're a good girl, and always want to please me, I know."

She kissed her, and went out softly.

In October three Americans came to Assisi. Two came to sketch the Giotto frescos in the church of St. Francis; the third came for her own entertainment; she read Symonds, and wandered about exploring the ancient town.

One day her wanderings led her to the little Guadagni house on the height. The back gate was open, and through it she saw an old woman staggering, then falling, under the weight of a sack of potatoes which she was trying to carry on her back.

The American rushed in to help her. "It's much too heavy for you," she said, indignantly, after she had given her assistance. "Oh dear—I mean, *è troppo grave*," she added, elevating her voice.

"Are you English?" said the old woman. "I'm an American myself; but I ain't deef. The sack warn't too heavy; it's only that I ain't so strong as I used to be—it's perfectly redeculous!"

"You're not strong at all," responded the stranger, still indignantly, looking at the wasted old face and trembling hands.

A week later Prudence was in bed, and an American nurse was in charge.

This nurse, whose name was Baily, was a calm woman with long strong arms, monotonous voice, and distinct New England pronunciation; her Italian (which was grammatically correct) was delivered in the vowels of Vermont.

One day, soon after her arrival, she remarked to Granmar, "That yell of yours, now—that yam—is a very unusual thing."

"My sufferings draw it from me," answered Granmar, flattered by the adjective used. "I'm a very pious woman; I don't want to swear."

"I think I have never heard it equalled, except possibly in lunatic asylums," Marilla Baily went on. "I have had a great deal to do with lunatic asylums; I am what is called an expert; that is, I find out people who are troublesome, and send them there; I never say much about it, but just make my observations; then, when I've got the papers out, whiff!—off they go."

Granmar put her hand over her mouth apprehensively, and surveyed her in silence. From that time the atmosphere of the kitchen was remarkably quiet.

Marilla Baily had come from Florence at the bidding of the American who had helped to carry the potatoes. This American was staying at the Albergo del Subasio with her friends who were sketching Giotto; but she spent most of her time with Prudence Wilkin.

"You see, I minded it because it was *him*," Prudence explained to her one day, at the close of a long conversation. "For I'd always been so fond of the boy; I had him first when he warn't but two years old—just a baby—and *so* purty and cunning! He always called me mamma—the only one of the children, 'cept poor Nounce there, that really seemed to care for me. And I cared everything for him. I went straight down to town and hunted all over. But he warn't to be found. I tried it the next day, and the next, not saying what I wanted, of course; but nobody knew where he was, and at last I made up my mind that he'd gone away. For three weeks I waited; I was almost dead; I couldn't do nothing; I felt as if I was broke in two, and only the skin held me together. Every morning I'd say to myself, 'There'll certainly come a letter to-day, and he'll tell me all about it.' But the letter didn't come, and didn't come. From the beginning, of course, I knew it was him—I couldn't help but know; Jo Vanny was the only person in the whole world that knew where it was. For I'd showed it to him one day—the work-box, I mean—and let him put it back in the hole behind the hay—'twas the time I took the money out for Patro. At last I did get a letter, and he said as how he'd meant to put it back the very next morning, sure. But something had happened, so he couldn't, and so he'd gone away. And now he was working just as hard as he could, he said, so as to be able to pay it back soon; he hardly played on his mandolin at all now, he said, he was working so hard. You see, he wasn't bad himself, poor little fellow, but he was led away by bad men; gambling's an awful thing, once you get started in it, and he was sort of *drove* to take that money, meaning all the while to pay it back. Well, of course I felt ever so much better just as soon as I got that letter. And I began to work again. But I didn't get on as well as I'd oughter; I can't understand why. That day, now, when I first saw you—when you ran in to help me—I hadn't been feeling sick at all; there warn't no sense in my tumbling down that way all of a sudden."

One lovely afternoon in November Prudence's bed was carried out to the front of the dark little house.

The cow-shed was gone. A straight path, freshly paved, led down to a swing gate set in a new paling fence, flower beds bordered the path, and in the centre of the open spaces on each side there was a large rose bush. The fence was painted a glittering white; there had been an attempt at grass; currant bushes in straight rows bordered the two sides.

Prudence lay looking at it all in peaceful silence. "It's mighty purty," she said at last, with grateful emphasis. "It's everything I planned to have, and a great deal nicer than I could have done it myself, though I thought about it goodness knows how many years!"

"I'm not surprised that you thought about it," the American answered. "It was the view you were longing for—fancy its having been cut off so long by that miserable stable! But now you have it in perfection."

"You mean the view of the garden," said Prudence. "There wasn't much to look at before; but now it's real sweet."

"No; I mean the great landscape all about us here,' responded the American, surprised. She paused. Then seeing that Prudence did not lift her eyes, she began to enumerate its features, to point them out with her folded parasol. "That broad Umbrian plain, Prudence, with those tall slender trees; the other towns shining on their hills, like Perugia over there; the gleam of the river; the velvety blue of the mountains; the color of it all—I do believe it is the very loveliest view in the whole world!"

"I don't know as I've ever noticed it much—the view," Prudence answered. She turned her eyes towards the horizon for a moment. "You see I was always thinking about my front yard."

"The front yard is very nice now," said the American. "I am so glad you are pleased; we couldn't get snowballs or Missouri currant, so we had to take roses." She paused; but she could not give up the subject without one more attempt. " You have probably noticed the view without being aware of it," she went on; " it is so beautiful that you must have noticed it. If you should leave it you would find yourself missing it very much, I dare say."

"Mebbe," responded Prudence. " Still, I ain't so sure. The truth is, I don't care much for these Eyetalian views; it seems to me a poor sort of country, and always did." Then, wishing to be more responsive to the tastes of this new friend, if she could be so honestly, she added, " But I like views, as a general thing; there was a very purty view from Sage's Hill, I remember."

" Sage's Hill?"

" Yes; the hill near Ledham. You told me you knew Ledham. You could see all the fields and medders of Josiah Strong's farm, and Deacon Mayberry's too; perfectly level, and not a stone in 'em. And the turnpike for miles and miles, with three toll-gates in sight. Then, on the other side, there were the factories to make it lively. It was a sweet view."

A few days afterwards she said: " People tell us that we never get what we want in this world, don't they? But I'm fortunate. I think I've always been purty fortunate. I got my front yard, after all."

A week later, when they told her that death was near, " My! I'd no idea I was so sick as that," she whispered. Then, looking at them anxiously, " What 'll become of Nounce?"

They assured her that Nounce should be provided for. " You know you have to be sorter patient with her," she explained; "but she's growing quicker-witted everyday."

Later, "I should like so much to see Jo Vanny," she murmured, longingly; "but of course I can't. You must get Bepper to send him my love, my dearest, dearest love."

Last of all, as her dulled eyes turned from the little window and rested upon her friend: "It seems a pity—But perhaps I shall find—"

NEPTUNE'S SHORE

I

OLD Mrs. Preston had not been able to endure the hotel at Salerno. She had therefore taken, for two months, this house on the shore.

"I might as well be here as anywhere, saddled as I am with the Abercrombies," she remarked to her cousin, Isabella Holland. "Arthur may really do something: I have hopes of Arthur. But as to Rose, Hildegarde, and Dorothea, I shall plainly have to drag them about with me, and drag them about with me, year after year, in the hope that the constant seeing of so many straight statues, to say nothing of pictures, may at last teach them to have spines. Here they are now; did you ever see such shoulders, or rather such a lack of them? Hildegarde, child, come here a moment," she added, as the three girls drew near. "I have an idea. Don't you think you could *hold* your shoulders up a little? Try it now; put them up high, as though you were shrugging them; and expand your chest too; you mustn't cramp that. There!—that is what I mean; don't you think, my dear, that you could keep yourself so?"

Hildegarde, with her shoulders elevated and her long chin run out, began to blush painfully, until her milk-white face was dyed red. "I am afraid I could not keep myself so *long*, aunt," she answered, in a low voice.

"Never mind; let them down, then: it's of no use," commented Mrs. Preston, despairingly. "Go and dance for twenty-five minutes in the upper hall, all of you. And dance as hard as you can."

The three girls, moving lifelessly, went down the echoing vaulted corridor. They were sisters, the eldest not quite sixteen, all three having the same lank figures with sloping shoulders and long thin throats, and the same curiously white, milk-white skin. Orphans, they had been sent with their brother Arthur to their aunt, Mrs. Octavia Preston, five years before, having come to her from one of the West India Islands, their former home.

"Those girls have done nothing but eat raw meat, take sea baths, and practise calisthenics and dancing ever since I first took charge of them," Mrs. Preston was accustomed to remark to intimate friends; "yet look at them now! Of course I could not send them to school—they would only grow lanker. So I take them about with me patiently, governess and all."

But Mrs. Preston was not very patient.

The three girls having disappeared, Isabella thought the occasion favorable for a few words upon another subject. "Do you like to have Paulie riding so often with Mr. Ash, Cousin Octavia? I can't help being distressed about it."

"Don't be Mistering John Ash, I beg; no one in the world but you, Isabella, would dream of doing it—a great swooping creature like that—the horseman in 'Heliodorus.'"

"You mean Raphael's fresco? Oh, Cousin Octavia,

how can you think so? Raphael — such a religious painter, and John Ash, who looks so dissipated!"

"Did I say he didn't look dissipated? I said he could ride. John Ash is one of the most dissipated-looking youths I have ever met," pursued Mrs. Preston, comfortably. "The clever sort, not the brutal."

"And you don't mind Paulie's being with him?"

"Pauline Euphemia Graham has been married, Pauline Euphemia Graham is a widow; it ill becomes those who have not had a tithe of her experience (though they may be *much* older) to set themselves up as judges of her conduct."

Mrs. Preston had a deep rich voice, and slow enunciation; her simplest sentences, therefore, often took on the tone of declamation, and when she held forth at any length, it was like a Gregorian chant.

"Oh, I didn't mean to judge, I'm sure," said Isabella; "I only meant that it would be such a pity— such a bad match for dear Paulie in case she should be thinking of marrying again. Even if one were sure of John Ash—and certainly the reverse is the case— look at his mother! I am interested, naturally, as Paulie is my first cousin, you know."

"Do you mean that your first cousin's becoming Mrs. John Ash might endanger your own matrimonial prospects?"

"Oh dear no," said poor little Isabella, shrinking back to her embroidery. She was fifty, small, plain, extremely good. In her heart she wished that people would take the tone that Isabella had "never cared to marry."

"Here is Pauline now, I think," said Mrs. Preston, as a figure appeared at the end of the hall.

Isabella was afraid to add, "And going out to ride again!" But it was evident that Mrs. Graham intended to ride: she wore her habit.

"I wish you were going, too," she said to Mrs. Preston, pausing in the doorway with her skirt uplifted. Her graceful figure in the closely fitting habit was a pleasant sight to see.

"Thanks, my dear; I should enjoy going very much if I were a little more slender."

"You are magnificent as you are," responded Pauline, admiringly.

And in truth the old lady was very handsome, with her thick silver hair, fine eyes with heavy black eyebrows, and well-cut aquiline profile. Her straight back, noble shoulders, and beautiful hands took from her massive form the idea of unwieldiness.

"Isabella—you who are always posing for enthusiasm—when will you learn to say anything so genuine as that?" chanted Cousin Octavia's deep voice. "I mention it merely on your account, as a question of styles conversational. Here is Isabella, who thinks John Ash so dissipated, Pauline; she fears that it may injure the family connection if you marry him. I have told her that no one here was thinking of marrying or of giving in marriage; if she has such ideas, she must have brought them with her from Florence. There are a great many old maids in Florence."

"I can only answer for myself: I certainly am not thinking of marriage," said Pauline, laughing, as she went down the stairs.

"Oh, Cousin Octavia, you have set Pauline against me!" exclaimed Isabella, in distress.

"Don't be an idiot; Pauline isn't against any one:

she doesn't care enough about it. She is a good deal for herself, I acknowledge; but she's not against any one. Pauline bears no malice; she is delightfully uncertain; she hasn't a theory in the world to live up to; in addition, to have her in the house is like going to the play all the time—she *is* such a stupendous liar!"

Isabella, who was punching round holes in a linen band with an implement of ivory, stopped punching. "I am sure poor Paulie—"

"Am I to sit through a defence of Pauline Euphemia Graham, born Preston, at your hands, Isabella? Pray spare me that. I am much more Pauline's friend than you ever can be. Did I say that she lied? Nature has given her a face that speaks one language and a mind that speaks another; she, of course, follows the language of her mind; but others follow that of her face, and this makes the play. Eh!—what noise is that?"

"We have come to pay you a visit, Aunt Octavia," called a boyish voice; its owner was evidently mounting the stairs three at a time: now he was in the room. "They're all down at the door—Freemantle and Gates and Beckett. And what do you think—we've got Griff!"

"Griff himself?" said Aunt Octavia, benevolently, as the lad, with a very pretty gallantry, bent to kiss her hand.

"Yes, Griff himself; you may be sure we're drawing like mad. Griff has come down from Paris for only three weeks, and he says he will go with us to Pæstum, and all about here—to Amalfi, Ravello, and everywhere. But of course Pæstum's the stunner."

"Yes, of course Pæstum's the stunner," repeated Aunt Octavia, as if trying it in Shakespearian tones.

"I say, may they come up?" Arthur went on.

They came up — three boys of seventeen and eighteen, and Griffith Carew, who was ten years older. These three youths, with Arthur Abercrombie, were studying architecture at the Beaux-Arts, Paris; this spring they had given to a tour in Italy for the purpose of making architectural drawings. Griffith Carew was also an architect, but a full-fledged one. His indomitable perseverance and painstaking accuracy caused all the younger men to respect him; the American students went further; they were sure that Griff had only to "let himself go," and the United States would bloom from end to end with City Halls of beauty unparalleled. In the mean time Griff, while waiting for the City Halls perhaps, was so kind-hearted and jovial and unselfish that they all adored him for that too. It was a master-treat, therefore, to Arthur and his companions, to have their paragon to themselves for a while on this temple-haunted shore.

Griff sat down placidly, and began to talk to Aunt Octavia. He was of medium height, his figure heavy and strong; he had a dark complexion and thick features, lighted by pleasant brown eyes, and white teeth that gleamed when he smiled.

Aunt Octavia was gracious to Griff; she had always distinguished him from "Arthur's horde." This was not in the least because the horde considered him the architect of the future. Aunt Octavia did not care much about the future; her tests were those of the past. She had known Griff's mother, and the persons whose mothers Aunt Octavia had known — ah, that was a certificate!

II

In the meanwhile Pauline Graham had left Salerno behind her, and was flying over the plain with John Ash.

Pauline all her life had had a passion for riding at breakneck speed; one of the explanations of her fancy for Ash lay in the fact that, having the same passion himself, he enabled her to gratify her own. Whenever she had felt in the mood during the past five weeks there had always been a horse and a mounted escort at her door. Upon this occasion, after what they called an inspiring ride (to any one else a series of mad gallops), they had dismounted at a farm-house, and leaving their horses, had strolled down to the shore. It was a lovely day, towards the last of March; the sea, of the soft misty blue of the southern Mediterranean, stretched out before them without a sail; at their feet the same clear water laved the shore in long smooth wavelets, hardly a foot high, whose gentle roll upon the sands had an indescribably caressing sound. There was no one in sight. It is a lonely coast. Pauline stood, gazing absently over the blue.

"Sit down for a moment," suggested Ash.

"Not now."

"Not now? When do you expect to be here again?"

She came back to the present, laughing. "True; but I did not mean that; I meant that you were not the ideal companion for sea-side musing; you never meditate. I venture to say you have never quoted poetry in your life."

"No; I live my poetry," John Ash responded.

"But for a ride you are perfect; for a rush over the plain, in the teeth of the wind, I have never had any one approaching you. You are a cavalier of the gods."

"Have you had many?"

"Cavaliers?—plenty. Of the gods?—no."

"Plenty! I reckon you have," said Ash, half to himself.

"Would you wish me to have had few? You must remember that I have been in many countries and have seen many peoples. I shouldn't have appreciated *you* otherwise; I should have thought you dangerous—horrible! There is Isabella, who has not been in many countries; Isabella is sure that you are 'so dissipated.'"

"Dissipated!—mild term!"

"Then you acknowledge it?"

"Freely."

Pauline looked about for a rock of the right height, and finding one, seated herself, and began to draw off her gloves. "Some time—in some other existence—will you come and tell me how it has paid you, please? You are so preternaturally intelligent, and you have such a will of your own, that you cannot have fallen into it from stupidity, as so many do." Her gloves off, she began to tighten the braids of her hair, loosened by the gallop.

"It pays as it goes; it makes one forget for a moment the hideous tiresomeness of existence. But you put your question off to some other life; you have no intention, then, of redeeming me in this?"

"I shouldn't succeed. In the first place, I have no influence—"

"You know I am your slave," said Ash; his voice suddenly deepened.

"And how much of a slave shall you be to the next pretty peasant girl you meet?" Mrs. Graham demanded, turning towards him, both hands still occupied with her hair.

"I don't deny that. But it has nothing to do with the subject."

"In one way I know it has not," she answered, after she had fastened the last braid in its place with a long gold pin.

"How right I was to like you! You understand of yourself the thing that so few women can ever be brought to comprehend. Well, if you acknowledge that it makes no difference—I mean about the peasant girls—we're just where we were; I am your slave, yet you have no desire to reclaim me. I believe you like me better as I am," he added, abruptly.

"Do you want me to tell you that you are impertinent?" demanded Pauline, with her lovely smile, that always contradicted in its sweetness any apparent rebuke expressed by her words. "Do I know what you are in reality, or care to know? I know what you seem, and what you seem is admirable, perfect, for these rides of ours, the most enchanting rides I have ever had."

"And the rides are to be the end of it? You wouldn't care for me elsewhere?"

"Ah!" said Pauline, rising and drawing on her gloves, "you wouldn't care for *me*. In Paris I am altogether another person; I am not at all as you see me here. In Paris you would call me a doll. Come, don't dissect the happy present; enjoy it as I do. 'He only is rich who owns the day,' and we own this—for our ride.

"'YOU KNOW I AM YOUR SLAVE'"

"'I hear the hoofs upon the hill;
I hear them fainter, fainter still,'"

she sang in her clear voice. "The idea of that old Virginia song coming to me here!"

"This talk about reclaiming and reforming is all bosh," remarked Ash, leaning back against a high fragment of rock, with his hands in his pockets. "I am what I am because I choose to be, that's all. The usual successes of American life, what are they? I no longer care a rap about them, because I've had them, or at least have seen them within my reach. I came up from nothing; I got an education—no matter now how I got it; I studied law. In ten years I had won such a position in my profession (my branch of it—I was never an office lawyer) that everything lay open before me. It was only a question of a certain number of years. Not only was this generally prophesied, but I knew it myself. But by that time I had found out the unutterable stupidity of people and their pursuits; I couldn't help despising them. I had made enough to make my mother comfortable, and there came over me a horror of a plodding life. I said to myself, 'What is the use of it?' Of pleasure there was no question. But I could go back to that plodding life to-morrow if I chose. Don't you believe it, Pauline?"

"Yes."

"Yet you don't say—try?"

"Try, by all means."

"At a safe distance from you!"

"Yes, at a safe distance from me," Pauline answered. "I should do you no good; I am not enough in earnest. I am never in earnest long about anything. I am changeable, too — you have no idea how changeable. There has been no opportunity to show you."

"Is that a threat? You know that I am deeply in love with you." He did not move as he said this, but his eyes were fixed passionately upon her face.

"I neither know it nor believe it; it is with you simply as it is with me—there is no one else here." She stood there watching the wavelets break at her feet. Nothing in her countenance corresponded in the least with the description she had just given of herself.

"How you say that! What am I to think of you? You have a face to worship: does it lie?" said Ash.

"Oh, my face!" She turned, and began to cross the field towards the farm.

"It shouldn't have that expression, then," he said, joining her, and walking by her side. "I don't believe you know what it is yourself, Pauline—that expression. It seems to say as you talk, coming straight from those divine lips, those sweet eyes: 'I could love you. Be good and I will.' Why, you have almost made *me* determine to be 'good' again, almost made *me* begin to dream of going back to that plodding life that I loathe. And you don't know what I am."

Mrs. Graham did not answer; she did not look up, though she knew that his head was bent beseechingly towards her.

John Ash was obliged to bend; he was very tall. His figure was rather thin, and he had a slouching gait; his broad shoulders and well-knit muscles showed that he had plenty of force, and his slouching step seemed to come from laziness, as though he found it too much trouble to plant his feet firmly, to carry his long length erect. He was holding his hat in his hand, and the light from the sea showed his face clearly, its good points and its bad. His head was well shaped, covered with thick brown hair, closely cut; but, in spite of the shortness, many silver threads could be seen on the brown—a premature silver, as he was not yet thirty-five. His face was beardless, thin, with a bold eagle-like outline, and strong, warm blue eyes, the blue eyes that go with a great deal of color. Ordinarily, Ash had now but little color; that is, there was but little red; his complexion had a dark brown hue; there were many deep lines. The mouth, the worst feature, had a cynical droop; the jaw conveyed suggestions that were not agreeable. The expression of the whole countenance was that of recklessness and cleverness, both of no common order. Of late the recklessness had often changed into a more happy merriment when he was with Pauline, the careless merriment of a boy; one could see then plainly how handsome he must have been before the lines, and the heaviness, and, alas! the evil, had come to darken his youth, and to sadden (for so it must have been) his silent, frightened-looking mother.

They reached the farm; he led out the horses, and mounted her. She gathered up the reins; but he still held the bridle. "How tired you look!" he said.

Her face was flushed slightly, high on the cheeks close under the eyes; between the fair eyebrows a perpendicular line was visible; for the moment, she showed to the full her thirty years.

"Yes, I am tired; and it's dangerous to tire me," she answered, smiling. She had recovered her light-hearted carelessness.

Ash still looked at her. A sudden conviction seemed to seize him. "Don't throw me over, Pauline," he pleaded. And as he spoke, on his brown, deeply lined face there was an expression which was boyishly young and trusting.

"As I told you, so long as there is no one else," Pauline answered.

The next moment they were flying over the plain.

III

The *table d'hôte* of the Star of Italy, the Salerno inn from whose mysteries (of eels and chestnuts) Mrs. Preston had fled—this unctuous *table d'hôte* had been unusually brilliant during this month of March; upon several occasions there had been no less than fifteen travellers present, and the operatic young landlord himself, with his affectionate smile, had come in to hand the peas.

The most unnoticed person was always a tall woman of fifty-five, who, entering with noiseless step, slipped into her chair so quickly and furtively that it seemed as if she were afraid of being seen standing upon her feet. Once in her place, she ate sparingly, looking neither to the right nor the left, holding her knife and fork with care, and laying them down cautiously, as though she were trying not to waken some one who was asleep. But the *table d'hôte* of the Star of Italy was never asleep; the travellers, English and American, could not help feeling that they were far from home on this shore where so recently brigands had prowled. It is well known that this feeling promotes conversation.

One evening a pink-cheeked woman, who wore a little round lace cap perched on the top of her smooth gray hair, addressed the silent stranger at her left hand. "You have been to Pæstum, I dare say?" she said, in her pleasant English voice.

"No."

"But you are going, probably? Directly we came, yesterday morning, we engaged horses and started at once."

"I don't know as I care about going."

"Not to see the temples?"

"I didn't know as there were temples," murmured the other, shyly.

"Fancy! But you really ought to go, you know," the pleasant voice resumed, doing a little missionary work (which can never come amiss). "The temples are well worth seeing; they are Greek."

"I've been ter see a good many buildings already: in Paris there were a good many; my son took me," the tall woman answered, her tone becoming more assured as she mentioned "my son."

"But these temples are—are rather different. I was saying to our neighbor here that she really ought on no account to miss going down to Pæstum," the fresh-faced Englishwoman continued, addressing her husband, who sat next to her on the right, for the moment very busy with his peas (which were good, but a little oily). "The drive is not difficult. And we found it most interesting."

"Interesting? It may well be interesting; finest Greek remains outside of Athens," answered the husband, a portly Warwickshire vicar. He bent forward a little to glance past his wife at this ignorer of temples at her other hand. "American," he said to himself, and returned to his peas.

to him that this nomad life abroad was causing her any suffering. Her shyness, her dread of being looked at, her dread of foreign servants, he did not fully see, because when he was present she controlled them; when he was present, also, in a great measure, they disappeared. He knew that she would not have had one moment's content had he left her behind him, even if he had left her in the finest house his money could purchase; so he took her with him, and travelled slowly, for her sake, making no journeys that she could not make, sending forward to engage the best rooms for her at the inns where he intended to stop.

That he had not taken her to Pæstum was not an evidence of neglect. During the first months of their wanderings he had been at pains to take her everywhere he had thought that she would enjoy it. But Mrs. Ash had enjoyed nothing—save the going about on her son's arm. If he left her alone amid the most exquisite scenery in the world, she did not even see the scenery; she thought a dusty jaunt in a horse-car "very pleasant" if John was there. So at last John gave her his simple presence often, but troubled her with descriptions and excursions no more.

Dumb, shy, hopelessly out of her element as she was, this mother had, on the whole, enjoyed her two years abroad. The reason was found in the fact that she could say to herself, or rather could hope to herself, that John was more "steady" over here.

The rustic term covered much—the days and the nights when John had not been "steady."

These six weeks at Salerno particularly had been a season of blessed repose to Azubah Ash; the days had gone by so peacefully that life had become almost comfortable to her again, in spite of the ordeal of dinner. She had even been beguiled into thinking a little of the future—of the farm she should like to have some day, with fruit and cream and vegetables—yes, especially vegetables; and she dreamed of an old pleasure of her youth, that of hunting for little round artichokes in the cool brown earth. John had been contented all the time, and his mood had been very tranquil. His mother liked this much better than high spirits. There was an element sometimes in John's high spirits that had made her tremble.

But on the day succeeding that last ride with Mrs. Graham, when they had dismounted and walked down to the shore, John had come back to the inn with a darkened face. The dark mood had lasted now for ten days. His mother began to lead her old sleepless, restless life again. Her awkward crochet-needle had stopped of itself; she went no more to her bench beside the asparagus. Instead, she remained in her room— her four rooms—every now and then peeping anxiously through the blinds. Nothing happened—so any one would have said; the sea continued blue and misty, the sky blue and clear; every one came and went as usual in the divine weather of the Italian spring. But John Ash's mother had, to use an old expression, her heart in her mouth all the time.

It choked her, and she gave up going to the *table d'hôte;* she let her son suppose that the meal was served in her sitting-room, but in reality she took no dinner at all. When he came in she was always there, always carefully dressed in the black silk whose rich texture the vicar's wife had noticed, with the "very good" diamonds fastening her collar and on her thin hands. She made a constant effort that her son should notice no change in her.

Azubah Ash had a gaunt frame with large bones; her chest was hollow, and she stooped a little as she walked. Yet, looking at her, one felt sure that she would live to be an old woman. Her large features were roughly moulded, her cheeks thin; her thick dusky hair was put plainly back from her face, and arranged with a high comb after a fashion of her youth. Her eyes, large, dark, and appealing, were sunken; they were beautiful eyes, if one could have removed from them their expression of apprehension, but that seemed now to have grown a part of them, to have become fixed by time. Observers of physiognomy who met Azubah during these two years of her sojourn abroad never forgot her —that tall gaunt woman with the awkward step and bearing, with the rich dress and diamonds, from whose timid face with its rough features those beautiful eyes looked appealingly out.

"Mother, I am going to Pæstum to-morrow," announced Ash on that eleventh day. "Perhaps you had better go with me." He had come in and thrown himself down upon the sofa, where he sat staring at the wall.

"Pæstum—yes, that's where that English lady said I'd oughter go," answered Mrs. Ash. Then, after a moment, "She said there were temples there." She had her hands folded tightly as she looked at her son.

"They're all going—old lady Preston, with her ghosts of Abercrombies, little Miss Holland, Mrs. Graham, and all. Those boys are sketching down there; they've been there some time."

"I shall be very glad ter go, John, if you are going.

AZUBAH ASH

Would you like ter have me—ter have me ride horseback?"

Ash, coming out of his abstraction, broke into a laugh. "I shall take you in the finest landau in Salerno, marmer," he said, coming across to kiss her; "old lady Preston will have to put up with the second best. You haven't forgotten, then, that you used to ride, marmer, have you?"

The mother's eyes had filled upon hearing the old name, the "marmer" of the days when he had been her devoted, constantly following, tyrannical, but very loving little boy. But she did not let the tears drop: she never made scenes of any kind before John. "Well, you've been riding horseback every day now for a long while; you haven't seemed to care at all for carriages. And I did use to ride horseback a good deal when I was a girl; I used to ride to the mill."

"I know you did. And carry the grist to be ground." He kissed her again. "Don't be afraid of anything or anybody to-morrow, marmer, I beg. You're the bravest and most sensible woman I know, and I want you to look what you are."

"Shall I wear my India shawl, then?"

"Wear the best you have; I wish it were a hundred times bester. You are handsomer than any of them as it is."

"Oh no, John; I ain't good-looking; I never was," said his mother, blushing. She put her hand up for a moment, nervously, over her mouth—a gesture habitual with her.

"Yes, you are, marmer. Look at your eyes. It's only that you have got into a way of not thinking so.

But I think so, and others shall." He went back to the sofa, and sank into abstraction again.

At length his mother broke the silence, which had lasted very long. " I hope they are all well over there to-day?" she asked, hesitatingly. " Over there " was her name for the house on the shore, the house where she knew her son had for many weeks spent all his time.

"Well? They're extraordinarily well," said Ash. He got up and walked restlessly about the room. After a while he stopped, and now he seemed to have forgotten his mother's presence, for his eyes rested upon her without seeing her. "One of them is a little too well," he said, menacingly ; "let him look to himself —that's all." And then into his face, his mother, watching him, saw coming slowly something she knew. The expression changed him so completely that the ladies who had seen so much of him would not have recognized their visitor. His mother recognized him. That expression on her son's face was her life's long terror.

He left the room. She listened as long as she could hear his steps; then, after sitting for some time with her head upon her arms on the table before her, she rose, and went slowly to put on her bonnet and shawl. Coming back, still slowly, she paused, and for five minutes stood there motionless. Then her hands dropped desparingly by her sides, and her worn face quivered. "O God, O our Father, I really don't know what ter do!" she murmured, breaking into helpless sobs, the stifled, difficult sobs of a person unaccustomed to self-expression, even the self-expression of grief.

She did not go out. Instead of that, she went back to the inner room and knelt down.

IV

The next morning three carriages and two persons on horseback were following the long road that stretches southward from Salerno to Pæstum.

In the first carriage old Mrs. Preston sat enthroned amid cushions and shawls; opposite she had placed her nephew Arthur, first because he was slim, second because he was a man (Mrs. Preston was accustomed to say, "Too much lady talk dries my brain"); the second carriage held Isabella Holland and the Abercrombie girls; in the third, a landau drawn by two spirited horses, were Mrs. Ash and her son. The two persons on horseback were Pauline Graham and Griffith Carew.

In the soft spring air the mountains that rise all the way on the left at no great distance from the road had in perfection the vague, dreamy outlines and violet hues that form so characteristic a feature of the Italian landscape. Up in the sky their peaks shone whitely, powdered with snow. The flat plain that stretches from the base of the mountains to the sea had beauty of another kind; often a fever-swept marsh, it possessed at this season all a marsh's luxuriance of waving reeds and flowers and tasselled jungles, with water birds rising from their feeding-places, and flying along, low down, with a slow motion of their broad wings, their feet stretched out behind. Troops of buffalo could be seen here and there. At rare intervals there was an oasis of cultivated ground, with a solitary farmhouse. On the right, all the way, the Mediterranean, meeting the flat land flatly, stretched forward from thence into space, going on bluely, and rising a little on the horizon line, as though it were surmounting a low hill.

Occasionally the carriages passed a little band of the small, quick-stepping Italian soldiers.

"Oh, I say, did you know, aunt, that people were murdered by brigands on this very bridge only ten years ago?" said Arthur, as they rolled across a stone causeway raised in the form of an arch over a sluggish stream.

"I should like very much to see the brigands who did it!" Mrs. Preston answered, smacking her lips contemptuously.

Arthur at least was very sure that no ten brigands could have vanquished his aunt.

"This, girls, is the ancient Tyrrhenian Gulf," began Isabella to her companions, waving one neatly gloved hand towards the sea. Isabella, owing to the singularly incessant death of relatives, was always in mourning; her neat gloves therefore were sable. "The temples we are about to visit are very ancient also, having been built ages ago by Greeks, who came from—from Greece, of course, naturally; and never ceased to regret it. And all this shore, and the temples also, were sacred to Neptune, or Poseidon, as he was called in Greek. And the Greeks lamented—but I will read you that later at the threshold of the temples; you cannot fail to be interested."

"I shall not be interested at all," said Hildegarde.

"Nor I," said Rose..

"*They* had nothing to lament about; *they* had no dancing to do," added Dorothea. And the three white faces glared suddenly and sullenly at their astonished companion.

"I am shocked," began Isabella.

"Shocked yourself," said Rose.

"You are a busybody," said Dorothea.

"And a gormandizer," added Hildegarde.

"And a *Worm!*" said Rose, with decision. "We have decided not to pretend any more before *you*, Worm! Dance yourself till your legs drop off, and see how you like it."

The three girls had weak soft voices; they possessed no other tones; the strong words they used, therefore, were all the more startling because so gently, almost sighingly, spoken.

In the landau there had been silence. Mrs. Ash, after respecting her son's sombre mood for more than an hour, at last spoke: "I guess you don't care very much about those triflin' temples, after all, do you, John? And it's going to be very long. Supposing we turn back?" She wore her India shawl and a Paris bonnet; she was sitting without touching the cushions of the carriage behind her. She had looked neither at the mountains nor at the sea; most of the time her eyes had rested on the blue cloth of the empty seat opposite. Occasionally, however, they had followed the two figures on horseback, and it was after these figures had passed them a second time, pushing on ahead in order to get a free space of road for a gallop, that she had offered her suggestion.

"Go back? Not for ten thousand dollars—not for ten thousand devils!" said John Ash. "What a lazy girl you are, marmer!" And he became gay and talkative.

His mother responded to his gayety as well as she could: she laughed when he did. Her laugh was eager. It was almost obsequious.

By-and-by the three temples loomed into view, standing in all their beauty on the barren waste, majestic, uninjured, extraordinary. Their rows of fluted columns, their brilliant tawny hues, their perfect Doric architecture, made the loneliness surrounding them even more lonely, made the sound of the sea breaking near by on the lifeless shore a melancholy dirge. When the party reached the great colonnades there were exclamations; there was even declamation, Mrs. Preston having been fitted by nature for that. Freemantle, Gates, and Beckett had come rushing forward to meet their arriving friends. In reality, however, it was Griff whom they had rushed to meet. Griff to their minds was the only important person present, even though the unimportant included Pauline.

"Hallo, Griff, old fellow! how are you?"

"Couldn't you stay, Griff? We've got a tent for you."

They laughed, and made jokes, and hovered about him, longing to drag him off immediately to show him their drawings, and to discuss with him a hundred disputed points. But though they thus paid small attention to Pauline, they were obliged to form part of her train; for as Griff remained with her, and they remained with Griff, naturally, as Isabella would have said, they made the tour of inspection in her company.

In the meanwhile Isabella, who had it upon her strictly kept conscience not to neglect her own duties in spite of the Abercrombie revolt, had taken her stand before the great temple of Neptune, with her instructive little book in her hand. "'The men of Poseidonia,' she began, "'having been at first true Greeks, had in process of time gradually become barbarized, changing to Romans.' Poseidonia, girls, was the ancient name of Pæstum," she interpolated in explanation, glancing over her glasses at her silent audience.

The Abercrombies could not retort this time, because Aunt Octavia was very near them, sitting at the base of one of the great columns of travertine with the air and manner of Neptune's only lawful wife. But their backs were towards her; she could not see their faces; they were able, therefore, to make grimaces at Isabella, and this they immediately proceeded to do in unison, flattening their thin lips over their teeth in a very ghastly way, and turning up their eyes so unnaturally far that Isabella was afraid the pupils would never come down again.

"'Yet they still observed one Hellenic festival,'" she read stumblingly on—stumblingly because she felt obliged from a sort of fascination to glance every now and then at the distorted countenances before her— "'one Hellenic festival, when they met together here to call to remembrance the old days and the old customs, and to weep upon each other's necks, and to lament drearily. And then, when the time of their mourning was over, they departed, each man in silence to his Roman home.'"

"Very fine," said Mrs. Preston, commendingly, from her column.

But Isabella had closed her book, and was walking away, wiping her forehead: those girls' faces were really too horrible.

"Where are you going, Isabella?" Mrs. Preston called.

"I suppose I may gather some asphodel?" Isabella responded, with some asperity.

But she did not gather much asphodel. Coming upon Mrs. Ash wandering about over the fallen stones, she stayed her steps to speak to her. She was not interested in Mrs. Ash, but she was so "happily relieved" that dear Paulie lately had given up her rides with the son, that she, as Paulie's cousin (first), could afford to be civil to the mother, in spite of that mother's bad judgment as to English and diamonds. Isabella disapproved of Mrs. Ash; she thought that "such persons" did great harm by their display of "mere vulgar affluence." No vulgar affluence oppressed Isabella. She had six hundred dollars a year of her own, and each dollar was well bred.

"We shall soon be having lunch, I suppose," she began, in a gracious tone. "It seems almost a desecration, doesn't it, to have it in the shrine itself, for I see they are arranging it there."

"Oh, is that a shrine?" said Mrs. Ash, vaguely. "I didn't know. But then I'm not a Catholic. They seem very large buildings. They seem wasted here."

Little Isabella looked up at her—she was obliged to look up, her companion was so tall. The anxious expression in Mrs. Ash's eyes had grown into anguish: she was watching her son, who had now joined Pauline and her train. Pauline had Carew on her right hand and John Ash on her left; the four boys walked stragglingly, now in front, now behind, but never far from Carew.

"You are not well," said Isabella; "the drive was too long for you. Pray take my smelling-salts; they are sometimes refreshing." And she detached from its black chain a minute funereal bottle.

"Thank you," answered Mrs. Ash, gazing down uncomprehendingly at the offering; "I am very well indeed. I was jest looking at your cousin, Mrs. Graham; she's very handsome."

"Yes," responded Isabella, gladly seizing this opportunity to convey to the Ash household a little light, "Pauline is handsome—in her own way. It is not the style that I myself admire. But then I know that my taste is severe. By ordinary people Pauline is considered attractive; it is therefore all the more to be deplored that she should be such a sad, sad flirt."

"A flirt?" said Mrs. Ash.

"Yes—I am sorry to say it. No matter how far she may go, it means nothing, absolutely nothing; she has not the slightest intention of allowing herself either to fall in love or to marry again; she prefers her position as it is. And I don't think she realizes sufficiently that what is but pastime to her may be taken more seriously by others; and naturally, I must say, after the way she sometimes goes on. *I* could never do so, no matter what the temptations were, and I must say I have never been able to understand it in Pauline. At present it is Mr. Carew; she is going to Naples with him to-morrow for the day. As you may imagine, it is against our wish—Cousin Octavia Preston's and mine. But Pauline being a widow, which *she* considers an advantage, and no longer young (she is thirty, though you may not think it; she shows her age very fully in the morning)—Pauline, under these circumstances, has for some time refused a chaperon. I don't think myself that she needs a chaperon exactly, but she might take a lady friend."

"Going to Naples with him to-morrow," murmured Mrs. Ash. She put her gloved hand over her mouth for a moment, the large kid expanse very different from Isabella's little black paw. "I might as well go over there," she said, starting off with a rapid step towards Pauline.

Pauline received her smilingly; Ash frowned a little. He frowned not at his mother—she was always welcome; he frowned at her persistence in standing so near Pauline, in dogging her steps. Mrs. Ash kept this up; she sat near Pauline at lunch; she followed her when she strolled down to the beach; she gathered flowers for her; in her India shawl and Paris bonnet she hovered constantly near.

Only once did John Ash find opportunity to speak to Pauline alone. The boys had at last carried off Griff by force to their camp; Griff was willing enough to go, the "force" applied to the intellectual effort necessary on the boys' part to detach him from a lady who wished to keep him by her side. They had all been strolling up and down in the shade of the so-called Basilica, amid the fern and acanthus. Left alone with her son and Mrs. Graham, Mrs. Ash, after remaining with them a few moments, turned aside, and entering the temple, sat down there. She was out of hearing, but still near.

"Ride with me to-morrow, Pauline," Ash said, immediately. "I have not had a chance to speak to you before. Don't refuse."

"I am afraid I must. I have an engagement."

"With Carew?"

"Yes."

"What is it?"

"I am very good-natured to tell you. I am going to Naples with him for the day."

"You are going— Damnation!"

"You forget yourself," said Pauline. Then, when she saw the look on his face—the face of this man with whom she had played—she was startled.

"Forget myself! I wish I could. You shall not go to Naples."

"And how can you prevent it?"

"Are you daring me?"

"By no means," answered Pauline; and this time she really tried to speak gently. "I was calling to your remembrance the fact that there is no tie between us, Mr. Ash; you have no shadow of authority over my actions; I am free to do as I please."

"I know you are; that is the worst of it," he said, almost with a groan. "Pauline, don't play with me now. I have given up hoping for anything for myself —if I ever really did hope; I am not worthy of you. Whether you could make me worthy I don't know; but I don't ask you that; I don't ask you to try; it would be too much. I only ask you to be as you have been; as you were, I mean, during all those many weeks, not as you have been lately. Only a few days are left when I can see you freely; be kind to me, then, during those few days, and then I will take myself off."

"I mean to be kind; I am kind."

"Then ride with me to-morrow; just this once more."

"But I told you it was impossible; I told you I was going to Naples."

The pleading vanished from Ash's face and voice. "*I* never asked you to do that—to go off with me for a whole day."

Pauline did not answer; she was arranging the flowers which Mrs. Ash had industriously gathered.

"So much the greater fool I!—is that what you are thinking?" Ash went on, laughing discordantly.

For the moment Pauline forgot to be angry in the vague feeling, something like fear, which took possession of her. All fear is uncomfortable, and she hated discomfort; she gave herself a little inward shake as if to shake it off. "I shall ask Cousin Oc to go back to Paris next week," was her thought. "I have had enough of Italy for the present—Italy and madmen!"

"You won't go?" asked Ash, bending forward eagerly, as though he had gained hope from her silence.

"To Paris?"

"Are we speaking of Paris? To Naples — to-morrow."

"Oh, I must go to Naples," she answered, gayly. In spite of her gayety she turned towards the Basilica; Mrs. Ash was the nearest person.

"You are going to my mother? She, at least, is a good woman; she would never have tarnished herself with such an expedition as you are planning!" cried Ash, in a fury.

Pauline turned white. "I am well paid for ever having endured you, ever having liked you," she said, in a low voice, as she hastened on. "I might have known—I might have known."

There was not much to choose now between the expression of the two faces, for the woman's sweet countenance showed in its pallor an anger as vivid as that which had flushed the face of the man beside her, with a red so dark that his blue eyes looked unnaturally light by contrast, as though they had been set in the face of an Indian.

Mrs. Ash had come hurriedly out to meet them. Her

son paid no attention to her; all his powers were evidently concentrated upon holding himself in check. "I shouldn't have said it, even if it were the plain brutal truth," he said. "But you madden me, Pauline. I mean what I say—you really do drive me into a kind of madness."

"I have no desire to drive you into anything; I have no desire to talk with you further," she answered.

"No, no, dearie, don't say that; talk ter him a little longer," said Mrs. Ash, coming forward, her face set in a tremulous smile. "I'm sure it's very pleasant here—beside these buildings. And John thinks so much of you; he means no harm."

"Poor mother!" said Ash, his voice softening. "She does not dare to say to you what she longs to say; she would whisper it if she could; and that is, 'Don't provoke him!' She has some pretty bad memories—haven't you, mother?— of times when I've— when I've gone a-hunting, as one may say. She'll tell you about them if you like."

"I don't want to hear about them; I don't want to hear about anything," answered Mrs. Graham, troubled out of all her composure, troubled even out of her anger by the strangeness of this strange pair. She looked about for some one, and, seeing Carew coming from the tents of the camp, she waved her hand to attract his attention and beckoned to him; then she went forward to meet him as he hastened towards her.

Ash disengaged himself from his mother, who, however, had only touched his arm entreatingly, for she had learned to be very cautious where her son was concerned; he strode forward to Pauline's side.

"I should rather see you dead before me than go with that man to-morrow."

"Pray don't kill me, at least till the day is over," Pauline answered, her courage, and her unconquerable carelessness too, returning in the approach of Carew. "It would be quite too great a disappointment to lose my day."

"You *shall* lose it!" said Ash, with a loud coarse oath.

"Oh!" said the woman, all her lovely delicate person shrinking away from him.

Her intonation had been one of disgust. She held the skirt of her habit closer, as if to avoid all contact.

V

At five o'clock of the same afternoon Freemantle, Gates, and Beckett, with Arthur Abercrombie, came running along the narrow streets of a village some miles from Pæstum.

The stone houses of which this village was composed stood like two solid walls facing each other, rising directly from the stone-paved road, which was barely ten feet wide; down this conduit water was pouring like a brook. The houses were about forty in number, twenty on each side, and this one short street was all there was of the town.

It was raining, not in drops, but in torrents, with great pats of water coming over, almost like stones, and striking upon the heads of those who were passing below; every two or three minutes there came a glare of blindingly white lightning, followed immediately by the crash of thunder, which seemed to be rolling on the very roofs of the houses themselves. The four boys must have been out in the storm for some time, for they paid no attention to it. Their faces were set, excited. Every thread of their clothing was wet through.

"This is the house," said Arthur.

They looked up, sheltering their eyes with their arms from the blows of the rain-balls. From the closed windows above, the faces of Isabella Holland and the three Abercrombie girls looked down at them, pressed flatly against the small panes, in order to see; for the storm had made the air so dark that the street lay in gloom.

The next moment the boys entered.

"No, we haven't found him," said Arthur, in answer to his white sisters' look. "But we're going to."

"Yes, we're going to," said the others. And then, walking on tiptoe in their soaked shoes, they went softly into an inner room.

Here on a couch lay Griffith Carew, dying.

An Italian doctor was still trying to do something for the unconscious man. He had an assistant, and the two were at work together. Near by, old Mrs. Preston sat waiting, her hands folded upon the knob of a cane which stood on the floor before her, her chin resting upon her hands. In this bent position, with her disordered white hair and great black eyes, she looked witchlike. Three candles burned on a table at the head of the bed, illumining Carew and the two doctors and the waiting old woman. The room was long, and its far end was in shadow. Was there another person present—sitting there silent and motionless? Yes—Pauline. The boys came to the foot of the bed and gazed with full hearts at Griff.

Griff had been shot by John Ash two hours before. The deed had been done just as they had reached the shelter of this village, swept into it almost by a tornado, which, preceding the darker storm, had driven them far from their rightful road. The darker storm had broken upon them immediately afterwards with a terrible sound and fury; but the boys had barely heard the crash in the sky above them as they carried Griff through the stony little street. They had found a doctor—two of them; they had done everything possible. Then they had been told that Griff must die, and they had gone out to look for the murderer.

He could not be far, for the village was small, and he could not have quitted the village, because the half-broken young horses that had brought him from Salerno, frightened by the incessant glare of the lightning, had become unmanageable, dragged their fastenings loose, and disappeared. In any case the plain was impassable; the roar of the sea, with the night coming on, indicated that the floods were out; they had covered the shore, and would soon be creeping inland; the road would be drowned and lost. Ash, therefore, could not be far.

Yet they had been unable to find him, though they had searched every house. And they had found no trace of his mother.

During these long hours four times the boys had sallied forth and hunted the street up and down. The Italians, crowded into their narrow dark dwellings from fear of the storm, had allowed them to pass freely in and out, to go from floor to floor; some of the men had even lighted their little oil lamps and gone down with them to search the shallow cellars. But the women did not look up; they were telling their beads or kneeling before their little in-door shrines, the frightened children clinging to their skirts and crying. For both the street and the dark houses were lighted every minute or two by that unearthly blinding glare.

The village version of the story was that the two *forestieri* had sprung at each other's throats, maddened by jealousy; poniards had been drawn, and one of them had fallen. One had fallen, indeed, but only one had attacked. And there had been no poniards: it was a well-aimed bullet from an American revolver that had struck down Griffith Carew.

The four boys, brought back each time from their search by a sudden hope that perhaps Griff might have rallied, and forced each time to yield up their hope at the sight of his death-like face, were animated in their grief by one burning determination: they would bring the murderer to justice. It was a foreign land and a remote shore; they were boys; and he was a bold, bad man with a wonderful brain—for they had always appreciated Ash's cleverness, though they had never liked him. In spite of all this he should not escape; they would hunt him like hounds — blood-hounds; and though it should take months, even years, of their lives, they would bring him to justice at the last.

This hot vow kept the poor lads from crying. They were very young, and their heads were throbbing with their unshed tears; there were big lumps in their throats when poor Griff, opening his dull eyes for a moment, knew them, and tried to smile in his cheery old way. But he relapsed into unconsciousness immediately. And the watch went on.

The gloomy day drew to its close; by the clocks,

evening had come. There was more breathing-space now between the lightning flashes and the following thunder; the wind was no longer violent; the rain still fell heavily; its torrent, striking the pavement below, sent up a loud hollow sound. One of the doctors left the house, and came back with a fresh supply of candles and various things, vaguely frightful, because hidden, concealed in a sheet. Then the other doctor went out to get something to eat. Finally they were both on guard again. And the real night began.

Then, to the waiting group in the lighted silent room, there entered a tall figure — Azubah Ash; drenched, without bonnet or shawl, she stood there before them. Her frightened look was gone forever: she faced them with unconscious majesty. "My son is dead"—this was her announcement.

She walked forward to the bed, and gazed at the man lying there. "Perhaps he will not die," she said, turning her head to glance at the others. "God is kind—sometimes; perhaps he will not die." She bent over and stroked his hair tenderly with her large hand. "Dear heart, live! Try ter live!" she said; "we want yer to, so much!"

Then she left him, and faced them again. "I thought of warning you," she began; "you"—and she looked at Mrs. Preston; "and you"—she turned towards the figure at the end of the room. "My son was not himself when he was in a passion—I have known it ever sence he was born. Even when he was a little fellow of two and three I used ter try ter guard him; but I couldn't do much—his will was stronger than mine. And he was always very clever, my son was—much cleverer than me. Twice before, three times before,

THE OLD WATCH-TOWER

I've ben afraid he'd take some one's life. You see, he didn't care about life so much as some people do; and now he has taken his own."

There was an involuntary stir among the boys.

Mrs. Ash turned her eyes towards them. "Would you like ter see him, so 's ter be sure? In one moment."

She went towards the bed again, and clasped her hands; then she knelt down, and began to pray beside the unconscious man in hushed tones. "O God, O our Father, give us back this life: do, Lord—O do. It's so dear ter these poor boys, and it's so dear ter many; and perhaps there's a mother too. O Lord, give it back to us! And when he's well again, help him ter be all that my poor son was not. For Christ's sake."

She rose and crossed to where the boys were standing. "Will you come now?" she said. "I'm taking him away at dawn." Then, very simply, she offered her hand to Mrs. Preston. "He was a great deal at your house; he told me that. I thank you for having ben so kind ter him. Good-bye."

"But I too will go with you," answered Mrs. Preston, in her deep tones. She rose, leaning on her cane. Mrs. Ash was already crossing the room towards the door.

The boys followed her; then came Mrs. Preston, looking bent and old. The figure of Pauline in her dark corner rose as they approached.

"No," said Mrs. Ash, seeing the movement. She paused. "Don't come, my dear; I really can't let you; you'd think of it all the rest of your life if you was ter see him now, and 'twould make you feel so bad. I know you didn't mean no harm. But you mustn't come."

And Pauline, shrinking back into the shadow, was held there by the compassion of this mother — this mother whose nobler nature, and large glance quiet in the majesty of sorrow, made her, made all the women present, fade into nothingness beside her. In the outer room Isabella and the excited, peering Abercrombies were like four unimportant, unnoticed ghosts, as the little procession went by them in silence, and descended the stairs. Then it passed out into the storm.

Mrs. Ash walked first, leading the way, the rain falling on her hair; the three boys followed; behind them came Mrs. Preston, leaning on her nephew's arm and helping herself with her cane. They passed down the narrow street, and the people brought their small lamps to the doorways to aid them in the darkness. The street ended, but the mother went on: apparently she was going out on the broad waste. They all followed, Mrs. Preston merely shaking her head when Arthur proposed that she should turn back.

At some distance beyond the town there was a grove of oaks; they went round an angle of this grove, stumbling in the darkness, and came to a mound behind it; on the summit of the mound there was something — a square structure of stone. Mrs. Ash went up, and entered a low door. Within there was but one room, empty save for a small lighted lamp standing on the dirt floor; a stairway, or rather a flight of stone steps, ascended to a room above. Mrs. Ash took the lamp and led the way up; Mrs. Preston's cane sounded on the stones as she followed.

The room above was square, like the one below; it was the whole interior of the ancient house, or rather the ancient watch-tower; its roof of beams was broken;

"THE CART WAS GOING SLOWLY ACROSS THE FIELDS, FOR THE ROAD WAS OVERFLOWED."

the rain came through in several places and dropped upon the floor. There was a second small lamp in the room besides the one which Mrs. Ash had brought; the two shed a dim ray over a peasant's rude bed, where something long and dark and straight was stretched out. Mrs. Ash went up to the bed, and motioning away the old peasant who was keeping watch there, she took both lamps and held them high above the still face. The others drew near. And then they saw that it was John Ash—dead!

There were no signs of the horror of it; his mother had removed them all; he lay as if asleep.

The mother held the lights up steadily for a long moment. Then she placed them on a table, and coming back, took her son's lifeless hand in hers.

"Now that you've seen him, seen that he's really gone, will you leave me alone with him?" she said. "I think there's nothing more."

There was a dignity in her face as she stood there beside her child which made the others feel suddenly conscious of the wantonness of further intrusion. As they looked at her, too, they perceived that she no longer thought of them, no longer even saw them: her task was ended.

Without a word they went out. Mrs. Preston's cane sounded on the stairway again; then there was silence.

At dawn they saw her drive away. Griff might live, the doctors had said. But for the moment the gazing group of Americans forgot even that. She was in a cart, with a man walking beside the horse; the cart was going slowly across the fields, for the road was overflowed. The storm had ceased; the sky was blue; the sun, rising, shed his fresh golden light on the tall, lonely figure with its dark hair uncovered, and on the long rough box at its feet.

Looking the other way, one could see in the south the beautiful temples of Pæstum, that have gazed over that plain for more than two thousand years.

A PINK VILLA

I

"YES, of the three, I liked Pierre best," said Mrs. Churchill. "Yet it was hard to choose. I have lived so long in Italy that I confess it would have been a pleasure to see Eva at court; it's a very pretty little court they have now at Rome, I assure you, with that lovely Queen Margherita at the head. The old Marchese is to resign his post this month, and the King has already signified his intention of giving it to Gino. Eva, as the Marchesa Lamberti, living in that ideal old Lamberti palace, you know—Eva, I flatter myself, would have shone in her small way as brightly as Queen Margherita in hers. You may think I am assuming a good deal, Philip. But you have no idea how much pains has been taken with that child; she literally is fitted for a court or for any other high position. Yet at the same time she is very childlike. I have kept her so purposely; she has almost never been out of my sight. The Lambertis are one of the best among the old Roman families, and there could not be a more striking proof of Gino's devotion than his having persuaded his father to say (as he did to me two months ago) that he should be proud to welcome Eva 'as she is,' which meant that her very small dowry would not be considered an objection. As to Eva herself, of course the

Lambertis, or any other family, would be proud to receive her," pursued Mrs. Churchill, with the quiet pride which in its unruffled serenity became her well. "But not to hesitate over her mere pittance of a portion, that is very remarkable; for the marriage-portion is considered a sacred point by all Italians; they are brought up to respect it—as we respect the Constitution."

"It's a very pretty picture," answered Philip Dallas —"the court and Queen Margherita, the handsome Gino and the old Lamberti palace. But I'm a little bewildered, Fanny; you speak of it all so appreciatively, yet Gino was certainly not the name you mentioned; Pierre, wasn't it?"

"Yes, Pierre," answered Mrs. Churchill, laughing and sighing with the same breath. "I've strayed far. But the truth is, I did like Gino, and I wanted to tell you about him. No, Eva will not be the Marchesa Lamberti, and live in the old palace; I have declined that offer. Well, then, the next was Thornton Stanley."

"Thornton Stanley? Has he turned up here? I used to know him very well."

"I thought perhaps you might."

"He is a capital fellow—when he can forget his first editions."

Mrs. Churchill folded her arms, placing one hand on each elbow, and slightly hugging herself. "He has forgotten them more than once in *this* house," she said, triumphantly.

"He is not only a capital fellow, but he has a large fortune — ten times as large, I venture to say, as your Lambertis have."

"I know that. But—"

"But you prefer an old palace. I am afraid Stanley could not build Eva an old castle. Couldn't you manage to jog on with half a dozen new ones?"

"The trouble with Thornton Stanley was his own uncertainty," said Fanny; "he was not in the least firm about staying over here, though he pretended he was. I could see that he would be always going home. More than that, I should not be at all surprised if at the end of five years—three even—he should have bought or built a house in New York, and settled down there forever."

"And you don't want that for your American daughter, renegade?"

Mrs. Churchill unfolded her arms. "No one can be a warmer American than I am, Philip — no one. During the war I nearly cried my eyes out; have you forgotten that? I scraped lint; I wanted to go to the front as nurse — everything. What days they were! We *lived* then. I sometimes think we have never lived since."

Dallas felt a little bored. He was of the same age as Fanny Churchill; but the school-girl, whose feelings were already those of a woman, had had her nature stirred to its depths by events which the lad had been too young to take seriously to heart. His heart had never caught up with them, though, of course, his reason had.

"Yes, I know you are flamingly patriotic," he said. "All the same, you don't want Eva to live in Fiftieth Street."

"In Fiftieth Street?"

"I chose the name at random. In New York."

"I don't see why you should be sarcastic," said Fanny. "Of course I expect to go back myself some time; I could not be content without that. But Eva—Eva is different; she has been brought up over here entirely; she was only three when I came abroad. It seems such a pity that all that should be wasted."

"And why should it be wasted in Fiftieth Street?"

"The very qualities that are admired here would be a drawback to her there," replied Mrs. Churchill. "A shy girl who cannot laugh and talk with everybody, who has never been out alone a step in her life, where would she be in New York?—I ask you that. While here, as you see, before she is eighteen—"

"Isn't the poor child eighteen yet? Why in the world do you want to marry her to any one for five years more at least?"

Mrs. Churchill threw up her pretty hands. "How little you have learned about some things, Philip, in spite of your winters on the Nile and your Scotch shooting-box! I suppose it is because you have had no daughters to consider."

"Daughters?—I should think not!" was Dallas's mental exclamation. Fanny, then, with all her sense, was going to make that same old mistake of supposing that a bachelor of thirty-seven and a mother of thirty-seven were of the same age.

"Why, it's infinitely better in every way that a nice girl like Eva should be married as soon as possible after her school-books are closed, Philip," Mrs. Churchill went on; "for then, don't you see, she can enter society—which is always so dangerous—safely; well protected, and yet quite at liberty as well. I mean, of course, in case she has a good husband. That is the mother's business, the mother's responsibility, and I think a mother who does not give her heart to it, her whole soul and energy, and choose *well*—I think such

a mother an infamous woman. In this case I am sure
I have chosen well; I am sure Eva will be happy with
Pierre de Verneuil. They have the same ideas; they
have congenial tastes, both being fond of music and
art. And Pierre is a very lovable fellow; you will
think so yourself when you see him."

"And you say she likes him?"

"Very much. I should not have gone on with it, of
course, if there had been any dislike. They are not
formally betrothed as yet; that is to come soon; but
the old Count (Pierre's father) has been to see me, and
everything is virtually arranged — a delightful man, the
old Count. They are to make handsome settlements;
not only are they rich, but they are not in the least narrow — as even the best Italians are, I am sorry to say.
The Verneuils are cosmopolitans; they have been everywhere; their estate is near Brussels, but they spend
most of their time in Paris. They will never tie Eva
down in any small way. In addition, both father and
son are extremely nice to *me*."

"Ah!" said Dallas, approvingly.

"Yes; they have the French ideas about mothers;
you know that in France the mother is and remains
the most important person in the family." As she
said this, Mrs. Churchill unconsciously lifted herself
and threw back her shoulders. Ordinarily the line
from the knot of her hair behind to her waist was long
and somewhat convex, while correspondingly the distance between her chin and her belt in front was surprisingly short: she was a plump woman, and she had
fallen into the habit of leaning upon a certain beguiling
steel board, which leads a happy existence in wrappings
of white kid and perfumed lace.

"Not only will they never wish to separate me from Eva," she went on, still abnormally erect, "but such a thought would never enter their minds; they think it an honor and a pleasure to have me with them; the old Count assured me of it in those very words."

"And now we have the secret of the Belgian success," said Dallas.

"Yes. But I have not been selfish; I have tried to consider everything; I have investigated carefully. If you will stay half an hour longer you can see Pierre for yourself; and then I know that you will agree with me."

In less than half an hour the Belgian appeared—a slender, handsome young man of twenty-two, with an ease of manner and grace in movement which no American of that age ever had. With all his grace, however, and his air of being a man of the world, there was such a charming expression of kindliness and purity in his still boyish eyes that any mother, with her young daughter's happiness at heart, might have been pardoned for coveting him as a son-in-law. This Dallas immediately comprehended. "You have chosen well," he said to Fanny, when they were left for a moment alone; "the boy's a jewel."

Before the arrival of Pierre, Eva Churchill, followed by her governess, had come out to join her mother on the terrace; Eva's daily lessons were at an end, save that the music went on; Mlle. Legrand was retained as a useful companion.

Following Pierre, two more visitors appeared, not together; one was an Englishman of fifty, small, meagre, plain in face; the other an American, somewhat younger, a short, ruddy man, dressed like an Englishman. Mrs. Churchill mentioned their names to Dallas: "Mr. Gordon-Gray." "Mr. Ferguson."

It soon appeared that Mr. Gordon-Gray and Mr. Ferguson were in the habit of looking in every afternoon, at about that hour, for a cup of tea. Dallas, who hated tea, leaned back in his chair and watched the scene, watched Fanny especially, with the amused eyes of a contemporary who remembers a different past. Fanny was looking dimpled and young; her tea was excellent, her tea-service elaborate (there was a samovar); her daughter was docile, her future son-in-law a Count and a pearl; in addition, her terrace was an enchanting place for lounging, attached as it was to a pink-faced villa that overlooked the sea.

Nor were there wanting other soft pleasures. "Dear Mrs. Murray-Churchill, how delicious is this nest of yours!" said the Englishman, with quiet ardor; "I never come here without admiring it."

Fanny answered him in a steady voice, though there was a certain flatness in its tone: "Yes, it's very pretty indeed." Her face was red; she knew that Dallas was laughing; she would not look in his direction. Dallas, however, had taken himself off to the parapet, where he could have his laugh out at ease: to be called Mrs. Murray-Churchill as a matter of course in that way— what joy for Fanny!

Eva was listening to the busy Mark Ferguson; he was showing her a little silver statuette which he had unearthed that morning in Naples, "in a dusty out-of-the-way shop, if you will believe it, where there was nothing else but rubbish—literally nothing. From the chasing I am inclined to think it's fifteenth century.

But you will need glasses to see it well; I can lend you a pair of mine."

"I can see it perfectly—thanks," said Eva. "It is very pretty, I suppose."

"Pretty, Miss Churchill! Surely it's a miracle!" Ferguson protested.

Pierre, who was sitting near the mother, glanced across and smiled. Eva did not smile in reply; she was looking vaguely at the blackened silver; but when he came over to see for himself the miracle, then she smiled very pleasantly.

Pierre was evidently deeply in love; he took no pains to conceal it; but during the two hours he spent there he made no effort to lure the young girl into the drawing-room, or even as far as the parapet. He was very well bred. At present he stood beside her and beside Mark Ferguson, and talked about the statuette. "It seems to me old Vienna," he said.

"Signor Bartalama," announced Angelo, Mrs. Churchill's man-servant, appearing at the long window of the drawing-room which served as one of the terrace doors; he held the lace curtains apart eagerly, with the smiling Italian welcome.

Fanny had looked up, puzzled. But when her eyes fell upon the figure emerging from the lace she recognized it instantly. "Horace Bartholomew! Now from what quarter of the heavens do you drop *this* time?"

"So glad you call it heaven," said the new-comer, as she gave him her hand. "But from heaven indeed this time, Mrs. Churchill—I say so emphatically; from our own great, grand country—with the permission of the present company be it spoken." And he bowed slightly to the Englishman and Pierre, his discriminating glance including even the little French governess, who smiled (though non-comprehendingly) in reply. "May I present to you a compatriot, Mrs. Churchill?" he went on. "I have taken the liberty of bringing him without waiting for formal permission; he is, in fact, in your drawing-room now. His credentials, however, are small and puny; they consist entirely of the one item —that I like him."

"That will do perfectly," said Fanny, smiling.

Bartholomew went back to the window and parted the curtains. "Come," he said. A tall man appeared. "Mrs. Churchill, let me present to you Mr. David Rod."

Mrs. Churchill was gracious to the stranger; she offered him a chair near hers, which he accepted; a cup of tea, which he declined; and the usual small questions of a first meeting, which only very original minds are bold enough to jump over. The stranger answered the questions promptly; he was evidently not original. He had arrived two days before; this was his first visit to Italy; the Bay of Naples was beautiful; he had not been up Vesuvius; he had not visited Pompeii; he was not afraid of fever; and he had met Horace Bartholomew in Florida the year before.

"I am told they are beginning to go a great deal to Florida," remarked Fanny.

"I don't go there; I live there," Rod answered.

"Indeed! in what part?" (She brought forward the only names she knew.) "St. Augustine, perhaps? Or Tallahassee?"

"No; I live on the southern coast; at Punta Palmas?"

"How Spanish that is! Perhaps you have one of those old Spanish plantations?" She had now exhausted all her knowledge of the State save a vague memory of her school geography: "Where are the Everglades?" "They are in the southern part of Florida. They are shallow lakes filled with trees." But the stranger could hardly live in such a place as that.

"No," answered Rod; "my plantation isn't old and it isn't Spanish; it's a farm, and quite new. I am over here now to get hands for it."

"Hands?"

"Yes, laborers—Italians. They work very well in Florida."

Eva and Mademoiselle Legrand had turned with Pierre to look at the magnificent sunset. "Did you receive the flowers I sent this morning?" said Pierre, bending his head so that if Eva should glance up when she answered, he should be able to look into her eyes.

"Yes; they were beautiful," said Eva, giving the hoped-for glance.

"Yet they are not in the drawing-room."

"You noticed that?" she said, smiling. "They are in the music-room; Mademoiselle put them there."

"They are the flowers for Mozart, are they not?" said Mademoiselle—"heliotrope and white lilies; and we have been studying Mozart this morning. The drawing-room, as you know, Monsieur le Comte, is always full of roses."

"And how do you come on with Mozart?" asked Pierre.

"As usual," answered Eva. "Not very well, I suppose."

Mademoiselle twisted her handkerchief round her

"'MRS. CHURCHILL, LET ME PRESENT TO YOU MR. DAVID ROD.'"

fingers. She was passionately fond of music; it seemed to her that her pupil, who played accurately, was not. Pierre also was fond of music, and played with taste. He had not perceived Eva's coldness in this respect simply because he saw no fault in her.

"I want to make up a party for the Deserto," he went on, "to lunch there. Do you think Madame Churchill will consent?"

"Probably," said Eva.

"I hope she will. For when we are abroad together, under the open sky, then it sometimes happens I can stay longer by your side."

"Yes; we never have very long talks, do we?" remarked Eva, reflectively.

"Do you desire them?" said Pierre, with ardor. "Ah, if you could know how I do! With me it is one long thirst. Say that you share the feeling, even if only a little; give me that pleasure."

"No," said Eva laughing, "I don't share it at all. Because, if we should have longer talks, you would find out too clearly that I am not clever."

"Not clever!" said Pierre, with all his heart in his eyes. Then, with his unfailing politeness, he included Mademoiselle. "She is clever, Mademoiselle?"

"She is good," answered Mademoiselle, gravely. "Her heart has a depth—but a depth!"

"I shall fill it all," murmured Pierre to Eva. "It is not that I myself am anything, but my love is so great, so vast; it holds you as the sea holds Capri. Some time—some time, you must let me try to tell you!"

Eva glanced at him. Her eyes had for the moment a vague expression of curiosity.

This little conversation had been carried on in French;

Mademoiselle spoke no English, and Pierre would have been incapable of the rudeness of excluding her by means of a foreign tongue.

II

The pink villa was indeed a delicious nest, to use the Englishman's phrase. It crowned one of the perpendicular cliffs of Sorrento, its rosy façade overlooking what is perhaps the most beautiful expanse of water in the world — the Bay of Naples. The broad terrace stretched from the drawing room windows to the verge of the precipice; leaning against its strong stone parapet, with one's elbows comfortably supported on the flat top (which supported also several battered goddesses of marble), enjoying the shade of a lemon-tree set in a great vase of tawny terra-cotta—leaning thus, one could let one's idle gaze drop straight down into the deep blue water below, or turn it to the white line of Naples opposite, shining under castled heights, to Vesuvius with its plume of smoke, or to beautiful dark Ischia rising from the waves in the west, guarding the entrance to the sea. On each side, close at hand, the cliffs of Sorrento stretched away, tipped with their villas, with their crowded orange and lemon groves. Each villa had its private stairway leading to the beach below;· strange dark passages, for the most part cut in the solid rock, winding down close to the face of the cliff, so that every now and then a little rock-window can let in a gleam of light to keep up the spirits of those who are descending. For every one does descend: to sit and read among the rocks; to bathe from the bathing-house

SORRENTO

on the fringe of beach; to embark for a row to the grottos or a sail to Capri.

The afternoon which followed the first visit of Philip Dallas to the pink villa found him there a second time; again he was on the terrace with Fanny. The plunging sea-birds of the terrace's mosaic floor were partially covered by a large Persian rug, and it was upon this rich surface that the easy-chairs were assembled, and also the low tea-table, which was of a construction so solid that no one could possibly knock it over. A keen observer had once said that that table was in itself a sufficient indication that Fanny's house was furnished to attract masculine, not feminine, visitors (a remark which was perfectly true).

"You are the sun of a system of masculine planets, Fanny," said Dallas. "After long years, that is how I find you."

"Oh, Philip—we who live so quietly!"

"So is the sun quiet, I suppose; I have never heard that he howled. Mr. Gordon-Gray, Mark Ferguson, Pierre de Vernueil, Horace Bartholomew, unknown Americans. Do they come to see Eva or you?"

"They come to see the view—as you do; to sit in the shade and talk. I give very good dinners too," Fanny added, with simplicity.

"O romance! good dinners on the Bay of Naples!"

"Well, you may laugh; but nothing draws men of a certain age—of a certain kind, I mean; the most satisfactory men, in short—nothing draws them so surely as a good dinner delicately served," announced Fanny, with decision. "Please go and ring for the tea."

"I don't wonder that they all hang about you," remarked Dallas as he came back, his eyes turning from the view to his hostess in her easy-chair. "Your villa is admirable, and you yourself, as you sit there, are the personification of comfort, the personification, too, of gentle, sweet, undemonstrative affectionateness. Do you know that, Fanny?"

Fanny, with a very pink blush, busied herself in arranging the table for the coming cups.

Dallas smiled inwardly. "She thinks I am in love with her because I said that about affectionateness," he thought. "Oh, the fatuity of women!"

At this moment Eva came out, and presently appeared Mr. Gordon-Gray and Mark Ferguson. A little later came Horace Bartholomew. The tea had been brought; Eva handed the cups. Dallas, looking at her, was again struck by something in the manner and bearing of Fanny's daughter. Or rather he was not struck by it; it was an impression that made itself felt by degrees, as it had done the day before—a slow discovery that the girl was unusual.

She was tall, dressed very simply in white. Her thick smooth flaxen hair was braided in two long flat tresses behind, which were doubled and gathered up with a ribbon, so that they only reached her shoulders. This school-girl coiffure became her young face well. Yes, it was a very young face. Yet it was a serious face too. "Our American girls are often serious, and when they are brought up under the foreign system it really makes them too quiet," thought Dallas. Eva had a pair of large gray eyes under dark lashes: these eyes were thoughtful; sometimes they were dull. Her smooth complexion was rather brown. The oval of her face was perfect. Though her dress was so childlike, her figure was womanly; the poise of her head was noble, her step light and free. Nothing could be more unlike the dimpled, smiling mother than was this tall, serious daughter who followed in her train. Dallas tried to recall Edward Churchill (Edward Murray Churchill), but could not; he had only seen him once. "He must have been an obstinate sort of fellow," he said to himself. The idea had come to him suddenly from something in Eva's expression. Yet it was a sweet expression; the curve of the lips was sweet.

"She isn't such a very pretty girl, after all," he reflected, summing her up finally before he dismissed her. "Fanny is a clever woman to have made it appear that she is."

At this moment Eva, having finished her duties as cup-bearer, walked across the terrace and stood by the parapet, outlined against the light.

"By Jove she's beautiful!" thought Dallas.

Fanny's father had not liked Edward Churchill; he had therefore left his money tied up in such a way that neither Churchill nor any children whom he might have should be much benefited by it; Fanny herself, though she had a comfortable income for life, could not dispose of it. This accounted for the very small sum belonging to Eva: she had only the few hundreds that came to her from her father.

But she had been brought up as though she had many thousands; studiedly quiet as her life had been, studiedly simple as her attire always was, in every other respect her existence had been arranged as though a large fortune certainly awaited her. This had been the mother's idea; she had been sure from the beginning that a large fortune did await her daughter. It now appeared that she had been right.

"I don't know what you thought of me for bringing a fellow-countryman down upon you yesterday in that unceremonious way, Mrs. Churchill," Bartholomew was saying. "But I wanted to do something for him — I met him at the top of your lane by accident; it was an impulse."

"Oh, I'm sure — any friend of yours —" said Fanny, looking into the teapot.

Bartholomew glanced round the little circle on the rug, with an expression of dry humor in his brown eyes. "You didn't any of you like him — I see that," he said.

There was a moment's silence.

"Well, he is rather a commonplace individual, isn't he?" said Dallas, unconsciously assuming the leadership of this purely feminine household.

"I don't know what you mean by commonplace; but yes, I do, coming from *you*, Dallas. Rod has never been abroad in his life until now; and he's a man with convictions."

"Oh, come, don't take that tone," said Mark Ferguson; "I've got convictions too; I'm as obstinate about them as an Englishman."

"What did your convictions tell you about Rod, then, may I ask?" pursued Bartholomew.

"I didn't have much conversation with him, you may remember; I thought he had plenty of intelligence. His clothes were — were a little peculiar, weren't they?"

"Made in Tampa, probably. And I've no doubt but that he took pains with them — wanted to have them appropriate."

"That is where he disappointed me," said Gordon-Gray — "that very appearance of having taken pains.

When I learned that he came from that—that place in the States you have just named—a wild part of the country, is it not?—I thought he would be more—more interesting. But he might as well have come from Clerkenwell."

"You thought he would be more wild, you mean; trousers in his boots; long hair; knives."

All the Americans laughed.

"Yes. I dare say you cannot at all comprehend our penchant for that sort of thing," said the Englishman, composedly. "And—er—I am afraid there would be little use in attempting to explain it to you. But this Mr. Rod seemed to me painfully unconscious of his opportunities; he told me (when I asked) that there was plenty of game there—deer, and even bears and panthers—royal game; yet he never hunts."

"He never hunts, because he has something better to do," retorted Bartholomew.

"Ah, better?" murmured the Englishman, doubtfully.

Bartholomew got up and took a chair which was nearer Fanny. "No—no tea," he said, as she made a motion towards a cup; then, without further explaining his change of position, he gave her a little smile. Dallas, who caught this smile on the wing, learned from it unexpectedly that there was a closer intimacy between his hostess and Bartholomew than he had suspected. "Bartholomew!" he thought, contemptuously. "Gray—spectacles—stout." Then suddenly recollecting the increasing plumpness of his own person, he drew in his out-stretched legs, and determined, from that instant, to walk fifteen miles a day.

"Rod knows how to shoot, even though he doesn't

hunt," said Bartholomew, addressing the Englishman. "I saw him once bring down a mad bull, who was charging directly upon an old man—the neatest sort of a hit."

"He himself being in a safe place meanwhile," said Dallas.

"On the contrary, he had to rush forward into an open field. If he had missed his aim by an eighth of an inch, the beast—a terrible creature—would have made an end of him."

"And the poor old man?" said Eva.

"He was saved, of course; he was a rather disreputable old darky. Another time Rod went out in a howling gale — the kind they have down there — to rescue two men whose boat had capsized in the bay. They were clinging to the bottom; no one else would stir; they said it was certain death; but Rod went out —he's a capital sailor—and got them in. I didn't see that myself, as I saw the bull episode; I was told about it."

"By Rod?" said Dallas.

"By one of the men he saved. As you've never been saved yourself, Dallas, you probably don't know how it feels."

"He seems to be a modern Chevalier Bayard, doesn't he?" said good-natured Mark Ferguson.

"He's modern, but no Bayard. He's a modern and a model pioneer—"

"Pioneers! oh, pioneers!" murmured Gordon-Gray, half chanting it.

None of the Americans recognized his quotation.

"He's the son of a Methodist minister," Bartholomew went on. "His father, a missionary, wandered down to Florida in the early days, and died there, leaving a sickly wife and seven children. You know the sort of man—a linen duster for a coat, prunella shoes, always smiling and hopeful—a great deal about 'Brethren.' Fortunately they could at least be warm in that climate, and fish were to be had for the catching; but I suspect it was a struggle for existence while the boys were small. David was the youngest; his five brothers, who had come up almost laborers, were determined to give this lad a chance if they could; together they managed to send him to school, and later to a forlorn little Methodist college somewhere in Georgia. David doesn't call it forlorn, mind you; he still thinks it an important institution. For nine years now—he is thirty—he has taken care of himself; he and a partner have cleared this large farm, and have already done well with it. Their hope is to put it all into sugar in time, and a Northern man with capital has advanced them the money for this Italian colonization scheme: it has been tried before in Florida, and has worked well. They have been very enterprising, David and his partner; they have a saw-mill running, and two school-houses already—one for whites, one for blacks. You ought to see the little darkies, with their wool twisted into twenty tails, going proudly in when the bell rings," he added, turning to Fanny.

"And the white children, do they go too?" said Eva.

"Yes, to their own school-house—lank girls, in immense sun-bonnets, stalking on long bare feet. He has got a brisk little Yankee school-mistress for them. In ten years more I declare he will have civilized that entire neighborhood."

"You are evidently the Northern man with capital," said Dallas.

"I don't care in the least for your sneers, Dallas; I'm not the Northern man, but I should like to be. If I admire Rod, with his constant driving action, his indomitable pluck, his simple but tremendous belief in the importance of what he has undertaken to do, that's my own affair. I do admire him just as he stands, clothes and all; I admire his creaking saw-mill; I admire his groaning dredge; I even admire his two hideously ugly new school-houses, set staring among the stumps."

"Tell me one thing, does he preach in the school-houses on Sundays and Friday evenings, say?" asked Ferguson. "Because if he does he will make no money, whatever else he may make. They never do if they preach."

"It's his father who was the minister, not he," said Bartholomew. "David never preached in his life; he wouldn't in the least know how. In fact, he's no talker at all; he says very little at any time; he's a doer— David is; he *does* things. I declare it used to make me sick of myself to see how much that fellow accomplished every day of his life down there, and thought nothing of it at all."

"And what were you doing 'down there,' besides making yourself sick, if I may ask?" said Ferguson.

"Oh, I went down for the hunting, of course. What else does one go to such a place for?"

"Tell me a little about that, if you don't mind," said the Englishman, interested for the first time.

"M. de Verneuil wants us all to go to the Deserto

some day soon," said Fanny; "a lunch party. We shall be sure to enjoy it; M. de Verneuil's parties are always delightful."

III

The end of the week had been appointed for Pierre's excursion.

The morning opened fair and warm, with the veiled blue that belongs to the Bay of Naples, the soft hazy blue which is so different from the dry glittering clearness of the Riviera.

Fanny was mounted on a donkey; Eva preferred to walk, and Mademoiselle accompanied her. Pierre had included in his invitation the usual afternoon assemblage at the villa—Dallas, Mark Ferguson, Bartholomew, Gordon-Gray, and David Rod.

For Fanny had, as Dallas expressed it, "taken up" Rod; she had invited him twice to dinner. The superfluous courtesy had annoyed Dallas, for of course, as Rod himself was nothing, less than nothing, the explanation must lie in the fact that Horace Bartholomew had suggested it. "Bartholomew was always wrong-headed; always picking up some perfectly impossible creature, and ramming him down people's throats," he thought, with vexation.

Bartholomew was walking now beside Fanny's donkey.

Mark Ferguson led the party, as it moved slowly along the narrow paved road that winds in zigzags up the mountain; Eva, Mademoiselle, Pierre, Dallas, and Rod came next. Fanny and Bartholomew were behind;

and behind still, walking alone and meditatively, came Gordon-Gray, who looked at life (save for the hunting) from the standpoint of the Italian Renaissance. Gordon-Gray knew a great deal about the Malatesta family; he had made a collection of Renaissance cloak clasps; he had written an essay on the colors of the long hose worn in the battling, leg-displaying days which had aroused his admiration, aroused it rather singularly, since he himself was as far as possible from having been qualified by nature to shine in such vigorous society.

Pierre went back to give some directions to one of the men in the rear of their small procession.

When he returned, "So the bears sometimes get among the canes?" Eva was saying.

"But then, how very convenient," said Pierre; "for they can take the canes and chastise them punctually." He spoke in his careful English.

"They're sugar-canes," said Rod.

"It's his plantation we are talking about," said Eva. "Once it was a military post, he says. Perhaps like Ehrenbreitstein."

"Exactly," said Dallas, from behind; "the same massive frowning stone walls."

"There were four one-story wooden barracks once," said Rod; "whitewashed; flag-pole in the centre. There's nothing now but a chimney; we've taken the boards for our mill."

"See the cyclamen, good folk," called out Gordon-Gray.

On a small plateau near by a thousand cyclamen, white and pink, had lifted their wings as if to fly away. Off went Pierre to get them for Eva.

ON THE WAY TO THE DESERTO

"Have you ever seen the bears in the canes yourself?" pursued Eva.

"I've seen them in many places besides canes," answered Rod, grimly.

"I too have seen bears," Eva went on. "At Berne, you know."

"The Punta Palmas bears are quite the same," commented Dallas. "When they see Mr. Rod coming they sit up on their hind legs politely. And he throws them apples."

"No apples; they won't grow there," said Rod, regretfully. "Only oranges."

"Do you make the saw-mill go yourself—with your own hands?" pursued Eva.

"Not now. I did once."

"Wasn't it very hard work?"

"That? Nothing at all. You should have seen us grubbing up the stumps—Tipp and I!"

"Mr. Tipp is perhaps your partner?" said Dallas.

"Yes; Jim Tipp. Tipp and Rod is the name of the firm."

"Tipp — and Rod," repeated Dallas, slowly. Then with quick utterance, as if trying it, "Tippandrod."

Pierre was now returning with his flowers. As he joined them, round the corner of their zigzag, from a pasture above came a troop of ponies that had escaped from their driver, and were galloping down to Sorrento; two and two they came rushing on, too rapidly to stop, and everybody pressed to one side to give them room to pass on the narrow causeway.

Pierre jumped up on the low stone wall and extended his hand to Eva. "Come!" he said, hastily.

Rod put out his arm and pushed each outside pony,

as he passed Eva, forcibly against his mate who had the inside place; a broad space was thus left beside her, and she had no need to leave the causeway. She had given one hand to Pierre as a beginning; he held it tightly. Mademoiselle meanwhile had climbed the wall like a cat. There were twenty of the galloping little nags; they took a minute or two to pass. Rod's outstretched hands, as he warded them off, were seen to be large and brown.

Eva imagined them "grubbing up" the stumps. "What is grubbing?" she said.

"It is writing for the newspapers in a street in London," said Pierre, jumping down. "And you must wear a torn coat, I believe." Pierre was proud of his English.

He presented his flowers.

Mademoiselle admired them volubly. "They are like souls just ready to wing their way to another world," she said, sentimentally, with her head on one side. She put her well-gloved hand in Eva's arm, summoned Pierre with an amiable gesture to the vacant place at Eva's left hand, and the three walked on together.

The Deserto, though disestablished and dismantled, like many another monastery, by the rising young kingdom, held still a few monks; their brown-robed brethren had aided Pierre's servant in arranging the table in the high room which commands the wonderful view of the sea both to the north and the south of the Sorrento peninsula, with Capri lying at its point too fair to be real —like an island in a dream.

"O la douce folie—
Aimable Capri!"

AT THE DESERTO

said Mark Ferguson. No one knew what he meant; he did not know himself. It was a poetical inspiration—so he said.

The lunch was delicate, exquisite; everything save the coffee (which the monks wished to provide: coffee, black-bread, and grapes which were half raisins was the monks' idea of a lunch) had been sent up from Sorrento. Dallas, who was seated beside Fanny, gave her a congratulatory nod.

"Yes, all Pierre does is well done," she answered, in a low tone, unable to deny herself this expression of maternal content.

Pierre was certainly a charming host. He gave them a toast; he gave them two; he gave them a song: he had a tenor voice which had been admirably cultivated, and his song was gay and sweet. He looked very handsome; he wore one of the cyclamen in his button-hole; Eva wore the rest, arranged by the deft fingers of Mademoiselle in a knot at her belt. But at the little feast Fanny was much more prominent than her daughter: this was Pierre's idea of what was proper; he asked her opinion, he referred everything to her with a smile which was homage in itself. Dallas, after a while, was seized with a malicious desire to take down for a moment this too prosperous companion of his boyhood. It was after Pierre had finished his little song. "Do you ever sing now, Fanny?" he asked, during a silence. "I remember how you used to sing Trancadillo."

"I am sure I don't know what you refer to," answered Fanny, coldly.

Another week passed. They sailed to Capri; they sailed to Ischia; they visited Pompeii. Bartholomew suggested these excursions. Eva too showed an almost passionate desire for constant movement, constant action. "Where shall we go to-day, mamma?" she asked every morning.

One afternoon they were strolling through an orange grove on the outskirts of Sorrento. Under the trees the ground was ploughed and rough; low stone copings, from whose interstices innumerable violets swung, ran hither and thither, and the paths followed the copings. The fruit hung thickly on the trees. Above the high wall which surrounded the place loomed the campanile of an old church. While they were strolling the bells rang the Angelus, swinging far out against the blue.

Rod, who was of the party, was absent-minded; he looked a little at the trees, but said nothing, and after a while he became absent-bodied as well, for he fell behind the others, and pursued his meditations, whatever they were, in solitude.

"He is bothered about his Italians," said Bartholomew; "he has only secured twenty so far."

Pierre joined Fanny; he had not talked with her that afternoon, and he now came to fulfil the pleasant duty. Eva, who had been left with Mademoiselle, turned round, and walking rapidly across the ploughed ground, joined Rod, who was sitting on one of the low stone walls at some distance from the party. Mademoiselle followed her, putting on her glasses as she went, in order to see her way over the heaped ridges. She held up her skirts, and gave ineffectual little leaps, always landing in the wrong spot, and tumbling up hill, as Dallas called it. "Blue," he remarked, meditatively. Every one glanced in that direction, and it was perceived that the adjective described the hue of Mademoiselle's birdlike ankles.

"For shame!" said Fanny.

But Dallas continued his observations. "Do look across," he said, after a while; "it's too funny. The French woman evidently thinks that Rod should rise, or else that Eva should be seated also. But her pantomime passes unheeded; neither Eva nor the backwoodsman is conscious of her existence."

"Eva is so fond of standing," explained Fanny. "I often say to her, 'Do sit down, child; it tires me to see you.' But Eva is never tired."

Pierre, who had a spray of orange buds in his hand, pressed it to his lips, and waved it imperceptibly towards his betrothed. "In everything she is perfect—perfect," he murmured to the pretty mother.

"Rod doesn't in the least mean to be rude," began Bartholomew.

"Oh, don't explain that importation of yours at this late day," interposed Dallas; "it isn't necessary. He is accustomed to sitting on fences probably; he belongs to the era of the singing-school."

This made Fanny angry. For as to singing-schools, there had been a time—a remote time long ago—and Dallas knew it. She had smiled in answer to Pierre's murmured rapture; she now took his arm. To punish Dallas she turned her steps—on her plump little feet in their delicate kid boots—towards the still seated Rod, with the intention of asking him (for the fifth time) to dinner. This would not only exasperate Dallas, but it would please Bartholomew at the same stroke. Two birds, etc.

When they came up to the distant three, Mademoiselle glanced at Mrs. Churchill anxiously. But in the presence of the mistress of the villa, Rod did at last lift his long length from the wall.

This seemed, however, to be because he supposed they were about to leave the grove. "Is the walk over?" he said.

Pierre looked at Eva adoringly. He gave her the spray of orange buds.

IV

A week later Fanny's daughter entered the bedroom which she shared with her mother.

From the girl's babyhood the mother had had her small white-curtained couch placed close beside her own. She could not have slept unless able at any moment to stretch out her hand and touch her sleeping child.

Fanny was in the dressing-room; hearing Eva's step, she spoke. "Do you want me, Eva?"

"Yes, please."

Fanny appeared, a vision of white arms, lace, and embroidery.

"I thought that Rosine would not be here yet," said Eva. Rosine was their maid; her principal occupation was the elaborate arrangement of Fanny's brown hair.

"No, she isn't there—if you mean in the dressing-room," answered Fanny, nodding her head towards the open door.

"I wanted to see you alone, mamma, for a moment. I wanted to tell you that I shall not marry Pierre."

Fanny, who had sunk into an easy-chair, at these words sprang up. "What is the matter? Are you ill?"

"Not in the least, mamma; I am only telling you that I cannot marry Pierre."

"You *must* be ill," pursued Fanny. "You have fever. Don't deny it." And anxiously she took the girl's hands. But Eva's hands were cooler than her own.

"I don't think I have any fever," replied Eva. She had been taught to answer all her mother's questions in fullest detail. "I sleep and eat as usual; I have no headache."

Fanny still looked at her anxiously. "Then if you are not ill, what can be the matter with you?"

"I have only told you, mamma, that I could not marry Pierre; it seems to me very simple."

She was so quiet that Fanny began at last to realize that she was in earnest. "My dearest, you know you like Pierre. You have told me so yourself."

"I don't like him now."

"What has he done—poor Pierre? He will explain, apologize; you may be sure of that."

"He has done nothing; I don't want him to apologize. He is as he always is. It is I who have changed."

"Oh, it is you who have changed," repeated Fanny, bewildered.

"Yes," answered Eva.

"Come and sit down and tell mamma all about it. You are tired of poor Pierre—is that it? It is very natural, he has been here so often, and stayed so long. But I will tell him that he must go away—leave Sorrento. And he shall stay away as long as you like, Eva; just as long as you like."

"Then he will stay away forever," the girl answered, calmly.

Fanny waited a moment. "Did you like Gino better? Is that it?" she said, softly, watching Eva's face.

"No."

"Thornton Stanley?"

"Oh no!"

"Dear child, explain this a little to your mother You know I think only of your happiness," said Fanny, with tender solicitude.

Eva evidently tried to obey. "It was this morning. It came over me suddenly that I could not possibly marry him. Now or a year from now. Never." She spoke tranquilly; she even seemed indifferent. But this one decision was made.

"You know that I have given my word to the old Count," began Fanny, in perplexity.

Eva was silent.

"And everything was arranged."

Eva still said nothing. She looked about the room with wandering attention, as though this did not concern her.

"Of course I would never force you into anything," Fanny went on. "But I thought Pierre would be so congenial." In her heart she was asking herself what the young Belgian could have done. "Well, dear," she continued, with a little sigh, "you must always tell mamma everything." And she kissed her.

"Of course," Eva answered. And then she went away.

Fanny immediately rang the bell, and asked for Mademoiselle. But Mademoiselle knew nothing about it. She was overwhelmed with surprise and dismay. She greatly admired Pierre; even more she admired the old Count, whom she thought the most distinguished of men. Fanny dismissed the afflicted little woman, and sat pondering. While she was thinking, Eva re-entered.

"Mamma, I forgot to say that I should like to have you tell Pierre immediately. To-day."

Fanny was almost irritated. "You have never taken that tone before, my daughter. Have you no longer confidence in my judgment?"

"If you do not want to tell him this afternoon, it can be easily arranged, mamma; I will not come to the dinner-table; that is all. I do not wish to see him until he knows."

Pierre was to dine at the villa that evening.

"What can he have done?" thought Fanny again.

She rang for Rosine; half an hour later she was in the drawing-room. "Excuse me to every one but M. de Verneuil," she said to Angelo. She was very nervous, but she had decided upon her course: Pierre must leave Sorrento, and remain away until she herself should call him back.

"At the end of a month, perhaps even at the end of a week, she will miss you so much that I shall have to issue the summons," she said, speaking as gayly as she could, as if to make it a sort of joke. It was very hard for her, at best, to send away the frank, handsome boy.

Poor Pierre could not understand it at all. He declared over and over again that nothing he had said, nothing he had done, could possibly have offended his betrothed. "But surely you know yourself that it is impossible!" he added, clasping his hands beseechingly.

"It is a girlish freak," explained the mother. "She is so young, you know."

"But that is the very reason. I thought it was only older women who say what they wish to do in that decided way; who have freaks, as you call it," said the

Belgian, his voice for a moment much older, more like the voice of a man who has spent half his life in Paris.

This was so true that Fanny was driven to a defence that scarcely anything else would have made her use. "Eva is different from the young girls here," she said. "You must not forget that she is an American."

At last Pierre went away; he had tried to bear himself as a gentleman should; but the whole affair was a mystery to him, and he was very unhappy. He went as far as Rome, and there he waited, writing to Fanny an anxious letter almost every day.

In the meanwhile life at the villa went on; there were many excursions. Fanny's thought was that Eva would miss Pierre more during these expeditions than at other times, for Pierre had always arranged them, and he had enjoyed them so much himself that his gay spirits and his gay wit had made all the party gay. Eva, however, seemed very happy, and at length the mother could not help being touched to see how light-hearted her serious child had become, now that she was entirely free. And yet how slight the yoke had been, and how pleasant! thought Fanny. At the end of two weeks there were still no signs of the "missing" upon which she had counted. She thought that she would try the effect of briefly mentioning the banished man. "I hear from Pierre almost every day, poor fellow. He is in Rome."

"Why does he stay in Rome?" said Eva. "Why doesn't he return home?"

"I suppose he doesn't want to go so far away," answered Fanny, vaguely.

"Far away from what? Home should always be the first place," responded the young moralist. "Of course you have told him, mamma, that I shall never be his wife? That it is forever?" And she turned her gray eyes towards her mother, for the first time with a shade of suspicion in them.

"Never is a long word, Eva."

"Oh, mamma!" The girl rose. "I shall write to him myself, then."

"How you speak! Do you wish to disobey me, my own little girl?"

"No; but it is so dishonest; it is like a lie."

"My dear, trust your mother. You have changed once; you may change again."

"Not about this, mamma. Will you please write this very hour, and make an end of it?"

"You are hard, Eva. You do not think of poor Pierre at all."

"No, I do not think of Pierre."

"And is there any one else you think of? I must ask you that once more," said Fanny, drawing her daughter down beside her caressingly. Her thoughts could not help turning again towards Gino, and in her supreme love for her child she now accomplished the mental somerset of believing that on the whole she preferred the young Italian to all the liberty, all the personal consideration for herself, which had been embodied in the name of Verneuil.

"Yes, there is some one else I think of," Eva replied, in a low voice.

"In Rome?" said Fanny.

Eva made a gesture of denial that was fairly contemptuous.

Fanny's mind flew wildly from Bartholomew to Dallas, from Ferguson to Gordon-Gray: Eva had no acquaintances save those which were her mother's also.

"It is David Rod," Eva went on, in the same low tone. Then, with sudden exaltation, her eyes gleaming, "I have never seen any one like him."

It was a shock so unexpected that Mrs. Churchill drew her breath under it audibly, as one does under an actual blow. But instantly she rallied. She said to herself that she had got a romantic idealist for a daughter— that was all. She had not suspected it; she had thought of Eva as a lovely child who would develop into what she herself had been. Fanny, though far-seeing and intelligent, had not been endowed with imagination. But now that she did realize it, she should know how to deal with it. A disposition like that, full of visionary fancies, was not so uncommon as some people supposed. Horace Bartholomew should take the Floridian away out of Eva's sight forever, and the girl would soon forget him; in the meanwhile not one word that was harsh should be spoken on the subject, for that would be the worst policy of all.

This train of thought had passed through her mind like a flash. "My dear," she began, as soon as she had got her breath back, "you are right to be so honest with me. Mr. Rod has not—has not said anything to you on the subject, has he?"

"No. Didn't I tell you that he cares nothing for me? I think he despises me—I am so useless!" And then suddenly the girl began to sob; a passion of tears.

Fanny was at her wits' end; Eva had not wept since the day of her baby ills, for life had been happy to her, loved, caressed, and protected as she had been always, like a hot-house flower.

"My darling," said the mother, taking her in her arms.

But Eva wept on and on, as if her heart would break. It ended in Fanny's crying too.

V

Early the next morning her letter to Bartholomew was sent. Bartholomew had gone to Munich for a week. The letter begged, commanded, that he should make some pretext that would call David Rod from Sorrento at the earliest possible moment. She counted upon her fingers; four days for the letter to go and the answer to return. Those four days she would spend at Capri.

Eva went with her quietly. There had been no more conversation between mother and daughter about Rod; Fanny thought that this was best.

On the fourth day there came a letter from Bartholomew. Fanny returned to Sorrento almost gayly: the man would be gone.

But he was not gone. Tranquillized, glad to be at home again, Mrs. Churchill was enjoying her terrace and her view, when Angelo appeared at the window: "Signor Ra."

Angelo's mistress made him a peremptory sign. "Ask the gentleman to wait in the drawing-room," she said. Then crossing to Eva, who had risen, "Go round by the other door to our own room, Eva," she whispered.

The girl did not move; her face had an excited look. "But why—"

"Go, child; go."

Still Eva stood there, her eyes fixed upon the long window veiled in lace; she scarcely seemed to breathe.

Her mother was driven to stronger measures. "You told me yourself that he cared nothing for you."

A deep red rose in Eva's cheeks; she turned and left the terrace by the distant door.

The mother crossed slowly to the long window and parted the curtains. "Mr. Rod, are you there? Won't you come out? Or stay—I will join you." She entered the drawing-room and took a seat.

Rod explained that he was about to leave Sorrento; Bartholomew had summoned him so urgently that he did not like to refuse, though it was very inconvenient to go at such short notice.

"Then you leave to-morrow?" said Fanny; "perhaps to-night?"

"No; on Monday. I could not arrange my business before."

"Three days more," Fanny thought.

She talked of various matters; she hoped that some one else would come in; but, by a chance, no one appeared that day, neither Dallas, nor Ferguson, nor Gordon-Gray. "What can have become of them?" she thought, with irritation. After a while she gave an inward start; she had become conscious of a foot-fall passing to and fro behind the half-open door near her— a door which led into the dining-room. It was a very soft foot-fall upon a thick carpet, but she recognized it: it was Eva. She was there—why? The mother could think of no good reason. Her heart began to beat more quickly; for the first time in her life she did not know her child. This person walking up and down be-

hind that door so insistently, this was not Eva. Eva
was docile; this person was not docile. What would
be done next? She felt strangely frightened. It was
a proof of her terror that she did not dare to close the
door lest it should be instantly reopened. She began
to watch every word she said to Rod, who had not perceived the foot-fall. She began to be extraordinarily
polite to him; she stumbled through the most irrele-
vant complimentary sentences. Her dread was, every
minute, lest Eva should appear.

But Eva did not appear; and at last, after long lin-
gering, Rod went away. Fanny, who had hoped to
bid him a final farewell, had not dared to go through
that ceremony. He said that he should come again.

When at last he was gone the mother pushed open
the half-closed door. "Eva," she began. She had intended to be severe, as severe as she possibly could be;
but the sight of Eva stopped her. The girl had flung
herself down upon the floor, her bowed head resting
upon her arms on a chair. Her attitude expressed a
hopeless desolation.

"What is it?" said Fanny, rushing to her.

Eva raised her head. "He never once spoke of me
—asked for me," she murmured, looking at her mother
with eyes so dreary with grief that any one must have
pitied her.

Her mother pitied her, though it was an angry pity,
too—a non-comprehending, jealous, exasperated feeling.
She sat down and gathered her child to her breast with
a gesture that was almost fierce. That Eva should suffer so cruelly when she, Fanny, would have made any
sacrifice to save her from it, would have died for her
gladly, were it not that she was the girl's only pro-

tector—oh, what fate had come over their happy life together! She had not the heart to be stern. All she said was, "We will go away, dear; we will go away."

"No," said Eva, rising; "let me stay here. You need not be afraid."

"Of course I am not afraid," answered Fanny, gravely. "My daughter will never do anything unseemly; she has too much pride."

"I am afraid I have no pride—that is, not as you have it, mamma. Pride doesn't seem to me at all important compared with— But of course I know that there is nothing I can do. He is perfectly indifferent. Only do not take me away again—do not."

"Why do you wish to stay?"

"Because then I can think—for three days more—that he is at least as near me as that." She trembled as she said this; there was a spot of sombre red in each cheek; her fair face looked strange amid her disordered hair.

Her mother watched her helplessly. All her beliefs, all her creed, all her precedents, the experience of her own life and her own nature even, failed to explain such a phenomenon as this. And it was her own child who was saying these things.

The next day Eva was passive. She wandered about the terrace, or sat for hours motionless staring blankly at the sea. Her mother left her to herself. She had comprehended that words were useless. She pretended to be embroidering, but in reality as she drew her stitches she was counting the hours as they passed: seventy-two hours; forty-eight hours. Would he ever be gone?

On the second day, in the afternoon, she discovered

"SHE SAT DOWN AND GATHERED HER CHILD TO HER BREAST"

that Eva had disappeared. The girl had been on the terrace with Mademoiselle; Mademoiselle had gone to her room for a moment, and when she returned her pupil could not be found. She had not passed through the drawing-room, where Fanny was sitting with her pretended industry; nor through the other door, for Rosine was at work there, and had seen nothing of her. There remained only the rock stairway to the beach. Mademoiselle ran down it swiftly: no one. But there was a small boat not far off, she said. Fanny, who was near-sighted, got the glass. In a little boat with a broad sail there were two figures; one was certainly David Rod, and the other—yes, the other was Eva. There was a breeze, the boat was rapidly going westward round the cliffs; in two minutes more it was out of sight.

Fanny wrung her hands. The French woman, to whom the event wore a much darker hue than it did to the American mother, turned yellowly pale.

At this moment Horace Bartholomew came out on the terrace; uneasy, for Fanny's missive had explained nothing, he had followed his letter himself. "What is it?" he said, as he saw the agitation of the two women.

"Your friend—*yours*—the man you brought here, has Eva with him at this moment out on the bay!" said Fanny, vehemently.

"Well, what of that? You must look at it with Punta Palmas eyes, Fanny; at Punta Palmas it would be an ordinary event."

"But my Eva is not a Punta Palmas girl, Horace Bartholomew!"

"She is as innocent as one, and I'll answer for Rod.

Come, be sensible, Fanny. They will be back before sunset, and no one in Sorrento—if that is what is troubling you so—need be any the wiser."

"You do not know all," said Fanny. "Oh, Horace—I must tell somebody—she fancies she cares for that man!" She wrung her hands again. "Couldn't we follow them? Get a boat."

"It would take an hour. And it would be a very conspicuous thing to do. Leave them alone—it's much better; I tell you I'll answer for Rod. Fancies she cares for him, does she? Well, he is a fine fellow; on the whole, the finest I know."

The mother's eyes flashed through her tears. "This from *you?*"

"I can't help it; he is. Of course you do not think so. He has got no money; he has never been anywhere that you call anywhere; he doesn't know anything about the only life you care for nor the things you think important. All the same, he is a man in a million. He is a man—not a puppet."

Gentle Mrs. Churchill appeared for the moment transformed. She looked as though she could strike him. "Never mind your Quixotic ideas. Tell me whether he is in love with Eva; it all depends upon that."

"I don't know, I am sure," answered Bartholomew. He began to think. "I can't say at all; he would conceal it from me."

"Because he felt his inferiority. I am glad he has that grace."

"He wouldn't be conscious of any inferiority save that he is poor. It would be that, probably, if anything; of course he supposes that Eva is rich."

"Would to Heaven she were!" said the mother. "Added to every other horror of it, poverty, miserable poverty, for my poor child!" She sat down and hid her face.

"It may not be as bad as you fear, nor anything like it. Do cheer up a little, Fanny. When Eva comes back, ten to one you will find that nothing at all has happened—that it has been a mere ordinary excursion. And I promise you I will take Rod away with me to-morrow."

Mrs. Churchill rose and began to pace to and fro, biting her lips, and watching the water. Mademoiselle, who was still hovering near, she waved impatiently away. "Let no one in," she called to her.

There seemed, indeed, to be nothing else to do, as Bartholomew had said, save to wait. He sat down and discussed the matter a little.

Fanny paid no attention to what he was saying. Every now and then broken phrases of her own burst from her: "How much good will her perfect French and Italian, her German, Spanish, and even Russian, do her down in that barbarous wilderness?"—"In her life she has never even buttoned her boots. Do they think she can make bread?"—"And there was Gino. And poor Pierre." Then, suddenly, "But it *shall* not be!"

"I have been wondering why you did not take that tone from the first," said Bartholomew. "She is very young. She has been brought up to obey you implicitly. It would be easy enough, I should fancy, if you could once make up your mind to it."

"Make up my mind to save her, you mean," said the mother, bitterly. She did not tell him that she was afraid of her daughter. "Should you expect *me* to live at Punta Palmas?" she demanded, contemptuously, of her companion.

"That would depend upon Rod, wouldn't it?" answered Bartholomew, rather unamiably. He was tired —he had been there an hour—of being treated like a door-mat.

At this Fanny broke down again, and completely. For it was only too true; it would depend upon that stranger, that farmer, that unknown David Rod, whether she, the mother, should or should not be with her own child.

A little before sunset the boat came into sight again round the western cliffs. Fanny dried her eyes. She was very pale. Little Mademoiselle, rigid with anxiety, watched from an upper window. Bartholomew rose to go down to the beach to receive the returning fugitives. "No," said Fanny, catching his arm, "don't go; no one must know before I do—no one." So they waited in silence.

Down below, the little boat had rapidly approached. Eva had jumped out, and was now running up the rock stairway; she was always light-footed, but to her mother it seemed that the ascent took an endless time. At length there was the vision of a young, happy, rushing figure—rushing straight to Fanny's arms. "Oh, mamma, mamma," the girl whispered, seeing that there was no one there but Bartholomew, "he loves me! He has told me so! he has told me so!"

For an instant the mother drew herself away. Eva, left alone, and mindful of nothing but her own bliss, looked so radiant with happiness that Bartholomew (being a man) could not help sympathizing with her.

"You will have to give it up," he said to Fanny, significantly. Then he took his hat and went away.

Fifteen minutes later his place was filled by David Rod.

"Ah! you have come. I must have a few words of conversation with you, Mr. Rod," said Fanny, in an icy tone. "Eva, leave us now."

"Oh no, mamma, not now; never again, I hope," answered the girl. She spoke with secure confidence; her eyes were fixed upon her lover's face.

"Do you call this honorable behavior, Mr. Rod?" Fanny began. She saw that Eva would not go.

"Why, I hope so," answered Rod, surprised. "I have come at once, as soon as I possibly could, Mrs. Churchill (I had to take the boat back first, you know), to tell you that we are engaged; it isn't an hour old yet—is it, Eva?" He looked at Eva smilingly, his eyes as happy as her own.

"It is the custom to ask permission," said Fanny, stiffly.

"I have never heard of the custom, then; that is all I can say," answered Rod, with good-natured tranquillity, still looking at the girl's face, with its rapt expression, its enchanting joy.

"Please to pay attention: I decline to consent, Mr. Rod; you cannot have my daughter."

"Mamma—" said Eva, coming up to her.

"No, Eva; if you will remain here—which is most improper—you will have to hear it all. You are so much my daughter's inferior, Mr. Rod, that I cannot, and I shall not, consent."

At the word "inferior," a slight shock passed over Eva from head to foot. She went swiftly to her lover, knelt down and pressed her lips to his brown hand, hiding her face upon it.

He raised her tenderly in his arms, and thus embraced, they stood there together, confronting the mother—confronting the world.

Fanny put out her hands with a bitter cry. "Eva!"

The girl ran to her, clung to her. "Oh, mamma, I love you dearly. But you must not try to separate me from David. I could not leave him—I never will."

"Let us go in, to our own room," said the mother, in a broken voice.

"Yes; but speak to David first, mamma."

Rod came forward and offered his arm. He was sorry for the mother's grief, which, however, in such intensity as this, he could not at all understand. But though he was sorry, he was resolute, he was even stern; in his dark beauty, his height and strength, he looked indeed, as Bartholomew had said, a man.

At the sight of his offered arm Mrs. Churchill recoiled; she glanced all round the terrace as though to get away from it; she even glanced at the water; it almost seemed as if she would have liked to take her child and plunge with her to the depths below. But one miserable look at Eva's happy, trustful eyes still watching her lover's face cowed her; she took the offered arm. And then Rod went with her, supporting her gently into the house, and through it to her own room, where he left her with her daughter. That night the mother rose from her sleepless couch, lit a shaded taper, and leaving it on a distant table, stole softly to Eva's side. The girl was in a deep slumber, her head pillowed on her arm. Fanny, swallowing her tears,

"FANNY PUT OUT HER HANDS WITH A BITTER CRY"

gazed at her sleeping child. She still saw in the face the baby outlines of years before, her mother's eye could still distinguish in the motionless hand the dimpled fingers of the child. The fair hair, lying on the pillow, recalled to her the short flossy curls of the little girl who had clung to her skirts, who had had but one thought—" mamma."

"What will her life be now? What must she go through, perhaps—what pain, privation—my darling, my own little child!"

The wedding was to take place within the month; Rod said that he could not be absent longer from his farm. Fanny, breaking her silence, suggested to Bartholomew that the farm might be given up; there were other occupations.

"I advise you not to say a word of that sort to Rod," Bartholomew answered. "His whole heart is in that farm, that colony he has built up down there. You must remember that he was brought up there himself, or rather came up. It's all he knows, and he thinks it the most important thing in life; I was going to say it's all he cares for, but of course now he has added Eva."

Pierre came once. He saw only the mother.

When he left her he went round by way of the main street of Sorrento in order to pass a certain small inn. His carriage was waiting to take him back to Castellamare, but there was some one he wished to look at first. It was after dark; he could see into the lighted house through the low uncurtained windows, and he soon came upon the tall outline of the young farmer seated at a table, his eyes bent upon a column of figures. The Belgian surveyed him from head to foot slowly. He stood there gazing for five minutes. Then he turned away. "*That*, for Americans!" he murmured in French, snapping his fingers in the darkness. But there was a mist in his boyish eyes all the same.

The pink villa witnessed the wedding. Fanny never knew how she got through that day. She was calm; she did not once lose her self-control.

They were to sail directly for New York from Naples, and thence to Florida; the Italian colonists were to go at the same time.

"Mamma comes next year," Eva said to everybody. She looked indescribably beautiful; it was the radiance of a complete happiness, like a halo.

By three o'clock they were gone, they were crossing the bay in the little Naples steamer. No one was left at the villa with Fanny—it was her own arrangement—save Horace Bartholomew.

"She won't mind being poor," he said, consolingly, "she won't mind anything—with *him*. It is one of those sudden, overwhelming loves that one sometimes sees; and after all, Fanny, it is the sweetest thing life offers."

"And the mother?" said Fanny.

THE STREET OF THE HYACINTH

I

It was a street in Rome—narrow, winding, not over-clean. Two vehicles meeting there could pass only by grazing the doors and windows on either side, after the usual excited whip-cracking and shouts which make the new-comer imagine, for his first day or two, that he is proceeding at a perilous speed through the sacred city of the soul.

But two vehicles did not often meet in the street of the Hyacinth. It was not a thoroughfare, not even a convenient connecting link; it skirted the back of the Pantheon, the old buildings on either side rising so high against the blue that the sun never came down lower than the fifth line of windows, and looking up from the pavement was like looking up from the bottom of a well. There was no foot-walk, of course; even if there had been one no one would have used it, owing to the easy custom of throwing from the windows a few ashes and other light trifles for the city refuse-carts, instead of carrying them down the long stairs to the door below. They must be in the street at an appointed hour, must they not? Very well, then—there they were; no one but an unreasonable foreigner would dream of objecting.

But unreasonable foreigners seldom entered the street of the Hyacinth. There were, however, two who lived there one winter not long ago, and upon a certain morning in the January of that winter a third came to see these two. At least he asked for them, and gave two cards to the Italian maid who answered his ring; but when, before he had time to even seat himself, the little curtain over the parlor door was raised again, and Miss Macks entered, she came alone. Her mother did not appear. The visitor was not disturbed by being obliged to begin conversation immediately; he was an old Roman sojourner, and had stopped fully three minutes at the end of the fourth flight of stairs to regain his breath before he mounted the fifth and last to ring Miss Macks's bell. Her card was tacked upon the door: "Miss Ettie F. Macks." He surveyed it with disfavor, while the little, loose-hung bell rang a small but exceedingly shrill and ill-tempered peal, like the barking of a small cur. "Why in the world doesn't she put her mother's card here instead of her own?" he said to himself. "Or, if her own, why not simply 'Miss Macks,' without that nickname?"

But Miss Macks's mother had never possessed a visiting-card in her life. Miss Macks was the visiting member of the family; and this was so well understood at home, that she had forgotten that it might not be the same abroad. As to the "Ettie," having been called so always, it had not occurred to her to make a change. Her name was Ethelinda Faith, Mrs. Macks having thus combined euphony and filial respect—the first title being her tribute to æsthetics, the second her tribute to the memory of her mother.

"I am so very glad to see you, Mr. Noel," said Miss

Macks, greeting her visitor with much cordial directness of voice and eyes. "I have been expecting you. But you have waited so long—three days!"

Raymond Noel, who thought that under the circumstances he had been unusually courteous and prompt, was rather surprised to find himself thus put at once upon the defensive.

"We are not always able to carry out our wishes immediately, Miss Macks," he replied, smiling a little. "I was hampered by several previously made engagements."

"Yes; but this was a little different, wasn't it? This was something important — not like an invitation to lunch or dinner, or the usual idle society talk."

He looked at her; she was quite in earnest.

"I suppose it to be different," he answered. "You must remember how little you have told me."

"I thought I told you a good deal! However, the atmosphere of a reception is no place for such subjects, and I can understand that you did not take it in. That is the reason I asked you to come and see me here. Shall I begin at once? It seems rather abrupt."

"I enjoy abruptness; I have not heard any for a long time."

"That I can understand, too; I suppose the society here is all finished off—there are no rough ends."

"There are ends. If not rough, they are often sharp."

But Miss Macks did not stop to analyze this; she was too much occupied with her own subject.

"I will begin immediately, then," she said. "It will be rather long; but if you are to understand me you ought, of course, to know the whole."

"My chair is very comfortable," replied Noel, placing his hat and gloves on the sofa near him, and taking an easy position with his head back.

Miss Macks thought that he ought to have said, "The longer it is, the more interesting," or something of that sort. She had already described him to her mother as "not over-polite. Not rude in the least, you know—as far as possible from that; wonderfully smooth-spoken; but yet, somehow—awfully indifferent." However, he was Raymond Noel; and that, not his politeness or impoliteness, was her point.

"To begin with, then, Mr. Noel, a year ago I had never read one word you have written; I had never even heard of you. I suppose you think it strange that I should tell you this so frankly; but, in the first place, it will give you a better idea of my point of view; and, in the second, I feel a friendly interest in your taking measures to introduce your writings into the community where I lived. It is a very intelligent community. Naturally, a writer wants his articles read. What else does he write them for?"

"Perhaps a little for his own entertainment," suggested her listener.

"Oh no! He would never take so much trouble just for that."

"On the contrary, many would take any amount just for that. Successfully to entertain one's self—that is one of the great successes of life."

Miss Macks gazed at him; she had a very direct gaze.

"This is just mere talk," she said, not impatiently, but in a business-like tone. "We shall never get anywhere if you take me up so. It is not that your remarks are not very cultivated and interesting, and all that, but simply that I have so much to tell you."

"Perhaps I can be cultivated and interesting dumbly. I will try."

"You are afraid I am going to be diffuse; I see that. So many women are diffuse! But I shall not be, because, I have been thinking for six months just what I should say to you. It was very lucky that I went with Mrs. Lawrence to that reception where I met you. But if it had not happened as it did I should have found you out all the same. I should have looked for your address at all the bankers', and if it was not there I should have inquired at all the hotels. But it was delightful luck getting hold of you in this way almost the very minute I enter Rome!"

She spoke so simply and earnestly that Noel did not say that he was immensely honored, and so forth, but merely bowed his acknowledgments.

"To go back. I shall give you simply heads," pursued Miss Macks. "If you want details, ask, and I will fill them in. I come from the West. Tuscolee Falls is the name of our town. We had a farm there, but we did not do well with it after Mr. Spurr's death, so we rented it out. That is how I come to have so much leisure. I have always had a great deal of ambition; by that I mean that I did not see why things that had once been done could not be done again. It seemed to me that the point was—just determination. And then, of course, I always had the talent. I made pictures when I was a very little girl. Mother has them still, and I can show them to you. It is just like all the biographies, you know. They always begin in childhood, and astonish the family. Well, I had my first lessons from a drawing-teacher who spent a summer in Tuscolee. I can show you what I did while with him. Then I attended, for four years, the Young Ladies' Seminary in the county-town, and took lessons while there. I may as well be perfectly frank and tell the whole, which is that everybody was astonished at my progress, and that I was myself. All sorts of things are prophesied out there about my future. You see, the neighborhood is a very generous-spirited one, and they like to think they have discovered a genius at their own doors. My telling you all this sounds, I know, rather conceited, Mr. Noel. But if you could see my motive, and how entirely without conceit my idea of myself really is, you would hold me free from that charge. It is only that I want you to know absolutely the whole."

"I quite understand," answered her visitor.

"Well, I hope you do. I went on at home after that by myself, and I did a good deal. I work pretty rapidly, you see. Then came my last lessons, from a third teacher. He was a young man from New York. He had consumption, poor fellow! and cannot last long. He wasn't of much use to me in actual work. His ideas were completely different from those of my other teachers, and, indeed, from my own. He was unreliable, too, and his temper was uneven. However, I had a good deal of respect for his opinion, and *he* told me to get your art-articles and read them. It wasn't easy. Some of them are scattered about in the magazines and papers, you know. However, I am pretty determined, and I kept at it until I got them all. Well, they made a great impression upon me. You see, they were new." She paused. "But I doubt,

Mr. Noel, whether we should ever entirely agree," she added, looking at him reflectively.

"That is very probable, Miss Macks."

Miss Macks thought this an odd reply. "He is so queer, with all his smoothness!" she said to her mother afterwards. "He never says what you think he will say. Now, any one would suppose that he would have answered that he would try to make me agree, or something like that. Instead, he just gave it right up without trying! But I expect he sees how independent I am, and that I don't intend to *reflect any* one.

"Well, they made a great impression," she resumed. "And as you seemed to think, Mr. Noel, that no one could do well in painting who had not seen and studied the old pictures over here, I made up my mind to come over at any cost, if it was a possible thing to bring it about. It wasn't easy, but—here we are. In the lives of all—almost all—artists, I have noticed—haven't you?—that there comes a time when they have to live on hope and their own pluck more than upon anything tangible that the present has to offer. They have to take that risk. Well, I have taken it; I took it when we left America. And now I will tell you what it is I want from *you*. I haven't any hesitation in asking, because I am sure you will feel interested in a case like mine, and because it was your writings really that brought me here, you know. And so, then, first: I would like your opinion of all that I have done so far. I have brought everything with me to show you. Second: I want your advice as to the best teacher; I suppose there is a great choice in Rome. Third: I should be glad if you would give a general oversight to all I do for the next year. And last, if you would be so kind, I should much enjoy making visits with you to all the galleries and hearing your opinions again by word of mouth, because that is always so much more vivid, you know, than the printed page."

"My dear Miss Macks! you altogether over-estimate my powers," said Noel, astounded by these far-reaching demands, so calmly and confidently made.

"Yes, I know. Of course it strikes you so—strikes you as a great compliment that I should wish to put myself so entirely in your hands," answered Miss Macks, smiling. "But you must give up thinking of me as the usual young lady; you must not think of me in that way any more than I shall think of you as the usual young gentleman. You will never meet me at a reception again; now that I have found *you*, I shall devote myself entirely to my work."

"An alarming girl!" said Noel to himself. But, even as he said it, he knew that, in the ordinary acceptation of the term at least, Miss Macks was not alarming.

She was twenty-two; in some respects she looked older, in others much younger, than most girls of that age. She was tall, slender, erect, but not especially graceful. Her hands were small and finely shaped, but thin. Her features were well cut; her face oval. Her gray eyes had a clear directness in their glance, which, combined with the other expressions of her face, told the experienced observer at once that she knew little of what is called "the world." For, although calm, it was a deeply confident glance; it showed that the girl was sure that she could take care of herself, and even several others also, through any contingencies that might arise. She had little color; but her smooth complexion was not pale—it was slightly brown. Her mouth was small, her teeth small and very white. Her light-brown hair was drawn back smoothly from her forehead, and drawn up smoothly behind, its thickness braided in a close knot on the top of her head. This compact coiffure, at a time when most feminine foreheads in Rome and elsewhere were shaded almost to the eyebrows by curling locks, and when the arched outline of the head was left unbroken, the hair being coiled in a low knot behind, made Miss Macks look somewhat peculiar. But she was not observant of fashion's changes. That had been the mode in Tuscolee; she had grown accustomed to it; and, as her mind was full of other things, she had not considered this one. One or two persons, who noticed her on the voyage over, said to themselves, "If that girl had more color, and if she was graceful, and if she was a little more womanly—that is, if she would not look at everything in such a direct, calm, impartial, impersonal sort of way—she would be almost pretty."

But Miss Macks continued without color and without grace, and went on looking at things as impersonally and impartially as ever.

"I shall be most happy, of course, to do anything that I can," Noel had answered. Then to make a diversion, "Shall I not have the pleasure of seeing Mrs. Macks?" he asked.

"Mrs. Macks? Oh, you mean mother. My mother's name is Spurr — Mrs. Spurr. My father died when I was a baby, and some years afterwards she married Mr. Spurr. She is now again a widow. Her health is not good, and she sees almost no one, thank you."

"I suppose you are much pleased with the picturesqueness of Roman life, and—ah—your apartment?" he went on.

"Pleased?" said Miss Macks, looking at him in wonder. "With our apartment? We get along with it because we must; there seems to be no other way to live in Rome. The idea of having only a story of a house, and not a whole house to ourselves, is dreadful to mother; she cannot get used to it. And with so many families below us—we have a clock-mender, a dress-maker, an engraver, a print-seller, and a cobbler —and only one pair of stairs, it does seem to me dreadfully public."

"You must look upon the stairway as a street," said Noel. "You have established yourselves in a very short time."

"Oh yes. I got an agent, and looked at thirty places the very first day. I speak Italian a little, so I can manage the house-keeping; I began to study it as soon as we thought of coming, and I studied hard. But all this is of secondary importance; the real thing is to get to work. Will you look at my paintings now?" she said, rising as if to go for them.

"Thanks; I fear I have hardly time to-day," said Noel. He was thinking whether it would be better to decline clearly and in so many words the office she had thrust upon him, or trust to time to effect the same without an open refusal. He decided upon the latter course; it seemed the easier, and also the kinder to her.

"Well, another day, then," said Miss Macks, cheerfully, taking her seat again. "But about a teacher?"

"I hardly know—"

"Oh, Mr. Noel! you *must* know."

And, in truth, he did know. It came into his mind to give her the name of a good teacher, and then put all further responsibilities upon him.

Miss Macks wrote down the name in a clear, ornamental handwriting.

"I am glad it isn't a foreigner," she said. "I don't believe I should get on with a foreigner."

"But it is a foreigner."

"Why, it's an English name, isn't it?—Jackson."

"Yes, he is an Englishman. But isn't an Englishman a foreigner in Rome?"

"Oh, you take that view? Now, to me, America and—well, yes, perhaps England, too, are the nations. Everything else is foreign."

"The English would be very much obliged to you," said Noel, laughing.

"Yes, I know I am more liberal than most Americans; I really like the English," said Miss Macks, calmly. "But we keep getting off the track. Let me see— Oh yes. As I shall go to see this Mr. Jackson this afternoon, and as it is not likely that he will be ready to begin to-morrow, will you come then and look at my pictures? Or would you rather commence with a visit to one of the galleries?"

Raymond Noel was beginning to be amused. If she had shown the faintest indication of knowing how much she was asking, if she had betrayed the smallest sign of a desire to secure his attention as Raymond Noel personally, and not simply the art authority upon whom she had pinned her faith, his disrelish for various other things about her would have been heightened into utter dislike, and it is probable that he would never have entered the street of the Hyacinth again. But she was so unaware of any intrusion, or any exorbitance in her demands, probably so ignorant of—certainly so indifferent to—the degree of perfection (perfection of the most quiet kind, however) visible in the general appearance and manner of the gentleman before her, that (he said to himself) he might as well have been one of her own Tuscolee farmers, for all she knew to the contrary. The whole affair was unusual; and Noel rather liked the unusual, if it was not loud—and Miss Macks was, at least, not loud; she was dressed plainly in black, and she had the gift of a sweet voice, which, although very clear, was low-toned. Noel was an observer of voices, and he had noticed hers the first time he heard her speak. While these thoughts were passing through his mind, he was answering that he feared his engagements for the next day would, unfortunately, keep him from putting himself at her service.

Her face fell; she looked much disappointed.

"Is it going to be like this all the time?" she asked, anxiously. "Are you always engaged?"

"In Rome, in the winter, one generally has small leisure. It will be the same with you, Miss Macks, when you have been here a while longer; you will see. As to the galleries, Mr. Jackson has a class, I think, and probably the pupils will visit them all under his charge; you will find that very satisfactory."

"But I don't want Mr. Jackson for the galleries; I want *you*," said Miss Macks. "I have studied your art criticisms until I know them by heart, and I have a thousand questions to ask about every picture you have mentioned. Why, Mr. Noel, I came to Europe to see you!"

Raymond Noel was rather at a loss what to answer to this statement, made by a girl who looked at him so soberly and earnestly with clear gray eyes. It would be of no avail again to assure her that his opinions would be of small use to her; as she had said herself, she was very determined, and she had made up her mind that they would be of great use instead of small. Her idea must wear itself out by degrees. He would try to make the degrees easy. He decided that he would have a little private talk with Jackson, who was a very honest fellow; and, for the present, he would simply take leave.

"You are very kind," he said, rising. "I appreciate it, I assure you. It has made me stay an unconscionable time. I hope you will find Rome all you expected, and I am sure you will; all people of imagination like Rome. As to the galleries, yes, certainly; a—ah—little later. You must not forget the various small precautions necessary here as regards the fever, you know."

"Rome will not be at all what I expected if *you* desert me," answered Miss Macks, paying no attention to his other phrases. She had risen, also, and was now confronting him at a distance of less than two feet; as she was tall, her eyes were not much below the level of his own.

"How can a man desert when he has never enlisted?" thought Noel, humorously. But he kept his thought to himself, and merely replied, as he took his hat: "Probably you will desert me; you will find out how useless I am. You must not be too hard upon us, Miss Macks; we Americans lose much of our native energy if we stay long over here."

"Hard?" she answered—"hard? Why, Mr. Noel, I am absolutely at your feet!"

He looked at her, slightly startled, although his face showed nothing of it; was she, after all, going to— But no; her sentence had been as impersonal as those which had preceded it.

"All I said about having contrary opinions, and all that, amounts to nothing," she went on, thereby relieving him from the necessity of making reply. "I desire but one thing, and that is to have you guide me. And I don't believe you are really going to refuse. You haven't an unkind face, although you *have* got such a cold way! Why, think of it: here I have come all this long distance, bringing mother, too, just to study, and to see you. I shall study hard; I have a good deal of perseverance. It took a good deal to get here in the first place, for we are poor. But I don't mind that at all; the only thing I should mind, the only thing that would take my courage away, would be to have you desert me. In all the troubles that I thought might happen, I assure you, I never once thought of *that*, Mr. Noel. I thought, of course, you would be interested. Why, in your books you are all interest. Are you different from your books?"

"I fear, Miss Macks, that writers are seldom good illustrations of their own doctrines," replied Noel.

"That would make them hypocrites. I don't believe you are a hypocrite. I expect you have a habit of running yourself down. Many gentlemen do that, and then they think they will be cried up. I don't believe you are going to be unkind; you *will* look at the pictures I have brought with me, won't you?"

"Mr. Jackson's opinion is worth a hundred of mine,

Miss Macks; my knowledge is not technical. But, of course, if you wish it, I shall take pleasure in obeying." He added several conventional remarks as filling-up, and then, leaving his compliments for "your mother" —he could not recall the name she had given—he went towards the little curtained door.

She had brightened over his promise.

"You will come Monday, then, to see them, won't you?—as you cannot come to-morrow," she said, smiling happily.

When she smiled (and she did not smile often), showing her little white, child-like teeth, she looked very young. He was fairly caught, and answered, "Yes." But he immediately qualified it with a "That is, if it is possible."

"Oh, *make* it possible," she answered, still smiling and going with him herself to the outer door instead of summoning the maid. The last he saw of her she was standing in the open doorway, her face bright and contented, watching him as he went down. He did not go to see her pictures on the following Monday; he sent a note of excuse.

Some days later he met her.

"Ah, you are taking one of the delightful walks?" he said. " I envy you your first impressions of Rome."

"I am not taking a walk—that is, for pleasure," she answered. "I am trying to find some vegetables that mother can eat; the vegetables here are so foreign! You don't know how disappointed I was, Mr. Noel, when I got your note. It was such a setback! Why couldn't you come right home with me now—that is, after I have got the vegetables—and see the pictures? It wouldn't take you fifteen minutes."

It was only nine o'clock, and a beautiful morning. He thought her such a novelty, with her urgent invitations, her earnest eyes, and her basket on her arm, that he felt the impulse to walk beside her a while through the old streets of Rome; he was very fond of the old streets, and was curious to see whether she would notice the colors and outlines that made their picturesqueness. She noticed nothing but the vegetable-stalls, and talked of nothing but her pictures.

He still went on with her, however, amused by the questions she put to the vegetable-dealers (questions compiled from the phrase-books), and the calm contempt with which she surveyed the Roman artichokes they offered. At last she secured some beans, but of sadly Italian aspect, and Noel took the basket. He was much entertained by the prospect of carrying it home. He remarked to himself that of all the various things he had done in Rome this was the freshest. They reached the street of the Hyacinth and walked down its dark centre.

"I see you have the sun," he said, looking up.

"Yes; that is the reason we took the top floor. We will go right up. Everything is ready."

He excused himself.

"Some other time."

They had entered the dusky hallway. She looked at him without replying; then held out her hand for the basket. He gave it to her.

"I suppose you have seen Mr. Jackson?" he said, before taking leave.

She nodded, but did not speak. Then he saw two tears rise in her eyes.

"My dear young lady, you have been doing too

much! You are tired. Don't you know that that is very dangerous in Rome?"

"It is nothing. Mother has been sick, and I have been up with her two nights. Then, as she did not like our servant, I dismissed her, and as we have not got any one else yet, I have had a good deal to do. But I don't mind that at all, beyond being a little tired; it was only your refusing to come up, when it seemed so easy. But never mind; you will come another day." And, repressing the tears, she smiled faintly, and held out her hand for good-bye.

"I will come now," said Noel. He took the basket again, and went up the stairs. He was touched by the two tears, but, at the same time, vexed with himself for being there at all. There was not one chance in five hundred that her work was worth anything; and, in the four hundred and ninety-nine, pray what was he to say?

She brought him everything. They were all in the four hundred and ninety-nine. In his opinion they were all extremely and essentially bad.

It was one of Raymond Noel's beliefs that, where women were concerned, a certain amount of falsity was sometimes indispensable. There were occasions when a man could no more tell the bare truth to a woman than he could strike her; the effect would be the same as a blow. He was an excellent evader when he chose to exert himself, and he finally got away from the little high-up apartment without disheartening or offending its young mistress, and without any very black record of direct untruth—what is more, without any positive promise as to the exact date of his next visit. But all this was a good deal of trouble to take for a girl he did not know or care for.

Soon afterwards he met, at a small party, Mrs. Lawrence.

"Tell me a little, please, about the young lady to whom you presented me at Mrs. Dudley's reception—Miss Macks," he said, after some conversation.

"A little is all I can tell," replied Mrs. Lawrence. "She brought a letter of introduction to me from a far-away cousin of mine, who lives out West somewhere, and whom I have not seen for twenty years; my home, you know, is in New Jersey. How they learned I was in Rome I cannot imagine; but, knowing it, I suppose they thought that Miss Macks and I would meet, as necessarily as we should if together in their own village. The letter assures me that the girl is a great genius; that all she needs is an opportunity. They even take the ground that it will be a privilege for me to know her! But I am mortally tired of young geniuses; we have so many here in Rome! So I told her at once that I knew nothing of modern art—in fact, detested it—but that in any other way I should be delighted to be of use. And I took her to Mrs. Dudley's *omnium gatherum.*"

"Then you have not been to see her?"

"No; she came to see me. I sent cards, of course; I seldom call. What did you think of her?"

"I thought her charming," replied Noel, remembering the night-vigils, the vegetables, the dismissed servant, and the two tears of the young stranger—remembering, also, her extremely bad pictures.

"I am glad she has found a friend in you," replied Mrs. Lawrence. "She was very anxious to meet you;

she looks upon you as a great authority. If she really has talent—of course *you* would know—you must tell me. It is not talent I am so tired of, but the pretence of it. She struck me, although wofully unformed and awkward, of course, as rather intelligent."

"She is intelligence personified," replied Noel, qualifying it mentally with "intelligence without cultivation." He perceived that the young stranger would have no help from Mrs. Lawrence, and he added to himself: "And totally inexperienced purity alone in Rome." To be sure, there was the mother; but he had a presentiment that this lady, as guardian, would not be of much avail.

The next day he went down to Naples for a week with some friends. Upon his return he stopped at Horace Jackson's studio one afternoon as he happened to be passing. His time was really much occupied; he was a favorite in Rome. To his surprise, Jackson seemed to think that Miss Macks had talent. Her work was very crude, of course; she had been brutally taught; teachers of that sort should simply be put out of existence with the bowstring. He had turned her back to the alphabet; and, in time, in time, they—would see what she could do.

Horace Jackson was English by birth, but he had lived in Italy almost all his life. He was a man of forty-five—short, muscular, his thick, rather shaggy, beard and hair mixed with gray; there was a permanent frown over his keen eyes, and his rugged face had marked lines. He was a man of strong individuality. He had the reputation of being the most incorruptibly honest teacher in Rome. Noel had known him a long time, and liked him, ill-tempered though he was. Jackson, however, had not shown any especial signs of a liking for Noel in return. Perhaps he thought that, in the nature of things, there could not be much in common between a middle-aged, morose teacher, who worked hard, who knew nothing of society, and did not want to know, and a man like Raymond Noel. True, Noel was also an artist—that is, a literary one. But he had been highly successful in his own field, and it was understood, also, that he had an income of his own by inheritance, which, if not opulence, was yet sufficiently large to lift him quite above the usual *res angusta* of his brethren in the craft. In addition, Jackson considered Noel a fashionable man; and that would have been a barrier, even if there had been no other.

As the Englishman seemed to have some belief in Miss Macks, Noel did not say all he had intended to say; he did, however, mention that the young lady had a mistaken idea regarding any use he could be to her; he should be glad if she could be undeceived.

"I think she will be," said Jackson, with a grim smile, giving his guest a glance of general survey that took him in from head to foot; "she isn't dull."

Noel understood the glance, and smiled at Jackson's idea of him.

"She is not dull, certainly," he answered. "But she is rather—inexperienced." He dismissed the subject, went home, dressed, and went out to dinner.

One morning, a week later, he was strolling through the Doria gallery. He was in a bad humor. There were many people in the gallery that day, but he was not noticing them; he detested a crowd. After a while some one touched his coat-sleeve from behind. He turned, with his calmest expression upon his face; when

he was in an ill-humor he was impassively calm. It was
Miss Macks, her eyes eager, her face flushed with pleasure.
"Oh, what good luck!" she said. "And to think
that I almost went to the Borghese, and might have
missed you! I am so delighted that I don't know
what to do. I am actually trembling." And she was.
"I have so longed to see these pictures with you," she
went on. "I have had a real aching disappointment
about it, Mr. Noel."

Again Noel felt himself slightly touched by her earnestness. She looked prettier than usual, too, on account of the color.

"I always feel a self-reproach when with you, Miss
Macks," he answered—"you so entirely over-estimate
me."

"Well, if I do, live up to it," she said, brightly.

"Only an archangel could do that."

"An archangel who knows about Art! I have been
looking at the Caraccis; what do you think of them?"

"Never mind the Caraccis; there are better things
to look at here." And then he made the circuit of the
gallery with her slowly, pointing out the best pictures.
During this circuit he talked to her as he would have
talked to an intelligent child who had been put in his
charge in order to learn something of the paintings; he
used the simplest terms, mentioned the marked characteristics, and those only of the different schools, and
spoke a few words of unshaded condemnation here and
there. All he said was in broad, plain outlines. His
companion listened earnestly. She gave him a close
attention, almost always a comprehension, but seldom
agreement. Her disagreement she did not express in

words, but he could read it in her eyes. When they had seen everything—and it took some time—

"Now," he said, "I want you to tell me frankly, and without reference to anything I have said, your real opinion of several pictures I shall name—that is, if you can remember?"

"I remember everything. I always remember."

"Very well. What do you think, then, of the Raphael double portrait?"

"I think it very ugly."

"And the portrait of Andrea Doria, by Sebastian del Piombo?"

"Uglier still."

"And the Velasquez?"

"Ugliest of all."

"And the two large Claude Lorraines?"

"Rather pretty; but insipid. There isn't any reality or meaning in them."

"The Memling?"

"Oh, *that* is absolutely hideous, Mr. Noel; it hasn't a redeeming point."

Raymond Noel laughed with real amusement, and almost forgot his ill-humor.

"When you have found anything you really admire in the galleries here, Miss Macks, will you tell me?"

"Of course I will. I should wish to do so in any case, because, if you are to help me, you ought to thoroughly understand me. There is one thing more I should like to ask," she added, as they turned towards the door, "and that is that you would not call me Miss Macks. I am not used to it, and it sounds strangely; no one ever called me that in Tuscolee."

"What did they call you in Tuscolee?"

"They called me Miss Ettie; my name is Ethelinda Faith. But my friends and older people called me just 'Ettie'; I wish you would, too."

"I am certainly older," replied Noel, gravely (he was thirty-three); "but I do not like Ettie. With your permission, I will call you Faith."

"Do you like it? It's so old-fashioned! It was my grandmother's name."

"I like it immensely," he answered, leading the way down-stairs.

"You can't think how I've enjoyed it," she said, warmly, at the door.

"Yet you do not agree with my opinions?"

"Not yet. But all the same it was perfectly delightful. Good-bye."

He had signalled for a carriage, as he had, as usual, an engagement. She preferred to walk. He drove off, and did not see her for ten days.

Then he came upon her again and again in the Doria gallery. He was fond of the Doria, and often went there, but he had no expectation of meeting Miss Macks this time; he fancied that she followed a system, going through her list of galleries in regular order, one by one, and in that case she would hardly have reached the Doria on a second round. Her list was a liberal one; it included twenty. Noel had supposed that there were but nine in Rome.

This time she did not see him; she had some sheets of manuscript in her hand, and was alternately reading from them and looking at one of the pictures. She was much absorbed. After a while he went up.

"Good-morning, Miss Macks."

She started; her face changed, and the color rose.

She was as delighted as before. She immediately showed him her manuscript. There he beheld, written out in her clear handwriting, all he had said of the Doria pictures, page after page of it; she had actually reproduced from memory his entire discourse of an hour.

There were two blank spaces left.

"There, I could not exactly remember," said Miss Macks, apologetically. "If you would tell me, I should be so glad; then it would be quite complete."

"I shall never speak again. I am frightened," said Noel. He had taken the manuscript, and was looking it over with inward wonder.

"Oh, please do."

"Why do you care for my opinions, Miss Macks, when you do not agree with them?" he asked, his eyes still on the pages.

"You said you would call me Faith. Why do I care? Because they are yours, of course."

"Then you think I know?"

"I am sure you do."

"But it follows, then, that you do not."

"Yes; and there is where my work comes in; I have got to study up to you. I am afraid it will take a long time, won't it?"

"That depends upon you. It would take very little if you would simply accept noncombatively."

"Without being convinced? That I could never do."

"You want to be convinced against your will?"

"No; my will itself must be convinced to its lowest depths."

"This manuscript won't help you."

"Indeed, it has helped me greatly already. I have

been here twice with it. I wrote it out the evening after I saw you. I only wish I had one for each of the galleries! But I feel differently now about asking you to go."

"I told you you would desert me."

"No, it is not that. But Mr. Jackson says you are much taken up with the fashionable society here, and that I must not expect you to give me so much of your time as I had hoped for. He says, too, that your art articles will do me quite as much good as you yourself, and more; because you have a way, he says, like all society men, of talking as if you had no real convictions at all, and that would unsettle me."

"Jackson is an excellent fellow," replied Noel; "I like him extremely. And when would you like to go to the Borghese?"

"Oh, will you take me?" she said, joyfully. "Any time. To-morrow."

"Perhaps Mrs.—your mother, will go, also," he suggested, still unable to recall the name; he could think of nothing but "stirrup," and of course it was not that.

"I don't believe she would care about it," answered the daughter.

"She might. You know we make more of mothers here than we do in America," he ventured to remark.

"That is impossible," said Miss Macks, calmly. Evidently she thought his remark frivolous.

He abandoned the subject, and did not take it up again. It was not his duty to instruct Miss Macks in foreign customs. In addition, she was not only not "in society," but she was an art student, and art students had, or took, privileges of their own in Rome.

"At what hour shall I come for you?" he said.

"It will be out of your way to come for me; I will meet you at the gallery," she answered, radiant at the prospect.

He hesitated, then accepted her arrangement of things. He would take her way, not his own. The next morning he went to the Borghese Palace ten minutes before the appointed time. But she was already there.

"Mother thought she would not come out—the galleries tire her so," she said; "but she was pleased to be remembered."

They spent an hour and a half among the pictures. She listened to all he said with the same earnest attention.

Within the next five weeks Raymond Noel met Miss Macks at other galleries. It was always very business-like—they talked of nothing but the pictures; in truth, her systematic industry kept him strictly down to the subject in hand. He learned that she made the same manuscript copies of all he said, and, when he was not with her, she went alone, armed with these documents, and worked hard. Her memory was remarkable; she soon knew the names and the order of all the pictures in all the galleries, and had made herself acquainted with an outline, at least, of the lives of all the artists who had painted them. During this time she was, of course, going on with her lessons; but as he had not been again to see Jackson, or to the street of the Hyacinth, he knew nothing of her progress. He did not want to know; she was in Jackson's hands, and Jackson was quite competent to attend to her.

In these five weeks he gave to Miss Macks only the odd hours of his leisure. He made her no promises;

but when he found that he should have a morning or half-morning unoccupied, he sent a note to the street of the Hyacinth, naming a gallery and an hour. She was always promptly there, and so pleased, that there was a sort of fresh aroma floating through the time he spent with her, after all—but a mild one.

To give the proper position to the place the young art student's light figure occupied on the canvas of Raymond Noel's winter, it should be mentioned that he was much interested in a French lady who was spending some months in Rome. He had known her and admired her for a long time; but this winter he was seeing more of her, some barriers which had heretofore stood in the way being down. Madame B—— was a charming product of the effects of finished cultivation and fashionable life upon a natural foundation of grace, wit, and beauty of the French kind. She was not artificial, because she was art itself. Real art is as real as real nature is natural. Raymond Noel had a highly artistic nature. He admired art. This did not prevent him from taking up occasionally, as a contrast to this lady, the society of the young girl he called "Faith." Most men of imagination, artistic or not, do the same thing once in a while; it seems a necessity. With Noel it was not the contrast alone. The French lady led him an uneasy life, and now and then he took an hour of Faith, as a gentle soothing draught of safe quality. She believed in him so perfectly! Now Madame appeared to believe in him not at all.

It must be added that, in his conversations with Miss Macks, he had dropped entirely even the very small amount of conventional gallantry that he had bestowed upon her in the beginning. He talked to her not as though she was a boy exactly, or an old woman, but as though he himself was a relative of mature age—say an uncle of benevolent disposition and a taste for art.

February gave way to March. And now, owing to a new position of his own affairs, Noel saw no more of Faith Macks. She had been a contrast, and he did not now wish for a contrast or a soothing draught, and a soothing draught was not at present required. He simply forgot all about her.

In April he decided rather suddenly to leave Rome. This was because Madame B—— had gone to Paris, and had not forbidden her American suitor to follow her a few days later. He made his preparations for departure, and these, of course, included farewell calls. Then he remembered Faith Macks; he had not seen her for six weeks. He drove to the street of the Hyacinth, and went up the dark stairs. Miss Macks was at home, and came in without delay; apparently, in her trim neatness, she was always ready for visitors.

She was very glad to see him; but did not, as he expected, ask why he had not come before. This he thought a great advance; evidently she was learning. When she heard that he had come to say good-bye her face fell.

"I am so very sorry; please sit as long as you can, then," she said, simply. "I suppose it will be six months before I see you again; you will hardly return to Rome before October." That he would come at that time she did not question.

"My plans are uncertain," replied Noel. "But probably I shall come back. One always comes back to Rome. And you — where do you go? To Switzerland?"

"Why—we go nowhere, of course; we stay here. That is what we came for, and we are all settled."

He made some allusion to the heat and unhealthiness.

"I am not afraid," replied Miss Macks. "Plenty of people stay; Mr. Jackson says so. It is only the rich who go away, and we are not rich. We have been through hot summers in Tuscolee, I can tell you!" Then, without asking leave this time, as if she was determined to have an opinion from him before he departed, she took from a portfolio some of the work she had done under Mr. Jackson's instruction.

Noel saw at once that the Englishman had not kept his word. He had not put her back upon the alphabet, or, if he had done so, he had soon released her, and allowed her to pursue her own way again. The original faults were as marked as ever. In his opinion all was essentially bad.

He looked in silence. But she talked on hopefully, explaining, comparing, pointing out.

"What does Mr. Jackson think of this?" he said, selecting the one he thought the worst.

"He admires the idea greatly; he thinks it very original. He says that my strongest point is originality," she answered, with her confident frankness.

"He means—ah—originality of subject?"

"Oh yes; my execution is not much yet. But that will come in time. Of course, the subject, the idea, is the important thing; the execution is secondary." Here she paused; something seemed to come into her mind. "I know *you* do not think so," she added, thoughtfully, "because, you know, you said"—and here she quoted a page from one of his art articles with her clear accuracy. "I have never understood what you meant by that, Mr. Noel; or why you wrote it."

She looked at him questioningly. He did not reply; his eyes were upon one of the sketches.

"It would be dreadful for me if you were right!" she added, with slow conviction.

"I thought you believed that I was always right," he said, smiling, as he placed the sketches on the table.

But she remained very serious.

"You are—in everything but that."

He made some unimportant reply, and turned the conversation. But she came back to it.

"It would be dreadful," she repeated, earnestly, with the utmost gravity in her gray eyes.

"I hope the long summer will not tire you," he answered, irrelevantly. "Shall I not have the pleasure of saying good-bye—although that, of course, is not a pleasure—to Mrs.—to your mother?"

He should have made the speech in any case, as it was the proper one to make; but as he sat there he had thought that he really would like to have a look at the one guardian this young girl was to have during her long, lonely summer in Rome.

"I will tell her. Perhaps when she hears that you are going away she will feel like coming in," said Miss Macks.

She came back after some delay, and with her appeared a matron of noticeable aspect.

"My mother," she said, introducing her (evidently Noel was never to get the name); "this is Mr. Noel, mother."

"And very glad I am to see you, sir, I'm sure," said

Mrs. Spurr, extending her hand with much cordiality. "I said to Ettie that I'd come in, seeing as 'twas you, though I don't often see strangers nowadays on account of poor health for a long time past; rheumatism and asthma. But I feel beholden to you, Mr. No-ul, because you've been so good to Ettie. You've been real kind."

Ettie's mother was a very portly matron of fifty-five, with a broad face, indistinct features, very high color, and a breathless, panting voice. Her high color — it really was her most noticeable feature — was surmounted by an imposing cap, adorned with large bows of scarlet ribbon; a worsted shawl, of the hue known as "solferino," decked her shoulders; under her low-necked collar reposed a bright blue necktie, its ends embroidered in red and yellow; and her gown was of a vivid dark green. But although her colors swore at each other, she seemed amiable. She was also voluble.

Noel, while shaking hands, was considering, mentally, with some retrospective amusement, his condition of mind if this lady had accepted his invitations to visit the galleries.

"You must sit down, mother," said Miss Macks, bringing forward an easy-chair. "She has not been so well as usual, lately," she said, explanatorily, to Noel, as she stood for a moment beside her mother's chair.

"It's this queer Eye-talian air," said Mrs. Spurr. "You see I ain't used to it. Not but what I ain't glad to be here on Ettie's account — real glad. It's just what she needs and oughter have."

The girl put her hand on her mother's shoulder with a little caressing touch. Then she left the room.

"Yes, I do feel beholden to you, Mr. No-ul. But,

then, she'll be a credit to you, to whatever you've done for her," said Mrs. Spurr, when they were left alone. "Her talunts are very remarkable. She was the head scholar of the Young Ladies' Seminary through four whole years, and all the teachers took a lot of pride in her. And then her paintings, too! I'm sorry you're going off so soon. You see, she sorter depends upon your opinion."

Noel felt a little stir at the edges of his conscience; he knew perfectly that his opinion was that Miss Macks, as an artist, would never do anything worth the materials she used.

"I leave her in good hands," he said.

After all, it was Jackson's responsibility, not his.

"Yes, Mr. Jackson thinks a deal of her. I can see that plain!" answered Mrs. Spurr, proudly.

Here the daughter returned, bringing a little notebook and pencil.

"Do you know what these are for?" she said. "I want you to write down a list of the best books for me to read this summer, while you are gone. I am going to work hard; but if I have books, too, the time won't seem so long."

Noel considered a moment. In one way her affairs were certainly none of his business; in another way they were, because she had thrust them upon him.

"I will not give you a list, Miss Macks; probably you would not be able to find the books here. But I will send you, from Paris or London, some things that are rather good, if you will permit me to do so."

She said he was very kind. Her face brightened.

"If she has appreciation enough to comprehend what

I send her," he thought, "perhaps in the end she will
have a different opinion about my 'kindness'!"

Soon afterwards he took leave. The next day he
went to Paris.

II

The events of Raymond Noel's life, after he left
Rome that spring, were various. Some were pleasant,
some unpleasant; several were quite unexpected. Their
combinations and results kept him from returning to
Italy the following winter, and the winter after that he
spent in Egypt. When he again beheld the dome of
St. Peter's he remembered that it lacked but a month
of two full years since he had said good-bye to it; it
was then April, and now it was March. He established
himself in some pleasant rooms, looked about him, and
then began to take up, one by one, the old threads of
his Roman life—such, at least, as remained unbroken.
He found a good many. Threads do not break in
Rome. He had once said himself that the air was so
soft and historic that nothing broke there—not even
hearts. But this was only one of his little speeches.
In reality he did not believe much in the breaking of
hearts; he had seen them stretch so!

It may be said with truth that Noel had not thought
of Miss Macks for months. This was because he had
had other things to think of. He had sent her the
books from Paris, with an accompanying note, a charming little note—which gave no address for reply. Since
then his mind had been otherwise occupied. But as
he never entirely forgot anything that had once interested him, even although but slightly (this was in real-

ity a system of his; it gave him many holds on life, and kept stored up a large supply of resources ready for use when wanted), he came, after a while, on the canvas of his Roman impressions, to the figure of Miss Macks. When he came to it he went to see her; that is, he went to the street of the Hyacinth.

Of course, she might not be there; a hundred things might have happened to her. He could have hunted up Horace Jackson; but, on the whole, he rather preferred to see the girl herself first—that is, if she was there. Mrs. Lawrence, the only person among his acquaintances who had known her, was not in Rome. Reaching the street of the Hyacinth, he interrogated the old woman who acted as portress at the lower door, keeping up at the same time a small commerce in fritters; yes, the Americans were still on the fourth floor. He ascended the dark stairway. The confiding little "Ettie" card was no longer upon the door. In its place was a small framed sign: "Miss Macks' School."

This told a story!

However, he rang. It was the same shrill, ill-tempered little bell, and when the door opened it was Miss Macks herself who opened it. She was much changed.

The parlor had been turned into a school-room—at present empty of pupils. But even as a school-room it was more attractive than it had been before. He took a seat, and spoke the usual phrases of a renewal of acquaintance with his accustomed ease and courtesy; Miss Macks responded briefly. She said that her mother was not very well; she herself quite well. No, they had not left Italy, nor indeed the neighborhood of Rome; they had been a while at Albano.

The expression of her face had greatly altered. The

old direct, wide glance was gone; gone also what he had called her over-confidence; she looked much older. On the other hand, there was more grace in her bearing, more comprehension of life in her voice and eyes. She was dressed as plainly as before; but everything, including the arrangement of her hair, was in the prevalent style.

She did not speak of her school, and therefore he did not. But after a while he asked how the painting came on. Her face changed a little; but it was more in the direction of a greater calm than hesitation or emotion.

"I am not painting now," she answered.

"You have given it up temporarily?"

"Permanently."

"Ah—isn't that rather a pity?"

She looked at him, and a gleam of scorn filtered into the glance.

"You know it is not a pity," she said.

He was a little disgusted at the scorn. Of course, the only ground for him to take was the ground upon which she stood when he last saw her; at that time she proposed to pass her life in painting, and it was but good manners for him to accept her intentions as she had presented them.

"I never assumed to be a judge, you know," he answered. "When I last had the pleasure of seeing you, painting was, you remember, your cherished occupation!"

"When you last had the pleasure of seeing me, Mr. Noel," said Miss Macks, still with unmoved calm, "I was a fool."

Did she wish to go into the subject at length? Or was that merely an exclamation?

"When I last had the pleasure of seeing you, you were taking lessons of Mr. Jackson," he said, to give a practical turn to the conversation. "Is he still here? How is he?"

"He is very well, now. He is dead."

(She was going to be dramatic then, in any case.)

He expressed his regret, and it was a sincere one; he had always liked and respected the honest, morose Englishman. He asked a question or two. Miss Macks replied that he had died here in the street of the Hyacinth—in the next room. He had fallen ill during the autumn following Noel's departure, and when his illness grew serious, they—her mother and herself—had persuaded him to come to them. He had lived a month longer, and died peacefully on Christmas Eve.

"He was one of the most honest men I ever knew," said Noel. Then, as she did not reply, he ventured this: "That was the reason I recommended him when you asked me to select a teacher for you."

"Your plan was made useless by an unfortunate circumstance," she answered, with an evident effort.

"A circumstance?"

"Yes; he fell in love with me. If I did not consider his pure, deep, and devoted affection the greatest honor of my life I would not mention it. I tell you because it will explain to you his course."

"Yes, it explains," said Noel. As he spoke there came across him a realization of the whole of the strength of the love such a man as Horace Jackson would feel, and the way in which it would influence him. Of course, he saw to the full the imperfection of her work, the utter lack of the artist's conception, the artist's eye and touch; but probably he had loved her from the beginning, and had gone on hoping to win her love in return. She was not removed from him by any distance; she was young, but she was also poor, friendless, and alone. When she was his wife he would tell her the truth, and in the greatness of his love the revelation would be naught. "He was a good man," he said. "He was always lonely. I am glad that at last he was with your mother and you."

"His goodness was simply unbounded. If he had lived he would have remained always a faithful, kind, and respectful son to my dear mother. That, of course, would have been everything to me." She said this quietly, yet her tone seemed to hold intention.

For a moment he thought that perhaps she had married the Englishman, and was now his widow. The sign on the door bore her maiden name, but that might have been an earlier venture.

"Had you opened your school at that time?" he asked. "I may speak of it, since, of course, I saw the sign upon the door."

"Not until two months later; I had the sign made then. But it was of little use; day-schools do not prosper in Rome; they are not the custom. I have a small class twice a week, but I live by going out as day-governess. I have a number of pupils of that kind; I have been very successful. The old Roman families have a fancy for English-speaking governesses, you know. Last summer I was with the Princess C——, at Albano; her children are my pupils."

"Her villa is a delightful one," said Noel; "you must have enjoyed that."

"I don't know that I enjoyed, but I learned. I

have learned a great deal in many ways since I saw you last, Mr. Noel. I have grown very old."

"As you were especially young when you saw me last it does not matter much," he answered, smiling.

"Yes, I was especially young." She looked at him soberly. "I do not feel bitterly towards you," she continued. "Strange! I thought I should. But now that I see you in person it comes over me that, probably, you did not intend to deceive me; that not only you tried to set me right by selecting Mr. Jackson as my teacher, but again you tried when you sent me those books. It was not much to do! But knowing the world as I now know it, I see that it was all that could have been expected. At first, however, I did not see this. After I went to Mr. Bellot, and, later, to Mr. Salviati, there were months when I felt very bitterly towards you. My hopes were false ones, and had been so from the beginning; you knew that they were, yet you did not set me right."

"I might have done more than I did," answered Noel. "I have a habit of not assuming responsibility; I suppose I have grown selfish. But if you went to Bellot, then it was not Jackson who told you?"

"He intimated something when he asked me to marry him; after that his illness came on, and we did not speak of it again. But I did not believe him. I was very obstinate. I went to Mr. Bellot the 1st of January; I wished him to take me as pupil. In answer he told me that I had not a particle of talent; that all my work was insufferably bad; that I better throw away my brushes and take in sewing."

"Bellot is always a brute!" said Noel.

"If he told the truth brutally, it was still the truth;

and it was the truth I needed. But even then I was not convinced, and I went to Mr. Salviati. He was more gentle; he explained to me my lacks; but his judgment was the same. I came home; it was the 10th of January, a beautiful Roman winter day. I left my pictures, went over to St. Peter's, and walked there under its bright mosaics all the afternoon. The next day I had advertisements of a day-school placed at the bankers' and in the newspapers. I thought that I could teach better than I could sew." All this she said with perfect calm.

"I greatly admire your bravery, Miss Macks. Permit me to add that I admire, even more, the clear, strong, good sense which has carried you through."

"I had my mother to think of; my—good sense might not have been so faithful otherwise."

"You do not think of returning to America?"

"Probably not; I doubt if my mother could bear the voyage now. We have no one to call us back but my brother, and he has not been with us for years, and would not be if we should return; he lives in California. We sold the farm, too, before we came. No; for the present, at least, it is better for us to remain here."

"There is one more question I should like to ask," said Noel, later. "But I have no possible right to do so."

"I will give you the right. When I remember the things I asked you to do for me, the demands I made upon your time, I can well answer a few questions in return. I was a miracle of ignorance."

"I always did you justice in those respects, Miss Macks; all that I understood at once. My question refers to Horace Jackson: I see you appreciated his worth — which was rare — yet you would not marry him."

"I did not love him."

"Did any of his relatives come out from England?" he said, after a moment of silence.

"After his death a cousin came."

"As heir to what was left?"

"Yes."

"He should have left it to you."

"He wished to do so. Of course, I would not accept it."

"I thank you for answering. My curiosity was not an idle one." He paused. "If you will permit me to express it, your course has been very brave and true. I greatly admire it."

"You are kind," said Miss Macks.

There was not in her voice any indication of sarcasm. Yet the fact that he immediately thought of it made him suspect that it was there. He took leave soon afterwards. He was smarting a little under the sarcasm he had divined, and, as he was, it was like him to request permission to come again.

For Raymond Noel lived up with a good deal of determination to his own standard of what was manly; if his standard was not set on any very fine elevation of self-sacrifice or heroism, it was at least firmly established where it did stand, and he kept himself fairly near it. If Miss Macks was sarcastic, he had been at fault somewhere; he would try to atone.

He saw her four times during the five weeks of his stay in Rome; upon three other occasions when he went to the street of the Hyacinth she was not at home. The third week in April he decided to go to

Venice. Before going he asked if there was not something he could do for her; but she said there was nothing, and he himself could think of nothing. She was well established in her new life and occupations, and needed nothing—at least, nothing that he could bestow.

The next winter he came back to Rome early in the season, before Christmas. By chance one of the first persons he encountered was Mrs. Lawrence. She began immediately to tell him a piece of American news, in which he, as an American, would of course be interested; the news was that "the brother of the Princess C——— —that is Count L———, you know—is determined to marry Ettie Macks. You remember her, don't you? I introduced you to her at the Dudley reception, three years ago."

Noel thought that probably he remembered her better than Mrs. Lawrence did, seeing that that lady had never troubled herself to enter the street of the Hyacinth. But he did her injustice. Mrs. Lawrence had troubled herself—lately.

"It seems that she has been out at Albano for two summers, as governess to his sister's children; it was there that he saw her. He has announced his determination to the family, and they are immensely disturbed and frightened; they had it all arranged for him to marry a second cousin down at Naples, who is rich— these Italians are so worldly, you know! But he is very determined, they say, and will do as he pleases in spite of them. He hasn't much money, but of course it's a great match for Ettie Macks. She will be a countess, and now, I suppose, more American girls will come over than ever before! Of course, as soon as I heard of it, I went to see her. I felt that she would need advice about a hundred things. In the beginning she brought a letter of introduction to me from a dear cousin of mine, and, naturally, she would rely upon me as her chief friend now. She is very much improved. She was rather silent; but, of course, I shall go again. The count is willing to take the mother, too, and that, under the circumstances, is not a small matter; she is a good deal to take. Until the other day I had not seen Mrs. Spurr! However, I suppose that her deficiencies are not apparent in a language she cannot speak. If her daughter would only insist upon her dressing in black! But the old lady told me herself, in the most cheerful way, that she liked 'a sprinkling of color.' And at the moment, I assure you, she had on five different shades of red!"

Noel had intended to present himself immediately at the street of the Hyacinth; but a little attack of illness kept him in for a while, and ten days had passed before he went up the dark stairway. The maid said that Miss Macks was at home; presently she came in. They had ten minutes of conversation upon ordinary topics, and then he took up the especial one.

"I am told that you are soon to be a countess," he said, "and I have come to give you my best good wishes. My congratulations I reserve for Count L——, with whom I have a slight acquaintance; he is, in my opinion, a very fortunate man."

"Yes, I think he is fortunate; fortunate in my refusal. I shall not marry Count L——."

"He is not a bad fellow."

"Isn't your praise somewhat faint?" This time the sarcasm was visible.

"Oh, I am by no means his advocate! All I meant was that, as these modern Romans go, he was not among the worst. Of course I should have expressed myself very differently if you had said you were to marry him."

"Yes; you would then have honored me with your finest compliments."

He did not deny this.

"Shall you continue to live in Rome?" he asked.

"Certainly. I shall have more pupils and patronage now than I know what to do with; the whole family connection is deeply obliged to me."

They talked awhile longer.

"We have always been unusually frank with each other, Miss Macks," he said, towards the end of his visit. "We have never stopped at conventionalities. I wonder if you will tell me why you refused him?"

"You are too curious. As to frankness, I have been frank with you; not you with me. And there was no conventionality, simply because I did not know what it was."

"I believe you are in love with some one in America," he said, laughing.

"Perhaps I am," answered Miss Macks. She had certainly gained greatly in self-possession during the past year.

He saw her quite frequently after this. Her life was no longer solitary. As she had said, she was overwhelmed with pupils and patronage from the friends of the Princess C——; in addition, the American girl who had refused a fairly-indorsed and well-appearing count was now something of a celebrity among the American visitors in Rome. That they knew of her refusal was not her fault; the relatives of Count L—— had announced their objections as loud and widely as the count had announced his determination. Apparently neither side had thought of a non-acceptance. Cards, not a few, were sent to the street of the Hyacinth; some persons even climbed the five flights of stairs. Mrs. Spurr saw a good deal of company—and enjoyed it.

Noel was very fond of riding; when in Rome he always rode on the Campagna. He had acted as escort to various ladies, and one day he invited Miss Macks to accompany him—that is, if she were fond of riding She had ridden in America, and enjoyed it; she would like to go once, if he would not be troubled by an improvised habit. They went once. Then a second time, an interval of three weeks between. Then, after a while, a third time.

Upon this occasion an accident happened, the first of Noel's life; his horse became frightened, and, skilled rider though he was, he was thrown. He was dragged, too, for a short distance. His head came against some stones, and he lost consciousness. When it came back it did not come wholly. He seemed to himself to be far away, and the girl who was weeping and calling his name to be upon the other side of a wide space like an ocean, over which, without volition of his own, he was being slowly wafted. As he came nearer, still slowly, he perceived that in some mysterious way she was holding in her arms something that seemed to be himself, although he had not yet reached her. Then, gradually, spirit and body were reunited, he heard what she was saying, and felt her touch. Even then it was only after several minutes that he was able to move and unclose his heavy eyes.

When she saw that he was not dead, her wild grief
was at once merged in the thought of saving him. She
had jumped from her horse, she knew not how; but he
had not strayed far; a shepherd had seen him, and was
now coming towards them. He signalled to another,
and the two carried Noel to a house which was not far
distant. A messenger was sent to the city; aid came,
and before night Noel was in his own rooms at the
head of the Via Sistina, near the Spanish steps.

His injuries proved to be not serious; he had lost
consciousness from the shock, and this, with his pallor
and the blood from the cuts made by the stones, had
given him the look of death. The cuts, however, were
not deep; the effect of the shock passed away. He
kept his bed for a week under his physician's advice; he had a good deal of time to think during that
week. Later his friends were admitted. As has been
said before, Noel was a favorite in Rome, and he had
friends not a few. Those who could not come in person
sent little notes and baskets of flowers. Among these
Miss Macks was not numbered. But then she was not
fashionable.

At the end of two weeks the patient was allowed to
go out. He took a short walk to try his strength, and,
finding that it held out well, he went to the street of
the Hyacinth.

Miss Macks was at home. She was "so glad" to
see him out again; and was he "really strong enough;"
and he "should be very prudent for a while;" and so
forth and so forth. She talked more than usual, and,
for her, quite rapidly.

He let her go on for a time. Then he took the conversation into his own hands. With few preliminaries,

and with much feeling in his voice and eyes, he asked her to be his wife.

She was overwhelmed with astonishment; she turned very white, and did not answer. He thought she was going to burst into tears. But she did not; she only sat gazing at him, while her lips trembled. He urged his point; he spoke strongly.

"You are worth a hundred of me," he said. "You are true and sincere; I am a dilettante in everything. But, dilettante as I am, in one way I have always appreciated you, and, lately, all other ways have become merged in that one. I am much in earnest; I know what I am doing; I have thought of it searchingly and seriously, and I beg you to say yes."

He paused. Still she did not speak.

"Of course I do not ask you to separate yourself from your mother," he went on, his eyes dropping for the moment to the brim of his hat, which he held in his hand; "I shall be glad if she will always make her home with us."

Then she did speak. And as her words came forth, the red rose in her face until it was deeply colored.

"With what an effort you said that! But you will not be tried. One gray hair in my mother's head is worth more to me, Mr. Noel, than anything you can offer."

"I knew before I began that this would be the point of trouble between us, Faith," he answered. "I can only assure you that she will find in me always a most respectful son."

"And when you were thinking so searchingly and seriously, it was *this* that you thought of—whether you could endure her! Do you suppose that I do not see the effort? Do you suppose I would ever place my mother in such a position? Do you suppose that you are of any consequence beside her, or that anything in this world weighs in my mind for one moment compared with her happiness?"

"We can make her happy; I suppose that. And I suppose another thing, and that is that we could be very happy ourselves if we were married."

"The Western girl, the girl from Tuscolee! The girl who thought she could paint, and could not! The girl who knew so little of social rules that she made a fool of herself every time she saw you!"

"All this is of no consequence, since it is the girl I love," answered Noel.

"You do not. It is a lie. Oh, of course, a very unselfish and noble one; but a lie, all the same. You have thought of it seriously and searchingly? Yes, but only for the last fourteen days! I understand it all now. At first I did not, I was confused; but now I see the whole. You were not unconscious out there on the Campagna; you heard what I said when I thought you were dying, or dead. And so you come —come very generously and self-sacrificingly, I acknowledge that—and ask me to be your wife." She rose; her eyes were brilliant as she faced him. "I might tell you that it was only the excitement, that I did not know or mean what I was saying; I might tell you that I did not know that I had said anything. But I am not afraid. I will not, like you, tell a lie, even for a good purpose. I did love you; there, you have it! I have loved you for a long time, to my sorrow and shame. For I do not respect you or admire you; you have been completely spoiled, and will always remain so. I shall make it the one purpose of my life from this moment to overcome the feeling I have had for you; and I shall succeed. Nothing could make me marry you, though you should ask me a thousand times."

"I shall ask but once," said Noel. He had risen also; and, as he did, he remembered the time when they had stood in the same place and position, facing each other, and she had told him that she was at his feet. "I did hear what you said. And it is of that I have been seriously thinking during the days of my confinement to the house. It is also true that it is what you said which has brought me here to-day. But the reason is that it has become precious to me—this knowledge that you love me. As I said before, in one way I have always done you justice, and it is that way which makes me realize to the full now what such a love as yours would be to me. If it is true that I am spoiled, as you say I am, a love like yours would make be better, if anything can." He paused. "I have not said much about my own feelings," he added; "I know you will not credit me with having any. But I think I have. I think that I love you."

"It is of little moment to me whether you do or not."

"You are making a mistake," he said, after a pause, during which their eyes had met in silence.

"The mistake would be to consent."

She had now recovered her self-possession. She even smiled a little.

"Imagine Mr. Raymond Noel in the street of the Hyacinth!" she said.

"Ah, I should hardly wish to live here; and my wife would naturally be with me."

"I hope so. And I hope she will be very charming and obedient and sweet." Then she dropped her sarcasms, and held out her hand in farewell. "There is no use in prolonging this, Mr. Noel. Do not think, however, that I do not appreciate your action; I do appreciate it. I said that I did not respect you, and I have not until now; but now I do. You will understand, of course, that I would rather not see you again, and refrain from seeking me. Go your way, and forget me; you can do so now with a clear conscience, for you have behaved well."

"It is not very likely that I shall forget you," answered Noel, "although I go my way. I see you are firmly resolved. For the present, therefore, all I can do is to go."

They shook hands, and he left her. As he passed through the small hall on his way to the outer door he met Mrs. Spurr; she was attired as opulently, in respect to colors, as ever, and she returned his greeting with much cordiality. He glanced back; Miss Macks had witnessed the meeting through the parlor door. Her color had faded; she looked sad and pale.

She kept her word; she did not see him again. If he went to the street of the Hyacinth, as he did two or three times, the little maid presented him with the Italian equivalent of "begs to be excused," which was evidently a standing order. If he wrote to her, as he did more than two or three times, she returned what he wrote, not unread, but without answer. He thought perhaps he should meet her, and was at some pains to find out her various engagements. But all was in vain; the days passed, and she remained invisible. Towards the last of May he left Rome. After leaving, he continued to write to her, but he gave no address for reply; she would now be obliged either to burn his letters or keep them, since she could no longer send them back. They could not have been called love-letters; they were friendly epistles, not long—pleasant, easy, sometimes amusing, like his own conversation. They came once a week. In addition he sent new books, and occasionally some other small remembrance.

In early September of that year there came to the street of the Hyacinth a letter from America. It was from one of Mrs. Spurr's old neighbors at Tuscolee, and she wrote to say that John Macks had come home —had come home broken in health and spirits, and, as he himself said, to die. He did not wish his mother to know; she could not come to him, and it would only distress her. He had money enough for the short time that was left him, and when she heard it would be only that he had passed away; he had passed from her life in reality years before. In this John Macks was sincere. He had been a ne'er-do-well, a rolling stone; he had not been a dutiful son. The only good that could be said of him, as far as his mother was concerned, was contained in the fact that he had not made demands upon her small purse since the sum he took from her when he first went away. He had written to her at intervals, briefly. His last letter had come eight months before.

But the Tuscolee neighbor was a mother herself, and, doing as she would be done by, she wrote to Rome. When her letter came Mrs. Spurr was overwhelmed with grief; but she was also stirred to an energy and determination which she had never shown before. For the first time in years she took the leadership, put her daughter decisively back into a subordinate place, and assumed the control. She would go to America. She must see her boy (the dearest child of the two, as the prodigal always is) again. But even while she was planning her journey illness seized her—her old rheumatic troubles, only more serious than before; it was plain that she could not go. She then required that her daughter should go in her place—go and bring her boy to Rome; this soft Italian air would give new life to his lungs. Oh, she should not die! Ettie need not be afraid of that. She would live for years just to get one look at him! And so it ended in the daughter's departure, an efficient nurse being left in charge; the physician said that although Mrs. Spurr would probably be crippled, she was in no danger otherwise.

Miss Macks left Rome on the 15th of September. On the 2d of December she again beheld the dome of St. Peter's rising in the blue sky. She saw it alone. John Macks had lived three weeks after her arrival at Tuscolee, and those three weeks were the calmest and the happiest of his unsuccessful—unworthy it may be —but also bitterly unhappy life. His sister did not judge him. She kissed him good-bye as he lost consciousness, and soon afterwards closed his eyes tenderly, with tears in her own. Although he was her brother, she had never known him; he went away when she was a child. She sat beside him a long time after he was dead, watching the strange, youthful peace come back to his worn face.

When she reached the street of the Hyacinth a carriage was before the door; carriages of that sort were not often required by the dwellers on the floors below their own, and she was rather surprised. She had heard from her mother in London, the nurse acting as amanuensis; at that time Mrs. Spurr was comfortable, although still confined to her bed most of the day. As she was paying her driver she heard steps on the stairway within. Then she beheld this: The nurse, carrying a pillow and shawls; next, her mother, in an invalid-chair, borne by two men; and last, Raymond Noel.

When Mrs. Spurr saw her daughter she began to cry. She had not expected her until the next day. Her emotion was so great that the drive was given up, and she was carried back to her room. Noel did not follow her; he shook hands with the new-comer, said that he would not detain her, and then, lifting his hat, he stepped into the carriage which was waiting and was driven away.

For two days Mrs. Spurr wished for nothing but to hear, over and over again, every detail of her boy's last hours. Then the excitement and renewed grief made her dangerously ill. After ten days she began to improve; but two weeks passed before she came back to the present sufficiently to describe to her daughter all "Mr. No-ul's kind attentions." He had returned to Rome the first of October, and had come at once to the street of the Hyacinth. Learning what had happened, he had devoted himself to her "most as if he was my real son, Ettie, I do declare! Of course, he couldn't never be like my own darling boy," continued the poor mother, overlooking entirely, with a mother's sublime forgetfulness, the small amount of devotion her boy had ever bestowed; "but he's just done everything he could, and there's no denying that."

"He has not been mentioned in your letters, mother."

"Well, child, I just told Mrs. Bowler not to. For he said himself, frankly, that you might not like it; but that he'd make his peace with you when you come back. I let him have his way about it, and I *have* enjoyed seeing him. He's the only person I've seen but Mrs. Bowler and the doctor, and I'm mortal tired of both."

During Mrs. Spurr's second illness Noel had not come in person to the street of the Hyacinth; he had sent to inquire, and fruits and flowers came in his name. Miss Macks learned that these had come from the beginning.

When three weeks had passed Mrs. Spurr was back in her former place as regarded health. One of her first requests was to be taken out to drive; during her daughter's absence Mr. Noel had taken her five times, and she had greatly enjoyed the change. It was not so simple a matter for the daughter as it had been for Mr. Noel; her purse was almost empty; the long journeys and her mother's illness had exhausted her store. Still she did it. Mrs. Spurr wished to go to the Pincio. Her daughter thought the crowd there would be an objection.

"It didn't tire me one bit when Mr. No-ul took me," said Mrs. Spurr, in an aggrieved tone; "and we went there every single time — just as soon as he found out that I liked it. What a lot of folks he does know, to be sure! They kept him a-bowing every minute."

The day after this drive Mr. Noel came to the street of the Hyacinth. He saw Miss Macks. Her manner was quiet, a little distant; but she thanked him, with careful acknowledgment of every item, for his kind attentions to her mother. He said little. After learning that Mrs. Spurr was much better he spoke of her own health.

"You have had two long, fatiguing journeys, and you have been acting as nurse; it would be well for you to give yourself entire rest for several weeks at least."

She replied, coldly, that she was perfectly well, and turned the conversation to subjects less personal. He did not stay long. As he rose to take leave, he said:

"You will let me come again, I hope? You will not repeat the 'not at home' of last spring?"

"I would really much rather not see you, Mr. Noel," she answered, after hesitating.

"I am sorry. But of course I must submit." Then he went away.

Miss Macks now resumed her burdens. She was obliged to take more pupils than she had ever accepted before, and to work harder. She had not only to support their little household, but there were now debts to pay. She was out almost the whole of every day.

After she had entered upon her winter's work Raymond Noel began to come again to the street of the Hyacinth. But he did not come to see her; his visits were to her mother. He came two or three times a week, and always during the hours when the daughter was absent. He sat and talked to Mrs. Spurr, or rather listened to her, in a way that greatly cheered that lady's monotonous days. She told him her whole history; she minutely described Tuscolee and its society; and, finally, he heard the whole story of "John." In addition, he sent her various little delicacies, taking pains to find something she had not had.

Miss Macks would have put an end to this if she had known how. But certainly Mr. Noel was not troubling *her*, and Mrs. Spurr resented any attempt at interference.

"I don't see why you should object, Ettie. He seems to like to come, and there's but few pleasures left to me, I'm sure! You oughtn't to grudge them!"

In this way two months passed, Noel continuing his visits, and Miss Macks continuing her lessons. She was working very hard. She now looked not only pale, but much worn. Count L——, who had been long absent, returned to Rome about this time. He saw her one day, although she did not see him. The result of this vision of her was that he went down to Naples, and, before long, the desirable second cousin with the fortune was the sister of the Princess C——.

One afternoon in March Miss Macks was coming home from the broad, new, tiresome piazza Indipendenza; the distance was long, and she walked with weariness. As she drew near the dome of the Pantheon she met Raymond Noel. He stopped, turned, and accompanied her homeward. She had three books.

"Give them to me," he said, briefly, taking them from her.

"Do you know what I have heard to-day?" he went on. "They are going to tear down your street of the Hyacinth. The Government has at last awakened to the shame of allowing all those modern accretions to disfigure longer the magnificent old Pagan temple. All the streets in the rear, up to a certain point, are to be destroyed. And the street of the Hyacinth goes first. You will be driven out."

"I presume we can find another like it."

He went on talking about the Pantheon until they entered the doomed street; it was as obstinately narrow and dark as ever. Then he dropped his Pagan temple.

"How much longer are you going to treat me in this way, Faith?" he said. "You make me very unhappy. You are wearing yourself out, and it troubles me greatly. If you should fall ill I think that would be the end. I should then take matters into my own hands, and I don't believe you would be able to keep me off. But why should we wait for illness? It is too great a risk."

They were approaching her door. She said nothing, only hastened her steps.

"I have been doing my best to convince you, without annoying you, that you were mistaken about me. And the reason I have been doing it is that I am convinced myself. If I was not entirely sure last spring that I loved you, I certainly am sure now. I spent the summer thinking of it. I know now, beyond the possibility of a doubt, that I love you above all and everything. There is no 'duty' or 'generosity' in this, but simply my own feelings. I could perfectly well have let the matter drop; you gave me every opportunity to do so. That I have not done it should show you—a good deal. For I am not of the stuff of which heroes are made. I should not be here unless I wanted to; my motive is the selfish one of my own happiness."

They had entered the dark hallway.

"Do you remember the morning when you stood here, with two tears in your eyes, saying 'Never mind; you will come another time'?" (Here the cobbler came down the stairs.) "Why not let the demolition of the street of the Hyacinth be the crisis of our fate?" he went on, returning the cobbler's bow. (Here the cobbler departed.) "If you refuse, I shall not give you up; I shall go on in the same way. But—haven't I been tried long enough?"

"You have not," she answered. "But, unless you will leave Rome, and—me, I cannot bear it longer."

It was a great downfall, of course; Noel always maintained that it was.

"But the heights upon which you had placed yourself, my dear, were too superhuman," he said, excusingly.

The street of the Hyacinth experienced a great downfall, also. During the summer it was demolished.

Before its demolition Mrs. Lawrence, after three long breaths of astonishment, had come to offer her congratulations—in a new direction this time.

"It is the most fortunate thing in the world," she said to everybody, "that Mrs. Spurr is now confined to her bed for life, and is obliged to wear mourning."

But Mrs. Spurr is not confined to her bed; she drives out with her daughter whenever the weather is favorable. She wears black, but is now beginning to vary it with purple and lavender.

A CHRISTMAS PARTY

In 188– the American Consul at Venice was occupying the second story of an old palace on the Grand Canal. It was the story which is called by Italians the *piano nobile*, or noble floor. Beneath this *piano nobile* there is a large low ground, or rather water, floor, whose stone pavement, only slightly above the level of the canal outside, is always damp and often wet. At the time of the Consul's residence this water-floor was held by another tenant, a dealer in antiquities, who had partitioned off a shallow space across its broad front for a show-room. As this dealer had the ground-floor, he possessed, of course, the principal entrance of the palace, with its broad marble steps descending into the rippling wavelets of the splendid azure street outside, and with the tall, slender poles, irregularly placed in the water, which bore testimony to the aristocracy of the venerable pile they guarded. One could say that these blue wands, ornamented with heraldic devices, were like the spears of knights; this is what Miss Senter said. Or one could notice their strong resemblance to barbers' poles; and this was what Peter Senter always mentioned.

Peter Senter was the American Consul, and his sister Barbara was the Consuless; for she kept house for her brother, who was a bachelor. And she not only kept house for him, but she assisted him in other ways, owing to her knowledge of Italian. The Consul, a man of fifty-seven, spoke only the language of his native place—Rochester, New York. That he could not understand the speech (gibberish, he called it) of the people with whom he was supposed to hold official relations did not disturb him; he thought it patriotic not to understand. There was a vice-consul, an Italian, who could attend to the business matters; and as for the rest, wasn't Barbara there—Barbara, who could chatter not only in Italian, but in French and German also, with true feminine glibness? (For Peter, in his heart, thought it unmasculine to have a polyglot tongue.) He knew how well his sister could speak, because he had paid her bills during the six years of her education abroad. These bills had been large; of course, therefore, the knowledge must be large as well.

Miss Senter was always chronically annoyed that she and her brother did not possess the state entrance. As the palace was at present divided, the tenants of the noble floor descended by an outside stairway to a large inner court, and from this court opened the second water-door. Their staircase was a graceful construction of white marble, and the court, with the blue sky above, one or two fretted balconies, and a sculptured marble well-curb in the centre, was highly picturesque. But this did not reconcile the American lady to the fact that their door was at the side of the palace; she thought that by right the gondola of the Consul should lie among the heraldic poles on the Grand Canal. But, in spite of right, nothing could be done; the antiquity-dealer held his premises on a long lease. Miss Senter, therefore, disliked the dealer.

Her dislike, however, had not prevented her from paying a visit to his establishment soon after she had taken possession of the high-ceilinged rooms above. For she was curious about the old palace, and wished to see every inch of it; if there had been cellars, she would have gone down to inspect them, and she was fully determined to walk "all over the roof." The dealer's name was Pelham—"Z. Pelham" was inscribed on his sign. How he came by this English title no one but himself could have told. He was supposed to be either a Pole or an Armenian, and he spoke many languages with equal fluency and incorrectness. He appeared to have feeble health, and he always wore large arctic overshoes; he was short and thin, and the most noticeable expression of his plain, small face was resignation. Z. Pelham conducted the Consuless through the dusky space behind his show-room, a vast, low, open hall with massive squat columns and arches, and the skeletons of two old gondolas decaying in a corner. At the back he opened a small door, and pointed out a flight of stone steps going up steeply in a spiral, enclosed in a circular shaft like a round tower. "It leads to the attic floor. Her Excellency wishes to mount?" he inquired, patiently. For, owing to the wares in which he dealt, he had had a large acquaintance with eccentric characters of all nations.

"Certainly," replied Miss Senter. "Carmela, you can stay below, if you like," she said to the servant who accompanied her.

But no; Carmela also wished to mount. Z. Pelham preceded them, therefore, carrying his small oil-lamp. They went slowly, for the steps were narrow, the spiral sharp. The attic, when they reached it, was a queer, ghostly place; but there was a skylight with a ladder, and the Consuless carried out her intention of traversing the roof, while Mr. Pelham waited calmly, seated on the open scuttle door. Carmela followed her mistress. She gave little cries of admiration; there never were such wonderful ladies anywhere as those of America, she declared. On the way down, the stairs were so much like a corkscrew that Miss Senter, feeling dizzy, was obliged to pause for a moment where there was a landing. "Isn't there a secret chamber?" she demanded of the dealer.

Z. Pelham shook his head. "I have not one found."

"Try again," said Miss Senter, laughing. "I'll make it worth your while, Mr. Pelham."

Z. Pelham surveyed the walls, as if to see where he could have one built. His eye passed over a crack, and, raising his lamp, he showed it to the Consuless. "One time was there a door, opening into the rooms of her Excellency. But it opens not ever now; it is covered on inside."

"Oh, *that* isn't a secret chamber," answered Miss Senter; "we have doors that have been shut up at home. What I want is something mysterious—behind a picture, or a sliding panel."

Partly in return for this expedition to the roof, and partly because she had a liking for wood-carvings, Miss Senter purchased from Mr. Pelham, shortly afterwards, his best antique cabinet. It was eight feet high, and its whole surface was beautifully sculptured in odd designs, no two alike. Within were many ingenious receptacles, and, better than these, a concealed drawer. "You see I have my secret chamber, after all," said the Consuless, making a joke. And there was a best even to this better; for after the cabinet had been placed in her own room, Miss Senter discovered within it a second hiding-place, even more perfectly concealed than the first. This was delightful, and she confided to its care all her loose money. She thought with disgust of the ugly green safe, built into the wall of Peter's Rochester house, where she was obliged to keep her gold and silver when at home. Not only was Miss Senter's own room in the old palace handsomely furnished, but all the others belonging to the apartment were rich in beautiful things. The Consuless had used her own taste, which was great, and her brother's fortune, which was greater, deferring to him only on one point—namely, warmth. In Peter's mind the temperature of his Rochester house remained a fixed standard, and his sister therefore provided in every room a place for a generous open fire, while in the great drawing-room, in addition to this fire, two large white Vienna stoves, like monuments, were set up, hidden behind screens. As this salon was eighty feet long and thirty feet high, it required all this if it was to be used—used by Peter, at least—in December, January, and February; for the Venetian winter, though short, is often sharp and raw.

On Christmas Eve of their third year in Venice this drawing-room was lighted for a party. At one end, concealed by a curtain, stood a Christmas-tree; for there were thirty children among their invited guests, who would number in all over fifty. After the tree had bestowed its fruit the children were to have a dance, and an odd little projection like a very narrow balcony high on the wall was to be occupied by five musicians. These musicians would have been much more comfortable below. But Miss Senter was sure that this shelf was intended for musicians; her musicians, therefore, were to sit there, though their knees would be well squeezed between the wall and the balustrade. Fifteen minutes before the appointed hour, which was an early one on account of the children, the Consuless appeared. She found her brother standing before the fire, surveying the room, with his hands behind him.

"Doesn't it look pretty?" said the sister, with pride; for she had a great faith in all her pots and pans, carvings and tapestries. Any one, however, could have had faith in the chandeliers of Venetian glass, from which came the soft radiance of hundreds of wax candles, lighting up the ancient gilding of the ceiling.

"Well, Barly, you know that personally I don't care much for all these second-hand articles you have collected," replied Peter. "And you haven't got the room very warm, after all—only 60°. However, I can stand it if the supper is all right—plenty of it, and the hot things really hot; not lukewarm, you know."

"We can trust Giorgio. But I'll go and have a final word with him, if you like," answered Miss Senter, crossing the beautiful salon, her train sweeping over the floor behind her. The Consuless was no longer young (the days when Peter had paid those school bills were now far distant), and she had never been handsome. But she was tall and slender, with pretty hands and feet, a pleasant expression in her blue eyes, and soft brown hair, now heavily tinged with silver. Her brother's use of "Barly" was a grief to her. She had tried to lead him towards the habit of calling her Barbe, the French form of Barbara, if nickname he must have. But he pronounced this Bob, and that was worse than the other.

On her way towards the kitchen the Consuless came upon Carmela. Carmela was the servant who had the general oversight of everything excepting the cooking. For Giorgio, the cook, allowed no interference in his department; in the kitchen he must be Cæsar or nothing. Carmela was not the house-keeper, for Miss Senter herself was the house-keeper. But the American would have found her task twenty times, fifty times more difficult if she had not had this skilful little deputy to carry out all her orders. Carmela was said to be middle-aged. But her short, slender figure was so erect, her little face so alert, her movements were so brisk, and her small black eyes so bright, that she seemed full of youthful fire; in fact, if one saw only her back, she looked younger than Assunta and Beppa, who were Venetian girls of twenty. Carmela was always attired in the French fashion, with tight corsets, a plain black dress fitting like a glove round her little waist, and short enough to show the neat shoes on her small feet; over this black dress there was a jaunty white apron with pockets, and upon her beautifully braided shining dark hair was perched a small spotless muslin cap. The younger servants asserted that the slight pink tint on the tidy little woman's cheeks was artificial. However that may have been, Carmela, as she stood, was the personification of trimness and activity. Untiring and energetic, she was a wonderful worker; Miss Senter, who had been much in Italy, appreciated her good-fortune in having secured for her Venetian house-keeping such a coadjutor as this. Carmela was scrupulously neat, and she was even more scrupulously honest, never abstracting so much as a pin; she economized for her mistress with her whole soul, and kept watch over every detail; she told the truth, she swept the corners, she dusted under everything; she worked conscientiously, in one way and another, all day long. Even Peter, who did not like foreign servants, liked Carmela; he said she was "so spry!"

"Is everything ready?" inquired Miss Senter, as she met her deputy.

"Yes, signorina, everything," answered Carmela, briskly. She was looking her very best and tightest, all black and white, with black silk stockings showing above her little high-heeled shoes. As she spoke she put her hands in their black lace mitts in the pockets of her apron, and, middle-aged though she was said to be, she looked at that moment like a smart French soubrette of the stage.

"I am going to the kitchen to have a word with Giorgio," said the Consuless, passing on.

"If the signorina permits, I carry the train," answered Carmela, lifting the satin folds from the floor. Thus they went on together, mistress and maid, through various rooms and corridors, until finally the kitchen was reached. It was a large, lofty place, brilliantly lighted, for Giorgio was old and needed all the radiance that could be obtained to aid his failing sight. He was a small man with a melancholy countenance. But this melancholy was an accident of expression; in reality, old Giorgio was cheerful and amiable, with a good deal of mild wit. He was the most skilful cook in Venice. But his health had failed some years before, and he had now very little strength; the Consul, who liked good dinners, paid him high wages, and gave him a young assistant.

"Well, Giorgio, all promises well, I trust?" said Miss

Senter as she entered, her steps somewhat impeded by the tightness with which Carmela held back her train. "The Consul is particular about having the hot things really hot, and constantly renewed, as it is such a cold night. The three men from Florian's will have charge of the ices and the other cold things, and will do all that is necessary in the supper-room. But for the hot dishes we depend upon you."

Giorgio, who was dressed entirely in white, bowed and waved his hand. "Mademoiselle need give herself no uneasiness," he said in French. For Giorgio had learned his art in Paris, and whenever Carmela was present he invariably answered his mistress in the language of that Northern capital, even though her question had been couched in Italian; it was one of his ways—and he had but few—of standing up, as it were, against the indefatigable little deputy. For, clever though Carmela was, she had never been out of her native land, and could speak no tongue but her own.

"Are you feeling well, Giorgio?" continued Miss Senter. "I see that you look pale. I am afraid you have been doing too much. Where is Luigi?" (Luigi was the cook's assistant.)

"He has gone home; ten minutes ago. I let him go, as it is a festival. He is young, and we can be young but once. *Che vuole!* In addition, all was done."

"No," said Miss Senter, who was now speaking French also; "there is still much to do, and it was not wise to let Luigi go. You are certainly very tired, Giorgio."

"Let not mademoiselle think of it," said the old man, straightening himself a little.

"But I *shall* think of it," said Miss Senter, kindly. "Carmela," she continued, speaking now in Italian, "go to my room and get my case of cordials."

Carmela divined that the cordial was for the cook. "And the signorina's train?" she said. "Surely I cannot leave it on this *dirty* floor! Will not the signorina return to the drawing-room to take her cordial? Eh —it is not for her? It is for Giorgio? A man? A *man* to be faint like a girl? Ha, ha! it makes me laugh!"

"Go and get it," repeated Miss Senter, taking the train over her own arm. She knew that Carmela did not like the cook. Jealousy was the one fault the hard-working little creature possessed. "She has tried to make me dismiss Giorgio more than once," she said to her brother, in confidence; "but I always pretend not to see the feeling that influences her. It is only Giorgio she is jealous of; she gets on perfectly well with Luigi, and with Assunta and Beppa; while for Ercole she can never do enough. She is devoted to Ercole!"

Giorgio had not taken up the slur cast upon his immaculate floor. All he said was, "*Comme elle est méchante!*" with a shrug.

"Where is Ercole?" said Miss Senter, while she waited.

"He is dressing," answered Giorgio. "He makes himself beautiful for the occasion."

Ercole was the chief gondolier—a tall, athletic young man of thirty, handsome and clever. Miss Senter had chosen Ercole to assist her with the Christmas-tree. The second gondolier, Andrea, was to be stationed at the end of the little quay or riva down below, outside of their own water-door; for here on the small canal were the steps used by arriving and departing gondolas, and here also floated the handsome gondola of the Consul, with its American flag. The two gondoliers also had picturesque costumes of white (woollen in winter, linen in summer), with blue collars, blue stockings, blue caps, and long fringed red sashes, the combination representing the American national colors. To-night Ercole, having to appear in the drawing-room, was making a longer stay than usual before his little mirror.

Carmela returned with the cordial-case. "Ah, yes, our cook *is* pale—pale as a young virgin!" she commented, as Miss Senter, unlocking the box, poured into one of the little glasses it contained a generous portion of a restorative whose every drop was costly.

Giorgio, taking off the white linen cap which covered his gray hair, made a bow, and then drank the draught with much appreciation. "It is true that I am pale," he remarked, slyly, in Italian. "I might, perhaps, try some rouge?"

And then the Consuless, to avert war, hastily bore her deputy away.

Half an hour later the guests had arrived; they included all the Americans in Venice, with a sprinkling of English, Italians, and Russians. The grown people assembled in the drawing-room. And presently they heard singing. Through the anterooms came the children, entering with measured step, two and two, led by three little boys in Oriental costumes. These three boys were singing as follows:

> "We three Kings of Orient are,
> Bearing gifts we've travelled from far,
> Field and fountain, moor and mountain,
> Following yonder star."

Here, from the high top branch of the Christmas-tree which rose above the concealing curtain, blazed out a splendid star. And then all the procession took up the chorus, as they marched onward:

> "Oh, star of wonder,
> Star of might,
> Star with royal
> Beauty bright!"

Ercole, who was behind the curtain, now drew it aside, and there stood the tree, blazing with fairy-lamps and glittering ornaments, while beneath it was a mound composed entirely of toys. The children behaved well; they kept their ranks and repeated their carol, as they had been told to do, ranging themselves meanwhile in a half-circle before the tree.

> "We three Kings of Orient are,"

chanted the three little kings a second time, though their eyes were fixed upon a magnificent box of soldiers, with tents and flags and cannon. The carol finished, Miss Senter, with the aid of her gondolier, distributed the toys and bonbons, and the room was filled with happy glee. When Ercole had detached the last package of sweets from the sparkling branches he disappeared. His next duty was to conduct the musicians up to their cage.

Miss Senter had allowed an hour for the inspection and trial of the toys before the dancing should begin. It was none too much, and the clamor was still great as this hour drew towards its close, so great that she herself was glad that the end was near. Looking up to see whether her musicians had assembled on their shelf, she perceived some one at the drawing-room door; it was Carmela, hiding herself modestly behind the portière, but at the same time unmistakably beckoning to her mistress as soon as she saw that she had caught her eye. Miss Senter went to the doorway.

"Will the signorina permit? A surprise of Ercole's," whispered Carmela, eagerly, standing on tiptoe to reach her mistress's ear. "He has dressed himself as a clown, and he *is* of a perfection! He has bells on his cap and his elbows, and if the signorina graciously allows, he will come in to amuse the children."

"A clown!" answered Miss Senter, hesitating. "I don't know; he ought to have told me."

"He has been dancing to show *me*. And oh! so beautifully, with bounds and leaps. He makes of himself also a statue," pursued Carmela.

"But I cannot have any buffoonery here, you know," said Miss Senter. "It would not do."

"Buffoonery! Surely the signorina knows that Ercole has the soul of a gentleman," whispered Carmela, reproachfully.

And it was true that Miss Senter had always thought that her chief gondolier possessed a great deal of natural refinement.

"Will the signorina step out for a moment and look at him?" pursued the deputy, her whisper now a little dejected. "If he is to be disappointed, poor fellow, may he at least have *that* pleasure?"

The idea of the gondolier's disappointment touched the amiable American. She turned her head and glanced into the drawing-room; all was going on gayly; no one had missed her. She slipped out under the portière, and followed Carmela to a room at the side.

Here stood the gondolier. He wore the usual white dress and white mask of a clown, and, as the Consuless entered, he cut a splendid caper, ringing all his bells.

"I had no idea that you were such a skilful acrobat, Ercole," said his mistress.

Ercole turned a light somerset, gave a high jump, and came down in the attitude of the Mercury of John of Bologna.

"Why, you are really wonderful!" said Miss Senter, admiringly.

And now he was dancing with butterfly grace.

Miss Senter was won. "But if I let you come in, Ercole, I hope you will remember where you are?" she said, warningly. "Can you breathe quite at ease in that mask?"

The gondolier opened his grotesque painted lips a little to show that he could part them.

"Yes, I see. Now listen; in the drawing-room you must keep your eye on me, and if at any time you see me raise my hand—so—you must dance out of the room, Ercole. For the sign will mean that that is enough. But, dear me! there's one thing we haven't thought of; who is to see to the musicians up-stairs, and to go back and forth, telling them what to play?"

"I can do that," said Carmela, who was now all smiles. "Does the signorina wish me to take them up? They are all ready. They are waiting in the wood-room."

The wood-room was a remote store-room for fuel; it was detached from the rest of the apartment. "Why did you put them *there?*" inquired Miss Senter, astonished.

"They are musicians—yes; but who knows what

else they may be? Thieves, perhaps!" said the deputy, shrewdly.

"Get them out immediately and take them up to the gallery," said Miss Senter. "And tell them to play something lively as a beginning."

Carmela, quick as usual, was gone before the words were ended.

"Now, Ercole, wait until you hear the music. Then come in," said the Consuless.

She returned to the drawing-room, making a motion with her hands as she advanced, which indicated that her guests were to move a little more towards the walls on each side, leaving the centre of the room free. And then, as the music burst out above, Ercole came bounding in. His dress was ordinary; Miss Senter was vexed anew that he had not told her of his plan, for if he had she could have provided a perfectly fresh costume. But no one noticed the costume; all eyes were fixed upon the gambols; for, keeping time to the music, he was advancing up the room, dancing, bounding, leaping, turning somersets, and every now and then striking an attitude with extraordinary skill. He was so light that his white linen feet made no sound, and so graceful that the fixed grin of his mask became annoying, clashing as it did with the beauty of his poses. This thought, however, came to the elders only; for to the children, fascinated, shouting with delight, the broad red smile was an important part.

"It's our gondolier," explained Miss Senter. "It's Ercole," she had whispered to her brother.

"You are always so fortunate in servants," said Lady Kay. "That little woman you have, too, Carmela—she is a miracle for an Italian."

Four times the clown made his pyrotechnic progress up and then down the long salon, never twice repeating the same pose, but always something new; then, after a final tremendous pigeon-wing, he let his white arms fall and his white head droop on his breast, as if saying that he was taking a moment for repose.

"Yes, yes; give him time to breathe, children," cried Peter. "I'll tell you what," he added to Sir William Kay; "I've never seen a better performance on any stage." And he slapped his leg in confirmation. The Consul was a man whose sole claim to beauty lay in the fact that he always looked extremely clean. He was meagre and small, with very short legs, but he was without consciousness of these deficiencies; in the presence of the Apollo Belvedere, for instance, it had never occurred to him to draw comparisons. Nature, however, will out in some way, and from childhood Peter Senter had had a profound admiration for feats of strength, vaulting, tumbling, and the like. "I'll tell you what," he repeated to Sir William; "I'll have the fellow exhibited; I'll start him at my own cost. Here all this time—two whole years—he has been our gondolier, Ercoly has, and nothing more; for I hadn't a suspicion that he had the least talent in this line. But, sir, he's a regular high-flier! And A Number One!"

Meanwhile the children were crowding closely round their clown, and peering up in order still to see his grin, which was now partly hidden, owing to his drooped head; the three Kings of Orient, especially, were very pressing in their attentions, pinching his legs to see if they were real.

"Come, children, this will be a good time for our second song," said Miss Senter, making a diversion.

"Take hands, now, in a circle; yes—round the clown, if you wish. There—that's right." She signalled to the music to stop, and then, beginning, led the little singers herself:

> "Though we're here on foreign shores,
> We are all devotion
> To our land of Stars and Stripes,
> Far across the ocean.
> Yankee doodle doodle doo,
> Yankee doodle dandy,
> Buckwheat cakes are very good,
> And so's molasses candy."

Singing this gayly to the well-known fife-like tune, round and round danced the children in a circle, holding each other's hands, the English and Italians generously joining with the little Americans in praise of the matutinal cakes which they had never seen; the Consuless had drilled her choir beforehand, and they sang merrily and well. The first four lines of this ditty had been composed by Peter himself for the occasion.

"I hear *you* haf written this vurra fine piece!" said a Russian princess, addressing him.

"Oh no," answered the Consul; ".I only wrote the first four lines; the chorus is one of our national songs, you know."

"But those first four lines—their sentiment ees so fine, so speerited!" said the princess.

"Well, they're *neat*," Peter admitted, modestly.

The clown, having recovered his breath, cut a caper. Instantly "Yankee Doodle" came to an end, and the children all stopped to watch him.

"Tell them to play a waltz," said Miss Senter to Carmela, who was in waiting at the door. The deputy must have flown up the little stairway leading to the gallery, for the waltz began in less than a minute. Then Ercole, selecting a pretty American child from among the group, began to dance with her in the most charming way, followed by all the little ones, two and two. Those who could waltz, did so; those who could not, held each other's hands and hopped about.

Supper followed. The hot things were smoking and delicious, and the supplies constantly renewed; old Giorgio was evidently on his mettle. It was the gondolier, still in his clown's dress, who brought in these supplies and handed them to the waiters from Florian's.

"You need not do that, Ercole," said Miss Senter, in an undertone; "these men can go to the kitchen for them."

Ercole bowed; it would not have been respectful to reply with his grinning linen lips. But he continued to fill the same office.

"Perhaps Giorgio won't have Florian's people in the kitchen!" the Consuless reflected.

As soon as supper was over, the children clamored for their clown, and he came bounding in a second time, and, after several astonishing capers, selected a beautiful English child with long golden curls and led a galop, followed again by all the others, two and two. Peter, his mind still occupied with his project of taking the young Italian to America as a star performer, moved from point to point, in order to get different views of him. One of these stations was in the doorway, and here Carmela spoke to him in a low tone, and asked him to come to the outer hall. He did not understand her words; but he comprehended her gesture and followed her. She was talking angrily, almost spluttering, as she led the way. But her talk was lost on her master, who, however, opened his eyes when he saw four policemen standing at his outer door. "What do you want here?" he said. "This is a private residence, and you are disturbing a Christmas party."

The chief officer told his tale. But Peter did not comprehend him.

"You should have gone to the Consulate," he went on. "The Consulate, you know—Riva Skevony. The vice-consul won't be there so late as this; but you'll find him early to-morrow morning, sure."

The policemen, however, remained where they were.

"There's no making them understand a word," said Peter to himself, in irritation. "Here, you go and call my sister," he said to Carmela, who, in her wrath over this intrusion, stood at a distance swallowing nothing in a series of gulps that made her throat twitch. "Let's see; sister, that's sorelly. Sorelly!" he repeated to Carmela. "Sorelly!"

The enraged little deputy understood. And she got Miss Senter out of the drawing-room without attracting notice. "The master wishes to see the signorina," she said, in a concentrated undertone. "I burn with indignation, for it is an insolent intrusion; it is an insult to his Excellency, who no doubt is a prince in his own country. But they *would* not go, in spite of all I could say. Nor would they tell me their errand—brutes!" And with her skirts quivering she led the way to the outer hall.

"Find out what these men want, Barly," said Peter, when his sister appeared.

And then the chief officer again told his story.

"Mercy!" said Miss Senter, "how dreadful. Somebody was killed, Peter, about seven o'clock this evening, in a café near the Rialto, and they say they have just found a clew which appears to track the assassin to this very door! And they wish to search."

"What an absurd idea! With the whole place crowded and blazing with lights, as it is to-night, a mouse couldn't hide," said Peter. "Tell them so."

"They repeat that they must search," said Miss Senter. "But if you will exert your authority, Peter—make use of your official position—I am sure we need not submit to such a thing."

Peter, however, was helpless without his vice-consul; he had no clear idea as to what his powers were or were not; he had never informed himself.

Carmela, greatly excited, had drawn Miss Senter aside. "There was a sixth man with those musicians!" she whispered. "I saw him. He did not play, but he sat behind them. And he has only just gone. Five minutes ago."

Miss Senter repeated the information to the chief officer. The officer immediately detached two men to follow this important clew; he himself, with the third, would remain to go through the apartment, as a matter of form.

"As the rooms are all open and lighted," said Miss Senter in English to her brother, "it will only take a few minutes, if go they must, and no one need know anything about it. But whom shall we send with them? If we call Ercole, it will attract attention; and Florian's men, who were due at another place, have already gone. We could have Andrea come up. But no; Giorgio will do best of all. Call Giorgio to go with these men," she added in Italian to Carmela.

"Let *me* conduct them!" answered the deputy.

"Yes; on the whole, she will be better than any one," said Miss Senter to Peter. "She is so angry at what she calls the insult to you, and so excited about the mysterious person who was with the musicians, that she will bully them and hurry them off to look for him in no time. They can begin with a peep into the drawing-room; I'll tell them to keep themselves hidden." She turned and explained her idea in Italian to the officer; they could glance into the drawing-room first, and then Carmela would take them through all the other rooms; the Consul, though he had the power of refusal, would permit this liberty in the cause of justice. Their search, however, would be unavailing; under the circumstances, it was impossible that any one should have taken refuge there, unless it was that one extra man who had been admitted with the musicians to the gallery. And he was already gone.

"Perhaps he only pretended to go?" suggested the officer. "With permission, I will lock this door." And he did so.

They went to the drawing-room, the policemen moving quietly, close to the wall. When the last anteroom was reached, the two men hid themselves behind the tapestries that draped the door, and, making loopholes among the folds, peeped into the ball-room. For it was at that moment a ball-room. The children had again taken up their whirling dance around Ercole, and the gondolier, who had now a small child perched on each of his shoulders, was singing with them in a clear

"A SMALL CHILD PERCHED ON EACH OF HIS SHOULDERS"

tenor, having caught the syllables from having heard them shouted about fifty times :

> "Yankee dooda dooda doo,
> Yankee dooda dandee,
> Barkeet cakar vera goo,
> Arso molarsa candee."

Miss Senter had sent Peter back to his guests. She herself, standing between the tapestries as though she were looking on from the doorway, named to the hidden policemen, as well as she could amid the loud singing within, all the persons present, one by one. Finally her list came to a close. "And that is Mr. Barlow, the American who lives at the Danieli; and the one near the Christmas-tree is Mr. Douglas, who has the Palazzo Dario. And the tall, large gentleman with silver hair is Sir William Kay. That is all, except the clown, who is our gondolier, and the five musicians up in the gallery; can you see them from here? If not, Carmela can take you up." And then she thought, with a sudden little shudder, that perhaps the officer's idea was not, after all, impossible; perhaps, indeed, that extra man had only pretended to go!

The policemen signified that this was enough as regarded the drawing-room; they withdrew softly, and waited outside the door.

"Now take them through all the other rooms, Carmela," whispered the Consuless. "Be as quiet about it as you can, so that no one need know. And when they have finally gone, come and stand for a moment between these curtains, as a sign. If, by any chance, they *should* discover any one—"

"The signorina need not be frightened; I saw the

man go myself! And he *could not* have re-entered without my knowledge. As for these beasts of policemen—" And Carmela's eyes flashed, while her set lips seemed to say, "Trust *me* to hustle them out!"

"Run up first and tell the musicians to play the music I sent them," said the Consuless. And then she rejoined her guests.

For the next dance was to be a Virginia Reel, and some of the elders were to join the children; the two lines, when arranged, extended down half the length of the long room. It began with great spirit, the clown and the three Kings of Orient dancing at the end of the file.

"It is really Sir Roger de Coverley, an English dance," said Lady Kay to the Russian princess, who was looking on from the chair next her own. "But the Senters like to call it a Virginia Reel, they are so patriotic. And we never contradict the Senters, you know," added the English lady, laughing; "we let them have their way."

"It seems to me a vurra good way," answered the princess, who was a plain-looking old woman with a charming smile. "I have nowhere seen so many reech toyees" (here she glanced at the costly playthings heaped on a table near by). "Nor haf I, in *Italy*, seen so many tings to eat. With so moche champagne."

"Yes, they always do that," answered the baronet's wife. "They are so very lavish. And very kind."

Miss Senter herself was dancing the reel. Once she thought there was a quaver in the music, and, glancing up quickly towards the gallery, she perceived the heads of the policemen behind the players. The players, however, recovered themselves immediately, and upon looking up again a moment afterwards she saw with relief that the sinister apparition had vanished. Ten minutes later the trim little figure of the deputy appeared between the tapestries of the doorway. Miss Senter, still dancing, nodded slightly, as a signal that she perceived her, and then Carmela, with an answering nod and one admiring look at Ercole, disappeared. After all, now that there had been a suspicion about that extra man, it *was* a comfort to have had the apartment searched; it would make the moment of going to bed easier, the American lady reflected.

It was now half-past eleven. By midnight the last sleepy child had been carried down the marble stairway, the music ceased, and the musicians departed. The elders, glad that the noise was over, remained half an hour longer; then they took leave. Only Lady Kay and her husband were left; they had waited to take a closer look at Miss Senter's Christmas present to her brother, which was a large and beautifully executed copy of Tintoretto's "Bacchus and Ariadne," from the Anticollegio of the Doge's Palace. It had been placed temporarily on the wall behind the Christmas-tree.

"How exquisite!" said Lady Kay, with a long sigh. "You are most fortunate, Mr. Senter."

"Oh yes. Though I don't quite know what they will think of it in Rochester, New York," answered Peter, chuckling.

Sir William and his wife intended to walk home. When it was cold they preferred to walk rather than go to and fro in a gondola; and as they were old residents, they knew every turn of the intricate burrowing chinks in all the quarters that serve as footways. When they took leave at one o'clock, Peter and Miss Senter, with

American friendliness, accompanied them to the outer door. Peter was about to open this door when it was swung back, and a figure reeled in—Ercole. He had taken off his clown's dress, and wore now his gondolier's costume; but this costume was in disorder, and his face was darkly red—a purple red.

"Why, Ercole, is it you? What is the matter?" said Miss Senter, as he staggered against the wall.

"Oh, her Excellency the Consuless, I have been *beaten!*"

"Beaten? Where have you been? I thought you were down at the landing with Andrea," said Miss Senter.

"The antiquity-dealer suffocates," muttered Ercole. "And Giorgio—dead!"

This "dead" (*morto!*) even Peter understood. "Dead! What is he saying, Barly?"

"The man is saying, Mr. Senter, that an antiquity-dealer is suffocating, and that somebody he calls Giorgio is dead," translated the pink-cheeked, portly Lady Kay, in her sweet voice. "It's your gondolier, isn't it—the one who played the clown so nicely? What a pity! He has been drinking, I fear."

While she was saying this, Sir William was leading Ercole farther away from the ladies.

"Yes, he is drunk," said Peter, looking at him. "Too bad! We must have help. Let's see; Andrea is down at the landing. I'll get him. And you call Giorgio, Barly."

Here Ercole, held by Sir William, gave a maddened cry, and threw his head about violently.

"Oh, don't leave my husband alone with him, Mr. Senter," said Lady Kay, alarmed. "He is a very powerful young man, and his eyes are dreadful. To me he looks as if he were mad. Those somersaults have affected his head."

And the gondolier's eyes were indeed strangely bloodshot and wild. Miss Senter had hurried to the kitchen. But Giorgio was not there. She came back, and found Ercole struggling with the Englishman and her brother.

"Let me try," she said. "I am not afraid of him. Ercole," she continued, speaking gently in Italian, "go to your room now, and go to bed quietly; everything will be all right to-morrow."

Ercole writhed in Sir William's grasp. "The antiquity-dealer! And Giorgio—dead!"

"Where *is* Giorgio, Barly?" said Peter, angrily, as he helped Sir William in securing the gondolier. "And where are the other servants? Where's Carmela? Find them, and send one down to the landing for Andrea, and the other for Giorgio. Quick!"

"Oh, Peter, I've been, and I couldn't find Giorgio or any one."

"Carmela was in your bedroom not long ago," said Lady Kay, watching the gondolier's contortions nervously; "she helped me put on my cloak."

Miss Senter ran to her bedroom, her train flying in the haste she made. But in a moment she was back again. "There is no one there. Oh, where *are* they all?"

Ercole, hearing her voice, peered at her with his crimsoned eyes, and then, breaking loose suddenly, he came and caught hold of her arm. "The antiquity-room. *Will* she come?"

Peter and Sir William dragged him away by main force.

"The gentlemen, then. Will *they* come?" said the gondolier, hoarsely. And again freeing himself with two strokes of his powerful arms, he passed out (for the door was still open), and began to descend the outside staircase.

"Oh, thank Heaven, he has gone!" "Oh, lock the door!" cried the two ladies together.

"We must follow him, Mr. Senter," said Sir William. "He is plainly mad from drink, and may do some harm."

"Yes; and down there Andrea can help us," answered Peter.

And the two gentlemen hastened down the staircase. It was a very long flight with three turns. The court below was brilliantly lighted by many wall lamps.

"I *don't* like my husband's going down," said Lady Kay, in a tremor, as she stood on the landing outside. "If they are going to seize him, the more of us the better; don't you think so? For while they are holding him, you and I could run across and get that other man in from the riva."

But Miss Senter was not there. She had rushed back into the house, and was now calling with all her strength: "Giorgio! Carmela! Assunta! Beppa!" There was no answer, and, seized with a fresh panic by the strangeness of this silence, she hastened out again and joined Lady Kay, who was already half-way down the stairs. The gondolier had not turned towards the water entrance; he had crossed the court in the opposite direction, and now he was passing through a broad, low door which led into the hall on the ground-floor behind the show-room of Z. Pelham, throwing open as he did so both wings of this entrance, so that the light from the court entered in a broad beam across the stone pavement.

"My dear, *don't* go in!" "Oh, Peter, stop! stop!" cried the two ladies, as they breathlessly descended the last flight.

But Peter and Sir William had paid no attention. Quickly detaching two of the lamps from the wall, they had followed the madman.

"The other gondolier!" gasped Lady Kay.

And the two women ran swiftly to the water-door and threw it open, Miss Senter calling, in Italian: "Andrea! come *instantly!*"

The little riva along the small canal was also brightly lighted. But there was no one there. And opposite there was only a long blank wall.

"Oh, we must not leave them a moment longer," said Lady Kay.

And again they rushed across the broad court, this time entering the dark water-story; for it was better to enter, dreadful though it was, than to remain outside, not knowing what might be happening within. Ercole meanwhile had made his way into Mr. Pelham's show-room, and here he had struck a match and lighted a candle. As he had left the door of the show-room open, those who were without could see him, and they stopped for a moment to watch what he would do next. It was now a group of four, for the ladies had joined the other two, Miss Senter whispering to her brother:

"Andrea isn't there!"

The gondolier bent down, and began to drag something across the floor and out to the open space behind. "Here!" he said, turning his purple face towards their lamps. "I can no more." And he sat down suddenly on the pavement, and let his head and arms fall forward over his knees.

Peter and Sir William, giving their lamps to the ladies, were approaching cautiously, in order to secure him while he was quiet, when they saw, to their horror, two human legs and feet protruding from the object which he had dragged forth.

"Why, it's the second-hand dealer; it's Z. Pelham!" said Peter, in fresh excitement. "I know his arctics. Bring the lamp, Barly. Quick!"

The two ladies came nearer, keeping one eye upon Ercole. Peter and Sir William with some difficulty cut the rope, and unwound two woollen coverlids and a sheet. Within, almost suffocated, with his hands tied behind him, was the dealer.

"I suppose *he* did this!" whispered Lady Kay to Miss Senter, her pink face white, as she indicated the motionless gondolier.

Sir William lifted the dealer's head, while Peter loosened his collar.

"Now will Excellencies look for Giorgio," muttered Ercole, without changing his position.

"He says now will you look for Giorgio," translated Lady Kay. "That he *tells* his crimes shows that he really *is* mad!" she added, in a whisper.

"No; I think he has come to for the moment, and that's why he tells," said Peter, hastily rubbing Z. Pelham's chest. "Ask him where we shall look, Barly; ask while he's lucid."

"Where must we look for Giorgio, Ercole?" quavered Miss Senter, her Italian coming out with the oddest pronunciation.

"Back stairs," answered the gondolier.

"Back stairs, he says," translated Lady Kay.

"There are no back stairs," replied Peter.

"I'll put this coverlid under his back. That will make him breathe better," said the Englishman, his sympathies roused by the forlorn plight of the little dealer, whose carefully strapped arctic shoes gave ironical emphasis to his helplessness.

Meanwhile Miss Senter, saying "Yes, there *are* stairs," had run across the pavement with her lamp, found the door at the back of the hall, and opened it. Z. Pelham began to breathe more regularly, although he had not yet opened his eyes. Sir William drew him farther away from the gondolier, and then he and Peter hastened across and looked up the spiral. "It goes to the attics," explained Miss Senter.

"You two stand here at the bottom with one lamp, and Sir William and I will go up with the other," said Peter. "Keep your eye on Ercole, Barly, and if he so much as *moves*, come right up and join us."

"Wait an instant," said the Englishman. "Stay here with Mr. Senter, Gertrude." Making a détour so as not to rouse the gondolier, he entered the antiquity-dealer's show-room and tried to open the outer door. But it was locked, and the key was not there. "No use," he said, coming hurriedly back; "I had hoped to get help from outside to watch him while we go up. Now remember, Gertrude, you and Miss Senter are to come up and join us *instantly* if he leaves his place." And then he and Peter ascended the winding steps, carrying one of the lamps. Round and round went the gleam of their light, and the two ladies at the bottom, standing with their skirts caught up ready to run, watched the still form of the gondolier in the distance, visible in the gleam of the candle burning in the showroom. It seemed an hour. But a full minute had not gone when Peter's voice above cried out:

"It's Giorgio! Good God! Killed! Bring up the other light."

And the two ladies rushed up together. There on the landing lay the poor old cook, his eyes closed, his face ghastly, his white jacket deeply stained with blood. Miss Senter, who was really attached to the old man, began to cry.

"He isn't quite dead," said Peter, who had been listening for the heart. "But we must get him out of this icy place. Then we'll tie up Ercoly—we can use that rope—and after he is secured, I can go for help. Here, you take his head and shoulders, Sir William; you are the strongest. And I'll take his body. Barly can take the feet."

"It will be difficult," said the Englishman. "These steep stairs—"

But Peter, when roused, was a veritable little lion. "Come on," he said; "we can do it."

"Please go down first and see if Ercole is still quiet," begged Miss Senter of Lady Kay. And the Englishwoman, who now had both lamps, went down and came back in thirty seconds; she never knew how she did it. "He has not stirred," she said. And then old Giorgio was borne down, and out to the brilliantly lighted court beyond.

"Now," said Peter, whose face was bathed with great drops of perspiration, "we'll first secure him," and he indicated Ercole by pointing his thumb backward over his shoulder towards the water-story, "and then I'll go for a doctor and the police."

But as he spoke, coming out of the door upon his hands and knees, appeared Z. Pelham, who, as soon as he saw the cook's prostrate body, called back, hoarsely, in Italian: "Ercole, get my brandy-flask."

"Oh, don't call him!" said Lady Kay, in terror, clapping a fold of her skirt tightly over the dealer's mouth and holding it there. "He is mad—quite mad!"

Mr. Pelham collapsed.

"Good heavens! Gertrude, don't suffocate the poor creature a second time," said Sir William, pulling his wife away.

Z. Pelham, released, raised his head. "Ercole has been bad beat, and that makes him not genteel," he explained. "Ercole, bring my brandy-flask," he called again, in Italian, and the effort he made to break through his hoarseness brought out the words in a sudden wild yell. "My voice a little deranged is," he added, apologetically, in English.

They could now hear the steps of the gondolier within, and the ladies moved to a distance as he appeared, walking unsteadily, the flask in his hand. "Not dead?" he said, trying to see Giorgio. But his eyes closed convulsively, and as soon as the dealer had taken the flask, down he went, or half fell, on the pavement as before, with his head thrown forward over his knees. Sir William placed himself promptly by his side, while Peter ran within to get the rope. Z. Pelham, uncorking the flask, poured a little brandy between Giorgio's pale lips. "You have all mistake," he said to Sir William as he did this. "Ercole was bad beat by a third partee who has done it all—me and he and this died cook; a third partee was done it all." And he chafed the cook's temples with brandy.

"A third party?" said Peter, who had returned with the rope. "Who?"

"I know not; they knocked me from behind. It was lightning to me, in *my* head also," answered Z. Pelham, going on with his chafing.

"Come here, Barly," said Peter, taking command. "Say what I tell you. Don't be afraid; Sir William and I will grab him if he stirs. Say, 'Ercoly, who hurt you?'"

"Ercole, who hurt you?" said Miss Senter, tremulously.

"*Non so. Un demonio*," answered the gondolier, his head still on his knees.

"He says he doesn't know. A demon," said Lady Kay.

"Ask when it happened."

"It was after he had taken the presents from the tree," translated Lady Kay again. "He was struck, dragged down the back stairs, gagged, and left in the antiquity-room. He has only just now been able to free himself."

"How could he act the clown, then?" pursued Peter.

"He says he hasn't been a clown or seen a clown. Oh, Peter, it was some one else disguised! Who could it have been?" cried Miss Senter, running away as if to fly up the staircase, and then in her terror running back again.

The cook's eyes had now opened. "He says see what is stoled," said Mr. Pelham, administering more brandy. Mr. Pelham was seated, tailor fashion, on the pavement, his feet in their arctics under him.

"Giorgio knows something about it, too," said Peter. "Ask him, Barly."

But Miss Senter was incapable of speaking; she had hidden her face on Lady Kay's shoulder, shuddering. The clown with whom she had talked, who had danced all the evening with the children, was an assassin! A strange and savage murderer!

"I'll do it," said the Englishman. And bending over Giorgio, he asked, in correct, stiff Italian: "Do you know who hurt you?"

"A tall, dark man. I never saw him before," answered the cook, or rather his lips formed those words. "He stabbed me after he had struck down Ercole."

"Now he is again gone," soliloquized Z. Pelham, as Giorgio's eyes closed; "I have fear this time he is truly died!" And he chafed the cook's temples anew.

"It's all clear now," said Peter, "and Ercoly isn't mad; only hurt in some way. So I'll go for help at once."

"Oh, Peter, you always get lost!" moaned his sister.

And it was true that the Consul almost invariably lost his way in the labyrinth of chinks behind the palace.

"I'll go," said the Englishman. "It's not very late" (he looked at his watch); "I shall be sure to find some one."

"You must let me go with you, my dear," urged Lady Kay.

In three minutes they were back with two men. "I've brought these two, and there's a doctor coming. And I sent word to the police," said the Englishman.

And following very soon came a half-dressed youth, a young American doctor, who had been roused by somebody. The cook was borne up the stairway and into the salon, where the chandeliers were shedding their soft radiance calmly, and where all the fairy-lamps were still burning on the Christmas-tree; for only twenty minutes had passed since the host and his guests had left the room. Behind the group of the two men from outside, who with Peter and the doctor were carrying Giorgio, came Sir William leading the gondolier, who seemed now entirely blind, while Z. Pelham followed, last of all, on his hands and knees.

"This old man has a deep cut—done with a knife; he has lost a good deal of blood; pretty bad case," said the doctor. "Your gondolier has been dreadfully beaten about the head, but it won't kill him; he is young and strong. This third man seems to be only sprained. Get me something for bandages and compresses, and bring cold water."

"Get towels, Barly," said the Consul.

"Oh, Peter, I'm afraid to go," said Miss Senter, faintly. "The man may still be hidden here somewhere. And I know he has murdered Carmela and the other servants, too!"

Peter ran to his own chamber, and came back with a pile of towels, a sheet from his bed, a large jug of water, and a scissors. "Now, doctor, you stay hear and do what you can for all three," he said, as he hurried round the great drawing-room, locking all the doors but one. "And the ladies will stay here with you. The rest of us will search the whole apartment immediately! Lock this last door as soon as we're out, will you?"

"Oh, Peter, don't go!" cried his sister. "Let those two men do it. Or wait for the police."

"My dear, pray consider," said Lady Kay to her husband; "if any one *is* hidden, it is some desperate character—"

But the Englishman and Peter were already gone, and the ladies were left with the doctor, who, comprehending everything quickly, locked the last door, and then hurried back to the cook. Old Giorgio's mind was now wandering; he muttered incoherently, and seemed to be suffering greatly. The gondolier, his head enveloped in wet towels, was lying in a stupor on one of the sofas. Z. Pelham quietly tied up his own sprained ankles with a portion of the torn sheet, and then assisted with much intelligence in the making of the bandages which the doctor needed for Giorgio.

Sir William, Peter, and the two men from outside began with the kitchen; no one. The pantries and store-rooms; no one. The supper-room; no one. The bedrooms; no one. The anterooms and small drawing-room; no one. As the whole house was still brightly lighted, this did not take long. They now crossed to four rooms on the north side; no one. Then came a large store-room for linen. This was not lighted, so they took in a lamp; no one.

"There's a second door here," said Sir William, perceiving one of those masked flat portals common in Italy, which are painted or frescoed so exactly like the wall that they seem a part of it.

"It opens into a little recess only a foot deep," said Peter, going on with the lamp to the second store-room. "No one could possibly hide there. Now after we have finished on this side, there is only the wood-room left; that is off by itself in a wing."

The Englishman had accompanied his host. But

having a strong bent towards thoroughness, he was not satisfied, and he quietly returned alone and opened that masked door. There, flattened against the wall, not clearly visible in the semi-darkness, was the outline of a woman's figure. His exclamation brought back the others with the lamp. It was Carmela.

She stood perfectly still for an instant or two, so motionless, and with such bright eyes staring at them, that she looked like a wax figure. Then she sprang from her hiding-place and made a swift rush down the corridor towards the outer door. They caught her. She fought and struggled dreadfully, still without a sound. So frantic were her writhings that her apron and cap were torn away, and the braids of her hair fell down and finally fell off, leaving only, to Peter's astonishment, a few locks of thin white hair in their place. It took the four men to hold her, for she threw herself from side to side like a wild-cat; she even dragged the four as far as the anteroom nearest the drawing-room in her desperate efforts to reach that outer door. But here, as she felt herself at last overpowered, a terrible shriek burst from her, her face became distorted, her eyes rolled up, and froth appeared on her lips.

The shriek, an unmistakably feminine one, had brought the doctor and two ladies from the drawing-room.

"A fit!" exclaimed the doctor as soon as he saw the froth. "Here, get open that tight dress." He unbuttoned a few buttons of the black bodice, and tore off the rest. "Gracious! corsets like steel." He took out his knife, and hastily cutting the cashmere across the shoulders, he got his hand in and severed the corset strings. "Now, ladies, just help me to get her out of this harness."

And with trembling fingers Lady Kay and Miss Senter gave their aid, and after a moment the whole edifice— for it was an edifice — sank to the floor. What was left was an old, old woman, small and withered, her feeble chest rising and falling in convulsions under her coarse chemise, and the rest of her little person scantily covered with a patched, poverty-stricken underskirt.

"Oh, *poor* creature!" said Lady Kay, the tears filling her eyes as all the ribs of the meagre, wasted body showed in the straining, spasmodic effort of the lungs to get breath.

"Bring something to cover her, Barly," said Peter.

And Miss Senter, forgetting her fears, ran to her room, and brought back the first thing she could find—a large white shawl.

"All right now; she's coming to," said the doctor.

The convulsions gradually ceased, and Carmela's eyes opened. She looked at them all in silence as she sat, muffled in the shawl, where they had placed her. Finally she spoke. "The Consul is too late," she said, with mock respect. "The Consuless also. Did they admire the dancing of the clown? A fine fellow that clown! You need not hold me," she added to the two men from outside, who were acting as guards. "I have nothing more to do. My son is safe, and that was all I cared for. They will never find him; he is far from here now. He is very clever, and he has, besides, to help him, all the money which the Consuless so kindly provided for him by keeping it in a secret drawer, whose 'secret' every Italian not an idiot knows. But the Consuless has always had a singular self-conceit. I had only to mention that extra man with the musicians—poor little Tonio the tailor it was—and she swallowed him down whole. I could have got away myself if I had cared to. But I waited, in order to keep back the alarm as long as possible; I waited. Oh yes, I helped all the ladies to put on their cloaks; I helped this English ladyship to put on hers last of all, as she knows. When their Excellencies went down to the water-story, I then tried to go; but I found that they could still see the staircase, so I came back. What matters it? They may do with me what they please. For myself I care not. My son is safe." On her old cheeks, under the falling white hair, were still the faint pink tinges of rouge, and from beneath the wretched petticoat came the two young-looking high-heeled shoes. She folded her thin hands on her lap, and refused to say more.

Assunta and Beppa were found in the wood-room, gagged and bound like the others, but not hurt. And in the morning the Consul's gondola was discovered floating out with the tide, and within it Andrea in the same helpless state. The man, who was an ex-convict, a burglar, suspected of worse crimes, after committing the murder at the café, had fled to the palace. Here he and his intrepid little mother had invented and carried out the whole scheme in the one hour which had followed the distribution of the presents from the tree, before the dancing began. Carmela had even left the house to obtain a clown's costume from a dealer in masquerade dresses who lived near by. And she had herself opened for her son's use the disused door which led to the spiral steps.

That son was never caught. His mother, who had worked for him indefatigably through her whole life— worked so hard that her hands were worn almost to claws—who had supported him and supplied him, who had made herself young and active like a girl, though she was seventy-four, in order to be able to send him money—his mother, who had allowed herself nothing in the world but the few smart clothes necessary for her disguise, who was absolutely honest, but who had stolen for him three thousand francs from the secret drawer, and had stood by and aided him when he beat, stabbed, and gagged her fellow-servants—this mother was not arrested. She should have been, of course. But somehow, very strangely, she escaped from the palace before morning.

Poor old Giorgio was never able to work again. But as Peter pensioned him handsomely, he led an easy life, while Ercole became a magnate among gondoliers.

It was not until three years afterwards, in Rochester, New York, that Peter, surrounded by Z. Pelham's entire collection (which he had purchased, though thinking it hideous, at large prices), confessed to his sister that he had connived at Carmela's escape. "Somehow I couldn't stand it, Barly. That thin white hair and those poor old arms of hers, and that wretched, wasted, gasping little chest—in prison!"

IN VENICE

"Yes, we came over again in February, and have been here in Venice since the last of March. For some reasons I was sorry to come back — one *is* so much more comfortable at home! What I have suffered in these wretchedly cold houses over here words, Mr. Blake, can never express. For in England, you know, they consider fifty-eight Fahrenheit quite warm enough for their drawing-rooms, while here in Italy — well, one never *is* so cold, I think, as in a warm climate. Yes, we should have been more comfortable, as far as *that* goes, in my own house in New York, reading all those delightful books on Art in a properly warmed atmosphere (and I must say a properly warmed spirit too), and looking at photographs of the pictures (you can have them as large as you like, you know), instead of freezing our feet over the originals, which half the time the eyes of a lynx could not see. But it is not always winter, of course. And then I have lived over here so long that I have, it seems, acquired foreign ways that are very unpopular at home. You may smile, and it *is* too ridiculous; but it is so. For instance, last summer we went to Carley Ledge (you know Carley; pretty little place), and we found out afterwards that the people came near mobbing us! Not exactly that, of course, but they took the most violent dislike to us;

and why? It is too comical. Because we had innocently treated Carley as we treat a pretty village over here. One lady said, and, I am told, with indignation, that we had been stopping, 'more than once, right in the main street, and standing there, in that *public* place, to look at a cloud passing over the mountain!' And another reported that she had herself discovered us 'sitting on the *grass*, no farther away from the main street than the open space in front of Deacon Seymour's, just as though it was out in the country!' That 'out in the country' is rather good, isn't it? Always that poor little main street!"

"Still, I think, on the whole, that the cold houses are worse than the village comments," replied Mrs. Marcy's visitor. "A New-Yorker I know, a confirmed European too, always goes home to spend the three months of winter. When he comes back in the spring his English friends say, 'I hear you have had so many degrees of frost over there — fancy!' — meaning, perhaps, zero or under. To which he assents, but always inflexibly goes back. They look upon him as a kind of Esquimau. But how does Miss Marcy like exile?"

"Oh, Claudia is very fond of Italy. You have not seen her, by-the-way, since she was a child, and she is now twenty. Do you find her altered?"

"Greatly."

"At home she was never thought pretty — when she was younger, I mean. She was thought too — too — vigorous is perhaps the best word; she had not that graceful slenderness one expects to see in a young girl. But over here, I notice, the opinion seems to be different," continued the lady, half questioningly. "And, of course, too, she has improved."

"My dear Miss Sophy—improved? Miss Marcy is a wonderfully beautiful woman."

"Yes, yes, I know; Mr. Lenox thinks so too, I believe," answered Mrs. Marcy, half pleased, half irritated. "It seems she is a Venetian—that is, of the sixteenth century; and dressed in dark-green velvet, with those great puffed Venetian sleeves coming down over her knuckles, a gold chain, and her hair closely braided, she would be, they tell me, a perfect Bonifazio. In fact, Mr. Lenox is painting her as one. Only he has to imagine the dress."

Mrs. Marcy was a widow, and fifty-five. It had pleased her to hear again the old "Miss Sophy" of their youth from Rodney Blake; but as she had been one of those tall, slender, faintly lined girls who are called lilies, and who are associated with pale blues and lavender, she naturally found it difficult to realize a beauty, even if it was that of a niece, so unlike her own. Mrs. Marcy was now less than slender; the blue eyes which had once mildly lighted her countenance were faded. But she still remained lily-like and willowy, and her attire adapted itself to that style; there was a gleam of the lavender still—she wore long shawls and scarfs.

In the easy-chair opposite, Rodney Blake leaned back. He was fifty-six, long and thin, with a permanent expression on his face of half-weary, half-amused cynicism, which, however, seemed to concern itself more with life in general than with people in particular, and thus prevented personal applications. He was well-to-do, well dressed. There was a generally received legend that he was rather brilliant. This was the more remarkable because he seldom said much. But perhaps that was the reason. Miss Marcy had entered as her aunt finished her sentence.

"The sitting is over, then," said the elder lady. "Has Mr. Lenox gone?"

"Not yet," answered the niece, giving her hand to Mr. Blake as he rose to greet her.

She was, as he had said, a beautiful woman. Yet at home there were still those who would have dissented from this opinion, as, secretly, her aunt dissented. She was of about medium height, with the form of a Juno. She had a rich complexion, slowly moving eyes of deep brown, and very thick, curling, low-growing hair of a bright gold color, which showed a warmer reddish tinge in the light. She was the personification of healthy life and vigor, but not of the nervous or active sort; of the reflective. Wherever the sun touched her it struck a color: whether the red of cheek or lip, or the beautiful tint of her forehead and throat, which was not fair but clear; whether the brown of her eyes, or the gold of eyebrows, eyelashes, and the heavy, low-coiled hair. Her features were fairly regular, but not of the pointed type; they were short rather than long, clearly, almost boldly, outlined. Her forehead was low; her mouth not small, the lips beautifully cut. She was attired in black velvet—she affected rich materials—and as she talked she twisted and untwisted a string of large pearls which hung loosely round her throat and down upon the velvet of her dress.

"Mr. Lenox does not have to imagine much, after all," observed Mr. Blake in his slow way to Mrs. Marcy. "In velvet, with those pearls, she does very well as it is."

"They are only Roman beads," said Claudia. "I don't know what you mean, of course."

"I had been telling Mr. Blake that they say that if you had a green velvet, with those big sleeves, you know, and your hair braided close to the head, to make it look too small in comparison with the shoulders, it would be a Bonifazio," explained the aunt.

"Your pearls are not so effective as they might be, Miss Marcy," continued the visitor, scanning her as she took a seat.

"I do not wear them in this way, but so." She unfastened the clasp, and rewound the long string in three close rows, one above the other, round her throat, above the high-coming black of her dress.

"That is better," said her critic.

"It feels like a piece of armor, so I unloosen it as soon as I can," she answered.

Here the artist came in, hat in hand. "I am on my way home," he said. "Good-morning, Mr. Blake. I have only stopped to ask about our expedition this afternoon, Mrs. Marcy."

"Oh, I suppose we shall go," answered that lady, "the day is so fine. How are they at home this morning, Mr. Lenox?"

"Elizabeth is quite well, thanks; Theocritus as usual. Shall I order gondolas, then?"

"If you will be so good; at four. Mr. Blake will, I hope, go with us."

And then Mr. Lenox bowed, and withdrew.

"Does the—the idyllic personage accompany us?" asked the gentleman in the easy-chair.

"It is only a child appended to the name," said Claudia, laughing. "For some reason Mrs. Lenox always pronounces it in full; she could just as well call him Theo."

"It is her nephew, and she is devoted to him," explained Mrs. Marcy. "He is nearly ten years old, but does not look more than five. His health is extremely delicate, and he is at times rather—rather babyish."

"Peevish, isn't it?" said Claudia. She had taken up two long black needles entangled in a mass of crimson worsted, and, disengaging them, was beginning to knit another row on an unfinished stripe. Her beautifully moulded hands, full and white, with one antique gem on each, contrasted with the tint of the wool. The thin fingers of Mrs. Marcy were decked with fine diamonds, and diamonds alone; in spite of the "foreign ways" of which that lady had accused herself, she remained sufficiently American for that. She could buy diamonds, and Claudia an antique ring or two; both aunt and niece enjoyed inherited incomes, that of Claudia being comfortable, that of Mrs. Marcy large.

These ladies occupied rooms on the third floor of a palace on the Grand Canal, not far below the Piazzetta. The palace was a stately example of Renaissance architecture, with three rows of majestic polished columns extending one above the other across its front. Between these columns the American tenant, who had once been called "the lily," and her niece, who was so like a Bonifazio, looked out upon the golden Venetian light—a light whose shadows are colors: mother-of-pearl, emerald, orange, amber, and all the changing gradations between them—thrown against and between the reds, browns, and fretted white marbles of the buildings rising from the water; that ever-moving water which mirrors it all—here a sparkling, glancing surface, there a mysterious darkness, both of them contrasting with the serene blue of the sky above, which is barred towards the riva by the long, lean, sharply defined lateen spars of the moored barks, and made even more deep in its hue over the harbor by the broad sails of the fishing-sloops outlined against it, as they come slowly up the channel, rich, unlighted sheets of tawny yellow and red, with a great cross vaguely defined upon them.

Next to the Renaissance palace was a smaller one, narrow and high, of mediæval Gothic, ancient and weather-stained; it had lancet-windows, adorned above with trefoil, and a little carved balcony like old Venetian lace cut in marble. Here Mr. and Mrs. Lenox occupied the floor above that occupied by the ladies in the larger palace. Communication was direct, however, owing to a hallway, like a little covered bridge, that crossed the canal which flowed between—a canal narrow, dark, and still, that worked away silently all day and all night at its life-long task of undermining the ponderous walls on each side; gaining perhaps a half-inch in a century, together with the lighter achievement of eating out the painted wooden columns which, like lances set upright in the sand at a tent's door, the old Venetians were accustomed to plant in the tide round their water-washed entrances. At four o'clock the little company started, the three from the Gothic palace having come across the hall bridge to join the others. Two gondolas were in waiting; as the afternoon was warm, they had light awnings instead of the antique black tops, with the sombre drapery sweeping out behind.

"I like the black tops better," observed Claudia. "Any one can have an awning, but the black tops are Venetian."

"They can easily be changed," said Lenox.

"Oh no; not in this heat," objected Mrs. Marcy. "We should stifle. Mr. Blake, shall you and I, as the selfish elders, take this one, and let the younger people go together in that?"

"I want to go in the one with the red awning—the *bright* red," said Theocritus. This was the one Mrs. Marcy had selected.

"No, no, my boy; the other will do quite as well for you," said Lenox.

"It won't," replied the child, in a decided little voice.

"It is not of the slightest consequence," graciously interposed Mrs. Marcy, signalling to the other gondola, and, with Blake's assistance, taking her place within it.

Mr. Lenox glanced at his wife. She was occupied in folding a shawl closely over the boy's little overcoat. "Come, then," he said, giving his hand first to Miss Marcy, then to his wife and the child. The gondolas floated out on the broad stream.

Claudia talked; she talked well, and took the Venetian tone. "The only thing that jars upon me," she said, after a while, "is that these Venetians of to-day—those men and women we are passing on the riva now, for instance—do not appreciate in the least their wonderful water-city—scarcely know what it is."

"They don't study 'Venice' because they are Venice—isn't that it?" said Mrs. Lenox. She had soothed the little boy into placidity, and he sat beside her quietly, with one gloved hand in hers, a small muffled figure, with a pale face whose delicate skin was lined like that of an old man. His eyes were narrow, deep-set, and dark under his faintly outlined fair eyebrows; his thin hair so light in hue and cut so closely to his head that it could scarcely be distinguished.

"I hope not," said Claudia, answering Mrs. Lenox's remark — "at least, I hope the old Venetians were not so; I like to think that they felt, down to their very finger-tips, all the richness and beauty about them."

"You may be sure the feeling was unconscious compared with ours," replied Mrs. Lenox. "They did not consult authorities about the pictures; they were the pictures. They did not study history; they made it. They did not read romances; they lived them."

"I wish I could have lived then," murmured Miss Marcy, her eyes resting thoughtfully on the red tower of San Giorgio, rising from the blue. No veil obscured the beautiful tints of her face; Claudia's complexion could brave the brightest light, the wind, and the sun. The dark-blue plume of the round hat she wore curled down over the rippled sunny braids of her hair. Mr. Lenox was looking at her. But Mr. Lenox was often looking at her.

"That would not be at all nice for us," said Mrs. Lenox, in her pleasant voice, answering the young lady's wish. "If you, Miss Marcy, can step back into the fifteenth century without trouble, we cannot; Stephen and I are very completely of this poor nineteenth."

"I don't know," said Claudia, slowly; she looked at "Stephen" with meditative eyes. "He could have been one of the soldiers. You remember that Venetian portrait in the Uffizi at Florence—General Gattamelata? Mr. Lenox does not look like it; but in armor he would look quite as well."

"I don't remember it," said Mrs. Lenox, turning to

see why Theocritus was beating upon her knees with his right fist.

"You must remember—it is so superb!" said Claudia.

"I want to sit on the other side," announced Theocritus.

"When we come back, dear. See, the church is quite near; we shall soon be there now," answered his aunt.

"You remember it, don't you?" said Claudia to Lenox.

"Perfectly."

"No—*now*," piped Theocritus. "The wind is blowing down my back."

"If he is cold, Stephen—" said Mrs. Lenox.

"I will change places with him," replied her husband. "Do not move, Miss Marcy."

"No; Aunt Lizzie must go too!" said the boy. He had wrinkled up his little face until he looked like an aged dwarf in a temper; he stretched back his lips over his little square white teeth, and glared at his uncle and Miss Marcy.

"Let me change—do," said Claudia, rising as she spoke. And Mrs. Lenox accepted the offer.

"When you have finished my portrait, suppose you paint yourself as a fifteenth-century Venetian general," continued Miss Marcy, taking up again the thread of conversation which had been broken by Theocritus's obstinacy. "The portrait of a man painted by himself is always interesting; you can see then what he thinks he is."

"And is not?" said Lenox.

"Possibly. Still, what he might be. It is his ideal

view of himself, and I believe in ideals. It is only our real, purified—what we shall all attain, I hope, in another world."

Thus she talked on. And the man to whom she talked thought it a loveliness of nature that she passed so naturally and unnoticingly over the demeanor of the spoiled child who accompanied them. Mrs. Lenox could, for the present take no further part in the conversation, as Theocritus had demanded that she should relate to him the legend of St. Mark, St. George, and St. Theodore climbing down from their places over the church porch, the palace window, and the crocodile column to fight the demons of the lagoons. This she did, but in so low a tone that the conversation of the others was not interrupted.

They reached the island and landed; Mrs. Marcy and Blake were already there, sitting on the sun-warmed steps of the church whose smooth white façade and red campanile are so conspicuous from Venice. "We were discussing the shape of the prow of the gondola," said Mrs. Marcy, as they came up. "To me it looks like the neck of a swan." Mrs. Marcy never sought for new terms; if the old ones were only poetical—she was a stickler for that—she used them as they were, contentedly.

Mr. Blake, who always took the key-note of the conversation in which he found himself, advanced the equally veteran comparison of the neck of a violin.

"It is the shining blade of St. Theodore, the patron of the gondolas," suggested Claudia.

"To me it looks a good deal like the hammer of a sewing-machine," observed Mrs. Lenox, lightly. This was so true that they all had to laugh.

"But this will never do, Mrs. Lenox," said Blake, turning to look at her as she stood on the broad marble step, holding the little boy's hand; "you will destroy all our carefully prepared atmosphere with your modern terms. Here we have all been reading up for this expedition, and we know just what Ruskin thinks; wait a bit, and you will hear us talk! And not one will be so rude as to recognize a single adjective."

"You admire him, then—Ruskin?" said the lady.

"Admire? That is not the word; he is the divinest madman! Ah, but he makes us work! In some always inaccessible spot he discovers an inscrutably beautiful thing, and then he goes to work and writes about it fiercely, with all his nouns in capitals, and his adjectives after the nouns instead of before them—which naturally awes us. But what produces an even deeper thrill is his rich way of spreading his possessive cases over two words instead of one, as, 'In the eager heart of him,' instead of 'In his eager heart.' This cows us completely."

"I want to go in the church. I don't want to stay out here any longer," announced Theocritus. And, as his aunt let him have his way, the others followed her, and they all went in together.

Compared with the warm sunshine without, the silent aisles seemed cool. After ten minutes or so Mrs. Marcy and Blake came out, and seated themselves on the step again. "You have known her for some time?" Blake was saying.

"Mrs. Lenox? No; only since we first met here, six —I mean seven—weeks ago. But Stephen Lenox I have always known, or rather known about; he is a distant connection of mine. His history has been rather unusual. His mother, a widow, managed to educate him, but that was all; they were really very poor, and Stephen was hard at work before he was twenty. He had some sort of a clerkship in an iron-mill, and was kept at it, I was told, twelve and thirteen hours a day. Before he was twenty-two he married. He worked harder than ever then, although he had, I believe, in time a better place. His wife had no money, either, and she was not strong. Their two little children died. Well, after twelve years of this, most unexpectedly, by the will of an uncle by marriage, he came into quite a nice little fortune; the uncle said, I was told, that he admired a man who, in these days, had never had or asked for the least help from his relatives. And so Stephen could at last do as he pleased, and very soon afterwards they came abroad. For he had been an artist at heart all this time, it seems—at least, he has a great liking for painting, and even, I think, some skill."

"I doubt if he is a creative artist," answered Blake. "He is too well balanced for that—a strong, quiet fellow. His wife is of about his age, I presume?"

"Yes; he is thirty-six, and she the same. They have been over here already nearly two years. She is a very nice little woman" (Mrs. Lenox was tall and slender; but Mrs. Marcy always patronized Mrs. Lenox), "although one *does* get extremely tired of that spoiled boy she drags about. Do you know," added the lady, deeply, "I feel sure it would be much better for Elizabeth Lenox if she would remember her present circumstances more; there is no longer any necessity for an invariable untrimmed gray gown."

"Doesn't she dress well?" said Blake. "I thought she always looked very neat."

"That is the very word—neat. But there is no flow, no richness. She has been rather pretty once; that is, in that style—gray eyes and dark hair; and she might be so still if she had the proper costumes. Of course, going about Venice in this way one does not want to dress much; but she has not even got anything put away."

"If one does not wear it, what difference does that make?" asked the gentleman.

"All the difference in the world!" replied Mrs. Marcy. "Let me tell you that the very *step* of a woman who knows she has two or three nice dresses in the bottom of her trunk is different from that of a woman who knows she hasn't."

"But perhaps Mrs. Lenox does not know that she 'hasn't,'" remarked Blake. This, however, went over Mrs. Marcy's head.

Within, the others were looking at the beautiful Tintorettos in the choir. After a while the ill-favored but gravely serene young monk who had admitted them approached and mentioned solemnly "the view from the campanile;" this not because he cared whether they went up or not, but simply as part of his duty.

"I should like to go," said Claudia; "I love to look off over the lagoons."

They turned to leave the choir. "*I* don't want to go," said Theocritus, holding back. "I want to stay here and see that picture some more; and I'm going to!"

This time Miss Marcy did not yield her wish. "Do not come with me," she said to Mr. and Mrs. Lenox; "it is not in the least necessary. I have been up before, and know the way. I will not be gone fifteen minutes."

"I really think that he ought not to climb all those stairs," said Mrs. Lenox to her husband, looking at the child, who had gone back to his station before the picture.

"Of course not," answered Lenox. Then, after a moment, "I will stay with him," he added; "you go up with Miss Marcy."

"I want Aunt Lizzie to stay—not Uncle Stephen!" called the boy, overhearing this, and turning round to scowl at them.

"He will not be good with any one but me," said Mrs. Lenox, in a low tone. "You two go up; I will wait for you here."

"The question is, Is he ever good, even with her?" said Claudia, following Lenox up the long flight of steps that winds in square turns up, up, to the top of the campanile.

"She says he is sometimes very sweet and docile—even affectionate," replied Lenox. "She thinks he has quite a remarkable mind, and will distinguish himself some day if we can only tide his poor, puny little body safely over its childish weakness, and give him a fair start."

"She is very fond of him."

"Yes; his mother was her dearest friend, his father her only brother."

Claudia considered that she had now given sufficient time to this subject (not an interesting one), and they talked of other things, but in short sentences, for they were still ascending. Twice she stopped to rest for a minute or two; then Lenox came down a step, and stood beside her. There was no danger; still, if a person should be seized with giddiness, the thought of the near open well in the centre, going darkly down, was a dizzy one.

At the top they had the view: wide green flatness towards the east, northeast, southeast, with myriad gleaming, silvery channels; the Lido and the soft line of the Adriatic beyond; towns shining whitely in the north; to the west, Venice, with its long bridge stretching to the mainland; in port, at their feet, a large Italian man-of-war; on the south side, the point of the Giudecca.

"'À Saint-Blaise, à la Zuecca,
Vous étiez bien aise;
À Saint-Blaise, à la Zuecca,
Nous étions bien là !'"

quoted Claudia. "I chant it because I have just discovered that the Zuecca means the Giudecca yonder."

"What is the verse?" said Lenox.

"Don't you know it? It is Musset."

"I have read but little, Miss Marcy."

"You have not had *time* to read," said Claudia, with a shade of emphasis; "your time has been given to better things."

"Yes, to iron rails!"

"To energy and to duty," she answered. Then she turned the subject, and talked of the tints on the water.

Down below, in the still church, the little boy sat beside his aunt, her arm round him, his head leaning against her. The monk had withdrawn.

"The angels were all there, no doubt," she was saying; "but only a few painters have ever tried to represent them in the picture. It is not easy to paint an angel if you have never seen one."

"Pooh! I have seen them," said Theocritus, "hundreds of times. I have seen their wings. They come floating in when the sunshine comes through a crack— all dusty, you know. How many of them there do you suppose saw the angels? Not that big girl with the plate, anyhow, *I* know!" Thus they talked on.

When the two from the campanile returned, and they went out to embark, a slight breeze had risen. The little boy lifted his shoulders uneasily, and seemed almost to shiver. Mrs. Lenox felt of his head and hands. "I think I had better take him back in one of those covered gondolas, Stephen," she said. "He seems to be cold; he might have a chill."

"Surely it is very warm," said Mrs. Marcy.

"Yes, but he is so delicate," replied the other lady.

"I will go with you, Mrs. Lenox," said Claudia.

"Oh no; the gondolas here are the small ones, I see, and Stephen could not come with us. Do not leave him to go back alone; if one of us sees to the child, that is enough."

It ended, therefore, according to her arrangement: she went back with Theocritus in a covered gondola, Mrs. Marcy and Blake returned as they had come, while Claudia and Lenox had the third boat to themselves.

Rodney Blake being added, this little party continued its Venetian life. Lenox made some progress with his portrait of Claudia, but it was not thought, at least by the others, that his wife made any with Theocritus, that child remaining as delicate as ever, and, if possible, more troublesome. In Mrs. Marcy's mind there had sprung up, since Mr. Blake's arrival, an aftermath of interest in Venetian art and architecture which was richer even than the first crop; she went contentedly to see the pictures, churches, and palaces a fourth and even fifth time.

Claudia had a great liking for St. Mark's. "But who has not?" said Mrs. Marcy, reproachfully, when Blake commented upon the younger lady's fancy.

"Yes; but it is not every liking that is strong enough to take its possessor there every day through eight long, slow weeks," answered the gentleman.

"Not so slow," said Claudia. "But how do you know? You have been here through only one of them."

"That leanest mosaic in the central dome is an old friend of mine; he has told me many things in his time (I am an inveterate Venetian lounger, you know), bending down from his curved abode, his glassy eyes on mine, and a long, thin finger pointed. Be careful; he has noticed you."

Several days later, strolling into the church, he found her there. "As usual," he said.

"Yes, as usual," she answered. Miss Marcy liked Blake; his slow remarks often amused her. And she liked to be amused—perhaps because she was not one of those young ladies who find everything amusing. She was sitting at the base of the last of the great pillars of the nave, where she could see the north transept with the star-lights of the chapel at the end, the old pulpit of colored marbles with its fretted top and angel, and the deep, gold-lined dimness of the choir-dome, into which the first horizontal ray of sunset light was now stealing—a light which would soon turn into miraculous splendor its whole expanse.

"It always seems to me like a cave set with gold and

gems," said Blake, taking a seat beside her. "And, in reality, that is what it is, you know—a wonderful robbers' cavern. As somebody has said, it is the church of pirates—of the greatest sea-robbers the world has ever known; and they have adorned it with the magnificent mass of treasure they stole from the whole Eastern hemisphere."

"I wish they had stolen a little for me—one of those Oriental chains, for instance. But what pleases me best here is the light. It isn't the bright, vast clearness of St. Peter's that makes one's small sins of no sort of consequence; it isn't the sombreness of the Duomo at Florence, where one soon feels such a dreadful repentance that the new virtue becomes acute depression. It is a darkness, I admit, but of such a warm, rich hue that one feels sumptuous just by sitting in it. I do believe that if some of our thin, anxious-faced American women could only be induced to come and sit here quietly several hours a day they would soon grow serene and physically opulent, like—"

"Like yourself?"

"Like the women of Veronese. (Of course I shall have to admit that I do not need this process. Unfortunately, I love it.) But those Veronese pictures, Mr. Blake—after all, what do they tell us? Blue sky and balconies, feasts and brocades, pages and dogs, colors and splendor, and those great fair women, with no expression in their faces—what does it all mean?"

"Simply beauty."

"Beauty without mind, then."

"A picture does not need mind. But, to be worth anything, beauty it must have."

"I don't know; a picture is a sort of companion.

One of those pictures would not be that; you might as well have a beautiful idiot."

"Ah, but a *picture* is silent," replied Blake.

Claudia laughed. "You are incorrigible." Then, going back to her first subject, "I wish Mrs. Lenox would come here more," she said.

"You think she needs this enriching process you have suggested?"

"In one way—yes. All this beauty here in Venice is so much to her husband; while she—is forever with that child!"

"But she does not keep him from the beauty."

"No; but she might make it so much more to him if she would."

"Why don't you suggest it to her?"

"There is no use. She does not understand me, I think. We speak a different language."

"That may be. But I fancy she understands you."

"Perhaps she does," answered Claudia, with the untroubled frankness which was one of her noticeable traits. She spoke as though she thought, indeed, that Claudia Marcy's nature was a thing which Mrs. Lenox, or any one, might observe. Claudia rather admired her nature. It was not perfect, of course, but at least it was large in its boundaries, and above the usual feminine pettinesses; she felt a calm pride in that. She was silent for a while. The first sunset ray had now been joined by others, and together they had lighted up one-half of the choir-dome; its gold was all awake and glistening superbly, and the great mosaic figure enthroned there began to glow with a solemn, mysterious life.

"Men should not marry until they are at least thirty,

I think," resumed Claudia; "and especially those of the imaginative or artistic temperament. Three-quarters of the incongruous marriages one sees were made when the husband was very young. It is not the wife's fault; at the time of the marriage she is generally the superior, the generous one; the benefit is conferred by her. But—she does not advance, and he does."

"What would you propose in the way of — of an amelioration?" asked her listener.

"There can, of course, be no amelioration in actual cases. But there might be a prevention. I think that a law could be passed,—such as now exists, for instance, against the marriage of minors. If a man could not marry until he was thirty or older, he would at that time naturally select a wife who was ten years or so his junior rather than one of his own age."

"And the women of thirty?"

"They would be already married to the men of fifty, you know."

Here a figure emerging from the heavy red-brown shadows of the north aisle, and seeming to bring some of them with it, as it advanced, crossed the billowy pavement, and stopped before them. It was Mr. Lenox. He took a seat on the other side of Blake, and they talked for a while of the way the chocolate-hued walls met the gold of the domes solidly, without shading, and of the total absence of white—two of the marked features of the rich interior of the old pirate cathedral. At length Blake rose, giving up his place beside Miss Marcy to the younger man. "I think we have still a half-hour before that jailer of a janitor jangles his keys," she said.

"Yes; but for the men of fifty it is time to be going," answered Blake. "They take cold rather easily, you know, those poor fellows of fifty."

He went away. Claudia and Lenox remained until the keys jangled.

Every day the weather and the water-city grew more divinely fair. June began. And now even Mrs. Marcy saw no objection to their utilizing the moonlight, and no longer spoke of "wraps." The evenings were haunted by music; everybody seemed to be floating about singing or touching guitars. The effect of the mingled light and shadows across the fronts of the palaces was enchanting; they could not say enough in its praise.

"Still, do you know sometimes I would give it all for the fresh odor of the fields at home, in the country, and the old scent of lilacs," said Mrs. Lenox.

"Do you care for lilacs?" said Claudia. "If you had said roses—"

"No, I mean lilacs—the simple country lilacs. And I want to see some currant bushes, too; yes, and even an old wooden garden fence," replied Mrs. Lenox, laughing, but nevertheless as if she meant what she said. She went with them only that once in the evening, for when she reached home she found that the little boy had been wakeful, and that he had refused to go to sleep again because she was not there. After this the others went without her in a gondola holding four. At last, although the moonlight lingers longer in Venice than anywhere else, there was, for that month at least, no more. Yet still the evening air was delicious, and the music did not cease; the effect of the shadows was even more marvellous than the mingled light and shade had been. They continued to go out and float about for an hour or two in the warm, peopled darkness. They went also, but by daylight, to Torcello, and this time Theocritus was of the party. During half of the day he was more despotic than he had ever been, but later he seemed very tired; he slept in his aunt's arms all the way home. Once she made an effort to transfer him to her husband, as the weight of his little muffled figure lay heavily on her slender arm; but Theocritus was awake immediately, and began to beat off his uncle's hands with all his might.

"Do let me take him, Elizabeth; he will soon fall asleep again," said Lenox. He looked annoyed. "You are overtaxing your strength; I can see that you are tired out."

"It will not harm me; I know when I am really too tired," answered his wife. She gave him a little trusting smile as she spoke, and his frown passed off.

They were all together in one of the large gondolas; Blake noted this little side-scene.

That night Theocritus had a slight attack of fever. Mrs. Lenox said that it came from over-fatigue, and that he must not go on any of the longer expeditions. When they went to Murano, therefore, and down to Chioggia, she did not accompany them, but remained at home with her charge.

Mrs. Marcy was enjoying this last month in Venice greatly. "Naturally, it is much pleasanter when one has some one to attend to one, and one too who knows one's tastes and looks after one's little comforts," she remarked to her niece, with some intricacy of impersonal pronouns. The lily did not observe that the attentions she found so agreeable were being offered to her niece also by another impersonal pronoun. As she would herself have said, "naturally," when they went here and there together, the two elders often sat down to rest awhile when Claudia and Lenox did not feel the need of it.

"Of course, with her beauty, her attractive qualities, and her fortune, Miss Marcy has had many suitors," said Blake to the aunt during one of these rests.

"Several," answered that lady, moderately. "But Claudia is not at all susceptible. Neither is she so— so generally attractive as you might suppose. She has too little thought for the opinions of others. She says, for instance, just what she thinks, and that, you know, is seldom agreeable."

"True; we much prefer that people should say what they don't. I have myself noticed some plainly evident faults in her: a most impolitic honesty; and, when stirred, an impulsiveness which is sure to be unremunerative in the long-run. I should say, too, that she had an empyrean sort of pride."

"Yes," replied the lily, not knowing what he meant, but concluding on the whole that he spoke in reprobation. "As I said before, she has not *quite* enough of that true feminine softness one likes so much to see—I mean, of course, in a woman."

"Her pride will be her bane yet. It will make her blind to the most obvious pitfall. However, I'll back her courage against it when once she sees where she has dropped."

"What?" said the lily.

"She will in time learn from you; she could not follow a more lovely example," said Blake, coming back from his reflections.

Towards the last of June a long expedition was
17

planned, an expedition into "Titian's country," which was to last three days. This little pilgrimage had been talked about for a long time, Mrs. Lenox being as much interested in it as the others. Whether she would have had the courage to take Theocritus, even in his best estate, is a question; but after the time was finally set and all the arrangements made, his worst asserted itself, and so markedly that it was plain to all that she could not go. Something was said about postponement, but it was equally plain that if they were to go at all they should go at once, as the weather was rapidly approaching a too great heat. Claudia wished particularly to take this little journey; she had set her heart upon seeing the Titians and reputed Titians said to be still left in that unvisited neighborhood. Blake asserted that she even expected to discover one. It was next proposed (although rather faintly) that Mr. Lenox should be excused from the pilgrimage. But it could not be denied that the little boy had been quite as ill (and irritable) several times before in Venice, and that he had always recovered in a day or two. Not that Mrs. Lenox denied it; on the contrary, she was the one to mention it. She urged her husband's going; it was the excursion of all others to please him the most. It ended in his consenting; it seemed, indeed, too much to give up for so slight a cause.

"She looks a little anxious," observed Blake, as they waited for him in the gondola which was to take them to the railway station. Lenox had said good-bye to her, and was now coming down the long stairway within, while she had stepped out on her balcony to see them start.

"Do you think so?" said Mrs. Marcy. "To me she always looks just the same, always so unmoved."

Lenox now came out, and the gondola started. Claudia looked back and waved her hand, Mrs. Lenox returning the salutation.

On the evening of the third day, at eleven o'clock, a gondola from the railway station stopped at the larger palace's lower door, and three persons ascended the dimly lighted stairs.

At the top Mrs. Lenox's servant was waiting for them. "Oh, where is signore? Is he not with you? He has not come? Oh, the poor signora—may the sweet Madonna help her now!" cried the girl, with tears in her sympathetic Italian eyes. "The poor little boy is dead."

They rushed up the higher stairway and across the hall bridge. But it was as the woman had said. There, on his little white bed, lay the child; he would be troublesome no more on this earth; he was quiet at last. Mrs. Lenox stood in the lighted doorway of her room as they came towards her. When she saw that her husband was not with them, when they began hurriedly to explain that he had not come, that he had stayed behind, that he had sent a note, she swayed over without a word and fainted away.

It was only over-fatigue, she explained later. The child had lain in her arms for thirty hours, most of the time in great pain, and she had suffered with him. She soon recovered consciousness and was quite calm —more calm than they had feared she would be. They were anxiously watchful; they tended her with the most devoted care. Blake did what he could, and then waited. After a while, when Mrs. Lenox had in a measure recovered, he softly beckoned Mrs. Marcy out.

"You must tell her that her husband will not be

back in time for—that he will not be back for at least six days, and very likely longer. And as his route was quite uncertain, we cannot reach him; there is no telegraph, of course, and even if I were to go after him I could only follow his track from village to village, and probably come back to Venice behind him."

"How can I tell her!" said the tearful lady. "Perhaps Claudia—"

"No, on no account. You are the one, and you must do it," replied Blake, and with so much decision that she obeyed him. Thus the wife was told.

What Blake had said was true; it was hopeless to try to reach Lenox before the time when he would probably be back of his own accord. He had started on a hunt after some early drawings of Titian's, of which they had unearthed dim legends. One was said to be in an old monastery, among others of no importance; two more were vaguely reported as now here, now there. Lenox had not been certain of his own route, but expected to be guided from village to village according to indications. It was not even certain whether he would come back by Conegliano or strike the railway at another point. "It certainly is an inexorable fate!" exclaimed poor Mrs. Marcy, in the emergency driven to unusual expressions.

But when Stephen Lenox's wife understood the position in which she was placed, she at once decided upon all that was to be done, and gave her directions clearly and calmly—directions which Blake executed with an attention and thoughtful care as complete as any one could possibly have bestowed.

The little boy was to be buried at Venice, in the

cemetery on the island opposite, early in the morning of the second day.

"She is *so* sensible!" Mrs. Marcy commented, admiringly. "Of course, under all the circumstances, it is the thing to do. But so many women would have insisted upon—all sorts of plans; and it would have been *so* hard."

"I would willingly carry out anything she wished for, no matter how difficult," replied Blake. "I greatly respect and admire Mrs. Lenox. But, as you say, the perfect balance of her character, her clear judgment and beautiful goodness, have at once decided upon the best course." (The lily had not quite said this; but in her present state of distressed sympathy she accepted it.)

Claudia, meanwhile, remained through all very silent. She assisted, and ably, in everything that was done, but said almost nothing.

The evening before the funeral the two ladies went across to Mrs. Lenox's rooms; they had left her some hours before, as she had promised to lie down for a while, but they thought that she was now probably awake again. They found her sitting beside the little white-shrouded form.

"Now this is not wise, Elizabeth," began Mrs. Marcy, chidingly.

"I think it is; I like to look at him," replied the watcher. "See, the peaceful expression I have been hoping for has come; it is not often needed on the face of a child, but it was with my poor little boy. Look."

And, sure enough, there shone upon the small, still countenance a lovely sweetness which had never been there in life. The face did not even seem thin; its lines had all passed away; it looked very fair and young, and very peacefully at rest.

"His mother would know him now at once; he was a very pretty little fellow the last time she saw him, when he was about a year old," she went on. "I was very fond of his mother, and his father, as probably you know, was my only brother. Their child was very dear to me," she resumed, after a short silence, which the others did not break. "His constant suffering made him unlike stronger, happier children, and I think that was the very reason I loved him the more. I wanted to make it up to him. But I could not. I suppose he never knew what it was to be entirely without pain—the doctors have told me so. He did not know anything else, or any other way, but to suffer more or less, and to be tired all the time. And he was so used to it, poor little fellow, that I suppose he thought that every one suffered too—that that was life. He has found a better now." Leaning forward, she took the small hands in hers. "All my loving care, dear child, was not enough to keep you here," she said, smoothing them tenderly. "But you are with your mother now; that is far better."

The funeral took place early the next morning. Then Mrs. Lenox came back to her empty rooms, and entered them alone. She preferred it so.

After the first explanation, the only allusion she had made to her husband's absence was to Rodney Blake. That gentleman had not expressed the shadow of a disapprobation. He had not told her that he had objected to Lenox's lengthened absence, and had done what he could to prevent it; he had stopped Mrs. Marcy sharply when she spoke of telling.

"Can't you see, Sophy, that that would be the worst of all for her?" he said; "to know that Lenox would go, in spite of my unconcealed opposition, just because Clau—just because he wanted those trivial drawings," he added, changing the termination of his sentence, but quite sure, meanwhile, that "Sophy" would never discover what he had begun to say.

Mrs. Lenox's remark was this. Blake had come in to speak to her about some necessary directions concerning the funeral, and when she had given them she said: "It will be a grief to Stephen when he comes back that he could not have seen the little boy, even if but for once more. And I hoped so that he would see him! I expected you back at eight—you know that was the first arrangement—and towards seven he seemed easier. Once he even smiled, and talked a little about that legend of St. Mark and St. Theodore, of which, you remember, he was so fond. Then it was half-past seven, and I still hoped. And then it grew towards eight, and he was in pain again. Still I kept listening for the sound of your gondola. But it did not come. And at half-past eight he died. But perhaps it was as well so," she continued, although her voice trembled a little. "Stephen would have felt his suffering so much. I was more used to it, you know, than he was."

"Yes," answered Blake.

But she seemed to know that he was not quite in accord with her. "Of course I feel it very deeply, Mr. Blake, on my own account, that my husband is not here; I depend upon him for everything, and feel utterly lonely without him. But his absence is one of those accidents which we must all encounter sometimes, and as to everything else—the outside help I needed—you have done all that even he could have done. You have been very good to me," and she held out her hand.

Blake took it, and thanked her. And in his words this time he put something that contented her. It was the sacrifice he made to his liking for Stephen Lenox's wife.

The evening after the funeral Mrs. Marcy, who had been made nervous and ill by all that had happened, went out at sunset for a change of air, and Blake accompanied her. Claudia preferred to stay at home. But five minutes after the departure of their gondola she went up the stairs and across the hall bridge that led to Mrs. Lenox's apartment. Mrs. Lenox was there, lying on the sofa. It was the first time since the return that the two had been alone together. She looked pale and ill, and there were dark shadows under her eyes; but she smiled and spoke in her usual voice, asking Claudia to sit beside her in an easy-chair that stood there. Claudia sat down, and they spoke on one or two unimportant subjects. But the girl soon paused in this.

"I have come to say," she began again, in a voice that showed the effort she made to keep it calm, "that I shall never forgive myself, Mrs. Lenox, for—for a great deal that I have thought about you, but especially for having had a part in the absence of your husband at such a time. If it had not been for me he would not have gone off on that foolish expedition. But I wanted those miserable drawings, or at least sketches of them, and so I kept talking about it. When I think of what you have had to go through, alone, in consequence of it, I am overwhelmed." Here her voice nearly broke down.

"You must not take it all upon yourself, Miss Marcy," answered the wife. "No doubt Stephen wanted to please you; no doubt he wanted to very much—to get you the drawings, if it was possible; of that I am quite sure."

But Claudia was not quieted. "If you knew how I have suffered—how I suffer now as I see you lying there so pale and ill"—here she stopped again. "I come to tell you how I feel your suffering, and I spend the time talking about my own," she added, abruptly. "I am a worthless creature!" And covering her face with her hands, she burst into tears.

Mrs. Lenox put out her hand and stroked the beautiful bowed head caressingly. "Do not feel so badly," she said. "You must not; it is not necessary."

"But it is—it is," said the girl, amid her tears. "If you knew—"

"I do know, Claudia. I know *you*."

"Oh, if you really do," said Claudia, lifting her head, her wet eyes turned eagerly upon the wife, "then it is better."

"It *is* better; it is well. My dear, I think I have understood you all along."

"But—I have not understood myself," replied Claudia. She had nerved herself to say it; but after it was spoken a deep blush rose slowly over her whole face until it was in a flame. Through all its heat, however, she kept her eyes bravely upon those of the wife.

"That I knew, too," rejoined Mrs. Lenox. "But I also knew that there was no danger," she added.

"There was not. It was unconscious. In any case,

I should in time have recognized it. And destroyed it, as I do now." These short sentences were brought out, each with a fresh effort. "I do not speak of—of the other side," the girl went on, with abrupt, heavy awkwardness of phrase. "There never was any other side—it was all mine." And then came the flaming blush again.

"But you are very beautiful, Claudia?" said the other woman, not as if disturbed at all in her own quiet calm, but half tentatively.

"Yes, I am beautiful," replied Claudia, with a sort of scorn. "But he is not that kind of man," she added, a quick, involuntary pride coming into her eyes. Then she turned her head away, shading her face with her hand. She said no more; it seemed as if she had stopped herself shortly there.

After a moment or two Mrs. Lenox began to speak. "All this life, here in Venice, has been so much to Stephen," she said, in her sweet, quiet voice. "You know he has worked very hard—he was obliged to; just so many hours of each long day, for long, hard years. He never had any rest; and the work was always distasteful to him, too. It was a slavery. And it was beginning to tell upon him; he could not have kept it up without being worn out both in body and mind. Judge, then, how glad I am that he has had all this change and pleasure—he needed it so! There is that side to his nature—a love of the beautiful, and a strong one. This has been always repressed and bound down; it is natural that it should break forth here. I have not the feeling myself—at least, not like his; but I understand it in him, and sympathize with it fully." She paused. Claudia did not speak.

"You have not been a wife, Claudia, and therefore there are some things you do not know," pursued the voice. "A wife becomes in time to her husband such a part of himself (that is, if he loves her) that she isn't a separate person to him any more, and he hardly thinks of her as one; she is himself. Many things become a matter of course to him—are taken for granted—on this very account. It does not occur to him that she may feel differently. He supposes that they feel alike. Often they do. Still, a woman's thoughts do not always run in the same channel as those of a man; we are more timid, more limited, more—afraid of things, you know; but the husband does not always remember that. But there are some things in which a husband and wife do feel alike, always and forever; there are ties which are eternal. And my own life holds them—ties and memories so precious that I can hardly explain them to you; memories of those early years of ours when we were so alone and poor, but so dear to each other that we did not mind it. We love each other just the same; but then we had nothing but our love—and it was enough. The coming, the short stay with us, and the fading away of our two little children, Claudia—these are ties deep down in our hearts which nothing can ever sunder. Stephen will go back to all that old grief of his when he comes home to find the little boy gone. For the greatest sorrow of his life, one he has never at heart overcome, was that he felt when we lost our own little boy. Stephen had loved the child passionately, and would not believe that he must go; and when he did he bowed his head in a silence so long that I was frightened. I had never seen him give up before. But even that is a dear tie between us, for then he had only me. Those early years of ours, with their joys and sorrows — I often think of them. A man does not dwell upon such memories, one by one, as a woman does. But they are none the less there, a part of his life and of him." She stopped. " Do not mind," she added, in a changed voice. " I am only—a little tired, I think."

Claudia, who had not moved, turned quickly. Mrs. Lenox's eyes were closed; she was very pale. But she did not faint; owing to Claudia's quick, efficient help, she was soon herself again. "You know what to do, don't you?" she said, smiling, when the faint feeling had passed.

" It is not that I know, so much as that I long to help you," answered Claudia. " I wish you would let me unbraid your hair, and make you ready for bed; you look so tired, and perhaps I could do it with a lighter touch than Bianca," she added, humbly.

" Very well," said the other, assentingly.

And with much care and skill the girl performed her task. " I will even put out the light," she said. " I will tell Bianca that you have gone to bed, and are not to be disturbed." When all was done and the light out, she paused for a moment by the bedside. " I am not going to talk any more," she said, " but I will just say this: aunt and I are going away. To-morrow, probably, or the day after. You will not be left alone, for Mr. Blake will stay."

There was a silence. Then Mrs. Lenox's voice said: " That is a mistake. It would be better to stay."

" I do not see it in that way," answered the girl. Then, " You must not ask too much," she added, in a lower voice.

Mrs. Lenox took her hands, which were hanging before her, tightly clasped. The touch shook Claudia; she sank down beside the bed and hid her face.

"Stay; it is far better," whispered the wife. "Then it will be over. By going away you will only think about it the more."

"Yes, I know. But—"

"I will answer for all. I know you better than—you know yourself. When you see us together, it will be different to you. Stay, to please me."

"Very well," murmured the girl.

They kissed each other, and she rose. When she had reached the door Mrs. Lenox spoke again. "Of course, you know that I quite understand that it is only a girl's fancy," she said, with a tender lightness. This was her offering to Claudia.

On the evening of the seventh day after the funeral Stephen Lenox came back; he had sent a despatch to his wife from Conegliano, and Blake was therefore able to meet him at Mestre, and tell him what had happened. He went directly home, and the others did not see him until the next evening. Then he came across to the larger palace. Blake was there; he kept himself rather constantly with Mrs. Marcy now, perhaps to direct that lady's somewhat wandering inspirations. For this occasion he had warned her that she must not be too sympathetic, that she must be on her guard. So Mrs. Marcy was "on her guard;" she only took out her handkerchief four times; she even talked of the weather. Claudia scarcely spoke. Blake himself conducted the conversation, and filled all the gaps. They could naturally say a good deal about the health of Mrs. Lenox, as that lady had been obliged to keep her room for the three preceding days. Lenox did not stay long; he said he must go back to his wife. As he rose he gave the small portfolio he had brought with him to Claudia. "I don't think they were Titians," he said. "But I sketched them for you as well as I could."

Mrs. Marcy thought this an opportunity; she took the portfolio, and exclaimed over each picture. Blake, too, put up his eye-glass to look at them. Lenox said a word or two about them and waited a moment longer; then he went away. Claudia had not glanced at them.

He never knew of her visit to his wife; those are the secrets women keep for each other, unto and beyond the grave.

What passed when he came home was simple enough. His wife cried when she saw him; she had not cried before. She told him the history of the little boy's last hours, and of all he had said, and of the funeral. Then they had talked a while of her health, and then of future plans.

"I ought to have remembered that you were anxious about him even before I went away," said Lenox, going back abruptly to the first subject. He was standing by the window, looking out; this was an hour after his return.

"But he had been ill so many times. No, it was something we could not foresee, and as such we must accept it. I wanted you to go—don't you remember? I urged your going. You must not blame yourself about it."

"But I do," answered her husband.

"I cannot allow you to; I shall never allow it. To

me, Stephen, all you do is right; I wish to hear nothing that could even seem otherwise. I trust you entirely, and always shall."

He turned. She was lying back in an easy-chair, supported by pillows. He came across and sat down beside her, his head bent forward, his elbows resting on his knees, his face in his hands. He did not speak.

"Because I know that I can," added the wife.

That was all.

They stayed on together in Venice through another two weeks. Mrs. Lenox improved daily, and was soon able to go about with them. She seemed, indeed, to bloom into a new youth. "It is the reaction after the long, wearing care of that child," explained Mrs. Marcy. "And isn't it beautiful to see how devoted he is to her, and how careful of her in every way? But I have always noticed what a devoted husband he was, haven't you?"

These two ladies and Mr. Blake were going to Baden-Baden. But the others were going back to America. "We may return some time," said Lenox; "but at present I think we want a home."

"I wish we could have stayed on together always, just as we are now," sighed the sentimental lily, smoothing the embroidered edge of her handkerchief. "*Such* a pleasant party, and of just the right size; these last two weeks have been so perfect!"

The time for parting came. The three who were going to Baden-Baden were to leave at dawn, and they had come across to Mrs. Lenox's parlor to spend a last hour. Claudia talked more than usual, and talked well; she looked brilliant.

At the end of the second hour the good-byes began

in earnest. Everything that was appropriate was said, Blake, in particular, delivering himself unblushingly of one long fluent commonplace after another. They were to meet again—oh, very soon; they were to visit each other; they were to write frequently—one would have supposed, indeed, that Blake intended to send a daily telegraphic despatch. At last the lily, having kept them all standing for twenty minutes, bestowed upon Mrs. Lenox a final kiss, and really did start, the two gentlemen and Claudia accompanying her down the long hall. But the hall was dark, and Claudia was behind; without the knowledge of the others she slipped back.

Mrs. Lenox was standing where they had left her. When she saw the girl returning, pale, repressed, all the sparkle gone, she went to her, and put her arms round her; Claudia laid her head down upon the other's shoulder. Thus they stood for several moments in silence. Then, still without speaking, Claudia went away.

When Mrs. Marcy reached the stairway which led down to her own apartment, on the other side of the hall bridge, "Why, where is Claudia?" she said.

"Here I am," said her niece, appearing from the darkness.

"You will come down with us for a moment, won't you, Mr. Lenox?" suggested the lily. "Just for one *last* look?"

"Do not ask him," said Claudia, smiling; "he is worn out! We have already extended that look over two long hours. Good-bye, Mr. Lenox; and this time, I think, is really the last."

By CONSTANCE F. WOOLSON.

HORACE CHASE. 16mo, Cloth, $1 25.
JUPITER LIGHTS. 16mo, Cloth, $1 25.
EAST ANGELS. 16mo, Cloth, $1 25.
ANNE. Illustrated. 16mo, Cloth, $1 25.
FOR THE MAJOR. 16mo, Cloth, $1 00.
CASTLE NOWHERE. 16mo, Cloth, $1 00.
RODMAN THE KEEPER. 16mo, Cloth, $1 00.

There is a certain bright cheerfulness in Miss Woolson's writing which invests all her characters with lovable qualities.—*Jewish Advocate*, N. Y.

Miss Woolson is among our few successful writers of interesting magazine stories, and her skill and power are perceptible in the delineation of her heroines no less than in the suggestive pictures of local life.—*Jewish Messenger*, N. Y.

Constance Fenimore Woolson may easily become the novelist laureate.—*Boston Globe.*

Miss Woolson has a graceful fancy, a ready wit, a polished style, and conspicuous dramatic power; while her skill in the development of a story is very remarkable.—*London Life.*

Miss Woolson never once follows the beaten track of the orthodox novelist, but strikes a new and richly-loaded vein which, so far, is all her own; and thus we feel, on reading one of her works, a fresh sensation, and we put down the book with a sigh to think our pleasant task of reading it is finished. The author's lines must have fallen to her in very pleasant places; or she has, perhaps, within herself the wealth of womanly love and tenderness she pours so freely into all she writes. Such books as hers do much to elevate the moral tone of the day—a quality sadly wanting in novels of the time.—*Whitehall Review*, London.

PUBLISHED BY HARPER & BROTHERS, NEW YORK.

☞ *The above works are for sale by all booksellers, or will be sent by the publishers, postage prepaid, to any part of the United States, Canada, or Mexico, on receipt of the price.*

By CHARLES DUDLEY WARNER

THE GOLDEN HOUSE. Illustrated by W. T. SMEDLEY. Post 8vo, Ornamental Half Leather, Uncut Edges and Gilt Top, $2 00.

It is a strong, individual, and very serious consideration of life; much more serious, much deeper in thought, than the New York novel is wont to be. It is worthy of companionship with its predecessor, "A Little Journey in the World," and keeps Mr. Warner well in the front rank of philosophic students of the tendencies of our civilization.—*Springfield Republican.*

A LITTLE JOURNEY IN THE WORLD. A Novel. Post 8vo, Half Leather, Uncut Edges and Gilt Top, $1 50; Paper, 75 cents.

THEIR PILGRIMAGE. Illustrated by C. S. REINHART. Post 8vo, Half Leather, Uncut Edges and Gilt Top, $2 00.

STUDIES IN THE SOUTH AND WEST, with Comments on Canada. Post 8vo, Half Leather, Uncut Edges and Gilt Top, $1 75.

OUR ITALY. Illustrated. 8vo, Cloth, Ornamental, Uncut Edges and Gilt Top, $2 50.

AS WE GO. With Portrait and Illustrations. 16mo, Cloth, Ornamental, $1 00. ("Harper's American Essayists.")

AS WE WERE SAYING. With Portrait and Illustrations. 16mo, Cloth, Ornamental, $1 00. ("Harper's American Essayists.")

THE WORK OF WASHINGTON IRVING. With Portraits. 32mo, Cloth, Ornamental, 50 cents.

PUBLISHED BY HARPER & BROTHERS, NEW YORK.

☞ *The above works are for sale by all booksellers, or will be sent by the publishers by mail, postage prepaid, to any part of the United States, Canada, or Mexico, on receipt of the price.*

By BRANDER MATTHEWS

VIGNETTES OF MANHATTAN. Illustrated by W. T. SMEDLEY. Post 8vo, Cloth, Ornamental, $1 50.

> In "Vignettes of Manhattan" Mr. Matthews renders twelve impressions of New York with admirable clearness and much grace. From the collection a vivid picture may be drawn of the great city.—*N. Y. Evening Post.*

AMERICANISMS AND BRITICISMS, with Other Essays on Other Isms. With Portrait. 16mo, Cloth, Ornamental, $1 00.

> A racy, delightful little book.... It is a long time since we have met with such a combination of keen yet fair criticism, genuine wit, and literary grace.—*Congregationalist,* Boston.

THE STORY OF A STORY, and Other Stories. Illustrated. 16mo, Cloth, Ornamental, $1 25.

STUDIES OF THE STAGE. With Portrait. 16mo, Cloth, Ornamental, $1 00.

THE ROYAL MARINE. An Idyl of Narragansett Pier. Illustrated. 32mo, Cloth, Ornamental, $1 00.

THIS PICTURE AND THAT. A Comedy. Illustrated. 32mo, Cloth, Ornamental, 50 cents.

THE DECISION OF THE COURT. A Comedy. Illustrated. 32mo, Cloth, Ornamental, 50 cents.

IN THE VESTIBULE LIMITED. A Story. Illustrated. 12mo, Cloth, Ornamental, 50 cents.

PUBLISHED BY HARPER & BROTHERS, NEW YORK.

☞ *The above works are for sale by all booksellers, or will be sent by the publishers by mail, postage prepaid, to any part of the United States, Canada, or Mexico, on receipt of the price.*

WILLIAM BLACK'S NOVELS
LIBRARY EDITION

Mr. Black knows so well just what to describe, and to what length, that the scenery of his novels—by comparison with that of many we are obliged to read—seems to have been freshened by soft spring rains. His painting of character, his conversations and situations, are never strongly dramatic and exciting, but they are thoroughly good. He never gives us a tame or a tiresome chapter, and this is something for which readers will be profoundly grateful.—*N. Y. Tribune.*

A DAUGHTER OF HETH.	STAND FAST, CRAIG-ROYS-
A PRINCESS OF THULE.	TON! Illustrated.
DONALD ROSS OF HEIMRA.	SUNRISE.
GREEN PASTURES AND PIC-	THAT BEAUTIFUL WRETCH.
CADILLY.	Illustrated.
IN FAR LOCHABER.	THE MAGIC INK, AND OTH-
IN SILK ATTIRE.	ER STORIES. Illustrated.
JUDITH SHAKESPEARE. Il-	THE STRANGE ADVENTURES
lustrated.	OF A HOUSE-BOAT. Ill'd.
KILMENY.	THE STRANGE ADVENTURES
MACLEOD OF DARE. Ill'd.	OF A PHAETON.
MADCAP VIOLET.	THREE FEATHERS.
PRINCE FORTUNATUS. Ill'd.	WHITE HEATHER.
SABINA ZEMBRA.	WHITE WINGS. Illustrated.
SHANDON BELLS. Illustrated.	YOLANDE. Illustrated.

12mo, Cloth, $1 25 per volume.

WOLFENBERG.—THE HANDSOME HUMES.
Illustrated. 12mo, Cloth, $1 50 per volume.

HIGHLAND COUSINS.
Illustrated. 12mo, Cloth, Ornamental, $1 75.

Complete Sets, 26 volumes, Cloth, $30 00; Half Calf, $57 00.

PUBLISHED BY HARPER & BROTHERS, NEW YORK.

☞ *The above works are for sale by all booksellers, or will be sent by the publishers, postage prepaid, to any part of the United States, Canada, or Mexico, on receipt of the price.*

www.ingramcontent.com/pod-product-compliance
Lightning Source LLC
Chambersburg PA
CBHW021956220426
43663CB00007B/831